KT-294-433

193 381

Rhetorics of Welfare

Also by Susan Kenny

COMMUNITIES FOR THE FUTURE: An Introduction to Community Development Theory and Practice in Australia

SOCIOLOGY: Australian Connections (*with R. Jureidini and M. Poole*)

Also by Bryan S. Turner

THE BLACKWELL COMPANION TO SOCIAL THEORY (*editor*)

CLASSICAL SOCIOLOGY

THE POLITICS OF J.-F. LYOTARD (*co-editor with C. Rojek*)

THE TALCOTT PARSONS READER (*editor*)

Rhetorics of Welfare

Uncertainty, Choice and Voluntary Associations

Kevin M. Brown
Lecturer in Sociology
Deakin University
Melbourne

Susan Kenny
Reader
School of Social Inquiry
Deakin University
Melbourne

Bryan S. Turner
Professor of Sociology
Cambridge University

with

John K. Prince
School of Social Inquiry
Deakin University
Melbourne

NORWICH CITY COLLEGE LIBRARY

Book No. 193381

Class 361. 37 BRO

Cat. Proc. I WL

palgrave

© Kevin M. Brown, Susan Kenny, Bryan S. Turner and John K. Prince 2000

All rights reserved. No reproduction, copy or transmission of this publication may be made without written permission.

No paragraph of this publication may be reproduced, copied or transmitted save with written permission or in accordance with the provisions of the Copyright, Designs and Patents Act 1988, or under the terms of any licence permitting limited copying issued by the Copyright Licensing Agency, 90 Tottenham Court Road, London W1P 0LP.

Any person who does any unauthorised act in relation to this publication may be liable to criminal prosecution and civil claims for damages.

The authors have asserted their rights to be identified as the authors of this work in accordance with the Copyright, Designs and Patents Act 1988.

Published by PALGRAVE
Houndmills, Basingstoke, Hampshire RG21 6XS and
175 Fifth Avenue, New York, N. Y. 10010
Companies and representatives throughout the world

PALGRAVE is the new global academic imprint of
St. Martin's Press LLC Scholarly and Reference Division and
Palgrave Publishers Ltd (formerly Macmillan Press Ltd).

Outside North America
ISBN 0–333–80359–0

In North America
ISBN 0–312–23203–9

This book is printed on paper suitable for recycling and made from fully managed and sustained forest sources.

A catalogue record for this book is available from the British Library.

Library of Congress Catalog Card Number: 99–088130 CIP

Transferred to Digital Printing 2002

Printed and bound in Great Britain by
Antony Rowe Ltd, Chippenham, Wiltshire

Contents

List of Figures and Tables

Figures

Tables

Acknowledgements

This book has developed from work made possible by a grant from the Australian Research Council.

Through the course of the research we have received help and advice from numerous people. We would particularly like to thank Wendy Taylor and Lauren Howe for their untiring support, advice and work on this project; Maria Anastasiadis for her help in the construction of the database; Linda Burke, for her organizational prowess in handling the focus group arrangements.

Thanks also to the people who participated in the focus groups and responded to the survey, without whom much of this work would not have been possible.

Part I

Towards a Theory of
Participatory Citizenship

1
Contested Rhetorics

Introduction: essentially contested concepts

This study examines the problems and issues of welfare institutions in a modern democracy within the context of a debate about the possibilities for active citizenship. Our inquiry is driven by one central question: can active citizenship survive the marketization of welfare provision through the medium of voluntary associations? The opportunities for the enhancement of social citizenship in contemporary societies are examined through an empirical study of the provision of welfare services by voluntary associations. These associations are the basic components of the third sector, namely those institutions which are neither parts of the private economy nor aspects of government. We believe that the relationship between these voluntary associations, the state and the economy has become increasingly complex and contested, because there have been major changes in government policies towards welfare provision in a post-Keynesian political environment. Because these relationships are uncertain and contested, there are various social rhetorics that attempt to describe, justify and promote different approaches to welfare management. Our study explores various types of welfare rhetorics in order to understand more precisely the possibilities for welfare and social citizenship in a deregulated economic environment. More specifically, we outline the contribution of voluntary associations to welfare provision and the development of active citizenship in contemporary Australia through a national survey, but we argue that these findings are generally relevant to a comparative understanding of the political significance of the third sector. As a result, we attempt to advance a general theory of these relationships, which is relevant to both political theory and sociology.

3

Many of the concepts and theories in this study are themselves contested. In this introductory chapter, we will attempt to clarify more exactly the central conceptual issues of our study. A more detailed analysis of voluntary associations, social citizenship and associative democracy will occupy subsequent chapters. The point of this initial discussion is to establish the broad parameters of our study and to place our analysis in the context of more general sociological concerns. For example, in Chapter 3 we will be specifically concerned to provide an account of the notion of 'voluntary association'. Although this notion is fast becoming part of everyday language with which the reader is familiar, it is important to note that on closer inspection it is quite complex. It is also contested, partly because the adjective 'voluntary' no longer necessarily refers to activities that are free, amateur, altruistic, unpaid or casual. The commonsense notion of voluntarism is that it is motivated by a sense of private responsibility to the needy and typically a leisure-time activity. Part of the drift of our research is that voluntary associations are increasingly professional in their orientation and managed by staff who are salaried and full time. Such people often want a career in third-sector organizations. One aspect of our argument then is that many nineteenth-century notions of charity and charitable organizations are becoming irrelevant for a comparative understanding of these associations, which are becoming an important sector of the economies of advanced societies (though other ideas of charity continue to find a place in current systems of meaning, as we discuss in Chapter 4). We also argue that voluntary associations are an essential part of what political theorists call 'civil society' and that such 'intermediary associations' which exist between the state and the market are an indispensable element of democracy. Throughout this book we use the term 'voluntary welfare sector' to denote the group of non-government, non-profit (or not-for-profit) organizations ('voluntary associations') primarily focused on welfare. They are voluntary in the sense of membership of and/or contribution to the organizations, but are often characterized by a mix of paid and unpaid (volunteer) work. Indeed, some voluntary associations are totally comprised of paid workers (see Chapters 3 and 6 for further discussions of these definitions).

The word 'rhetoric' is equally problematic. The term in commonsense usage suggests a mode of argument or debate which is deliberately artificial and misleading. For example, from a critical standpoint, advertizements are rhetorical devices to encourage us to want a commodity that in fact we do not need. In this study, however, it refers to any public argument or discourse by which a particular perspective is organized and presented. It has for us therefore a more neutral significance as a mode of argumentation by which values and perspectives are promoted. Rhetorics of welfare exist because the ways by which welfare could be funded, managed and delivered in contemporary societies are numerous. What constitutes an appropriate social policy for welfare is unclear, ambiguous and contested in terms of economics, politics and administration. The post-war welfare mixture of government planning, centralized provision, direct taxation, compulsory retirement and guaranteed superannuation has been largely abandoned. The economies of the advanced societies have been deregulated, retirement policies are more flexible, and full employment is rarely an overt commitment by governments. The consequences of post-Keynesian strategies are wholly uncertain and even the terminology by which this new environment could be described is disputed. Is the deregulation of welfare and the creation of welfare marketization best characterized as 'economic rationalism', or managerialism, or Reagonomics, or Thatcherism, or post-Fordism?

The issue is complex, because many authors would argue that genuine markets in the welfare sector cannot be created, and at best we can expect the creation of 'quasi-markets' (Flynn, 1997). There are well-known problems in attempting to treat health as a commodity. It is difficult in welfare contexts to make assumptions about consumer sovereignty; clients are often too sick to exercise any effective entitlement without third-party intervention. There are legal and moral difficulties with marketization of the human body. The European Community has legislated against markets for the sale of body parts, and the sale of eggs for IVF is heavily controlled. Markets tend to offend against bioethical norms of research and treatment, because they compromise the professional relationship between doctor and patient. Furthermore, while customers can select personal services such as a haircut by experimentally sampling providers, open-heart surgery is typically a one-off health service. Clients find it difficult rationally to select their surgeon in advance of an operation, because they cannot compare surgical success rates of different surgeons with respect to their own heart operation. Comparisons of different welfare regimes are equally problematic from the point of view of customers, because long-term effects can only be judged effectively across generational cohorts. Probably all that can be said with some degree of confidence is that, from a Keynesian point of view, we are all dead in the long run. Given the contested and uncertain nature of these economic and political issues, a range of rhetorical responses has been developed to articulate, promote and advocate different solutions and strategies.

Because we believe that these disputes are genuine rather than merely fashionable, and that the underlying political and social problems do not have neat economic solutions, we have adopted the term 'rhetoric' rather than 'ideology'. The term 'ideology' has frequently been employed to describe the illusory nature of welfare promises in the past (Clarke et al., 1987). In the current situation, to describe 'managerialism' as an ideology of welfare cutbacks is problematic, partly because it is premature. If 'managerialism' simply means in practice 'accountability', then there can be little rational objection to this management strategy. We are not yet in a position to make such a categorical judgement and in addition we accept that the welfare difficulties, to which some forms of managerialism are a possible solution, are real problems: they include such changes as the greying populations, increasing health demands, rising expectations about service, welfare bureaucracy and over-staffing, the erosion of community as a basis of care, the social isolation of the elderly through family transformations, the decline of familial and kinship obligations, the decline of work, and the rising cost of medical provision with technological innovation. Managerialism may well be an ideology of welfare cutbacks resulting in the pauperization of large sections of the population, but this judgement should be an empirical question and not an assumption of our research. To assume that welfare systems prior to neo-liberalism were a roaring success in terms of delivery and client satisfaction is merely nostalgic.

There is an additional reason for being more comfortable with 'rhetoric' rather than 'ideology'. The current social and economic situation of welfare is changing very rapidly and the general context of economic growth is problematic, given the uncertainty surrounding the global economy. Solutions to welfare are likely to be temporary and proximate solutions from a range of options. The notion of 'risk society' (Beck, 1992) is an important addition to the vocabulary of modern society, because it points to the uncertainties of an unregulated, global system. It takes note of the fact that all governments are forced to manage societies that are subject to uncontrollable global economic pressures and that as a result the policy environment is highly contingent. Risks are increasingly global and complex. Neither corporations nor governments can easily control or effectively respond to these rapid global changes. As the problems become more complex, expert opinion becomes more divided and uncertain. Sociologists have argued the modernity as a consequence becomes more reflexive and contested (Giddens, 1990).

Within both government and industry, we live in a world that, as a result of global changes and increasing competitive pressures, is being constantly restructured. Organizational structures tend to be temporary, middle management is subject to constant change and appraisal, and organizational and business mergers are constant features of the business sector. Universities that traditionally were sheltered from such pressures now operate under quasi-market conditions. To meet these new challenges, university mission statements are written, evaluated and rewritten. Organizational fluidity can be seen in this respect as a response to growing social complexity. Institutional contingency is a function of increasing global economic competition, the growing scale and complexity of social problems and social change brought about by constant technological innovation in the electronic information society.

These changes are compounded by the managerial need for control, accountability and transparency. Alongside a risk society, we now have the 'audit society' (Power, 1998). Organizational change and instability have produced a countervailing set of social forces which seek to measure, regulate and control through auditory and accounting mechanisms. Modern societies can be seen in terms of a tension between deregulation (resulting in risky environments) and regulation (resulting in McDonaldization, audits and quality control regimes). The consequence of these contradictory pressures is a hybrid social environment which verges simultaneously on social anomie and authoritarian control (Turner, 1999). Welfare systems are subject to the same pressures and exhibit the same pattern of organizational malaise: constant restructuring and replanning is accompanied by an endless round of managerial inspections, quality audits and measurement of customer satisfaction. Organizational stress and fatigue creates a social context of managerial uncertainty, where organizational leaders are inclined to embrace whatever fashion is currently promoted by academic managerial theory: neo-Taylorism, postmodernism, rational choice theory, just-in-time management, public relations theory and so forth. The malaise produces rhetorics which propose strategically appropriate responses. We argue, therefore, that rhetorics are a function of competing and incommensurable systems of expert knowledge; rhetorics flourish because there is no obvious process of closure. Finally, we prefer to use the notion of rhetoric to discuss the uncertainty of modern welfare systems rather than a concept of the 'postmodern', partly because we believe that the term has been used promiscuously (Leonard, 1997).

It would be an easy but ultimately pointless argument to suggest that all one can do in this situation is to describe the various policy options and simply list the various rhetorical responses. We do want to develop a distinctive position, which is driven by a commitment to active citizenship. In the conclusion of this chapter, we explore a number of welfare scenarios which we attempt to evaluate in terms of policy criteria which are derived from a particular value position that is defined by the contemporary notion of citizenship. In order to present this argument, we need to consider a typology of political theories about citizenship that provides the underlying structure of this study.

A typology of citizenship and political regimes

In order to provide a framework for the analysis of our study of third-sector welfare in Australia, we develop a typology that describes four political regimes. In the social sciences, we can conceptualize social theory as organized around and articulated in terms of four basic concepts, which often stand in dichotomous relationships: state, market, individual and community. It is possible to regard these concepts as the principal building blocks of all social theory. The claim is that any social theory will explicitly or implicitly hold a view as to the empirical and normative connections between these four elements. For example, in classical liberal theory, it is the individual who is privileged over the community or the state. By contrast, communitarianism has attempted to restore the balance between these concepts, arguing amongst other things that only certain versions of individualism (such as utilitarian individualism) are hostile to communal obligations. Similarly, we can conceive versions of market relations that give scope to choice and flexibility in resource distribution without a concomitant basis in profit. These kinds of 'civil' or social market mechanisms will almost certainly be important within any project that seeks to 'democratize social democracy' (see for example Walzer, 1992).

In this introduction, we propose to examine four combinations: (a) individual and state; (b) individual and market; (c) community and state; and (d) market and community. We argue that an exploration of this field of concepts provides us with a distinctive framework for this study and with a normative position with respect to the rhetorics of welfare.

(a) Fascism: individual and state

Some social theories have often regarded the relationship between the individual and the state as fundamental to an understanding of society. Where the individual is regarded as morally corrupt, weak or dangerous to social order, there is a parallel tendency to regard to state as therefore the guardian of civilization and social order. The function of the state is to express the values of the nation, to promote national culture and to regulate or subordinate the individual to this political objective. There are many versions of this type of theory. In this introduction, we shall simply refer to the legacy of Lutheran theology in German political theory. The German Protestant churches in the immediate aftermath of Luther's articles discovered through the peasant wars (Engels, 1956) that unrestrained and uncontrolled interpretations of biblical authority resulted in endless schism and sectarian conflict. Both Lutheran and Calvinistic doctrines of political power came to regard the state as a necessary institution: that is, an institution which had to play a significant role in the moral regulation of the individual in the interests of the public good. We could regard this outcome as one version of the Hobbesian problem of order. Men are rational (but not necessarily moral), and they will tend to argue with each other, producing social (religious) divisions. The state is created as the ultimate and rational arbitration of public debate. In German idealism, this position tended to argue paradoxically that men are free when their actions express the intentions of the state and its laws. Freedom of action is maximized when it is compatible with the laws of the state.

The logical result of this position is authoritarianism, because the implication is that there can be no legitimate opposition to the state. In terms of theories of citizenship, an extreme version of this argument is what we might call 'organic fascism', in which the identity of the individual is completely submerged in the identity of the state. The individual finds their true identity in selfless service of the state, for example through loyalty to a leader. This argument has been expressed in the notion of leader-democracy and found its embodiment in the charismatic leadership of Hitler. Because the state cannot be questioned, it became difficult to argue from the constitution that the Nazi state was not a legitimate political institution (Krieger, 1957). In Max Weber's political theory (Turner, 1989), we find a watered-down version of this argument in his notion of plebiscitary democracy. Through the influence of Roberto Michels' critical theory of mass politics, Weber came to the pessimistic conclusion that a grass-roots democracy is not a viable political solution for a modern state. He was also conscious of the failures of German political leadership after the disastrous outcome of the First World War. As a result he came to the conclusion that democracy was simply a mechanism for selecting a leader with some degree of public legitimacy. However, once in office, an effective leader should not be constrained by any need to consult with the electorate. Bismarck, who had created a powerful and integrated German state through a process of Prussianization, was the obvious example. Two important consequences flow from this tradition. Plebiscitary democracy implies passive not active citizenship, and indeed suggests that the proper arena for moral actions on the part of the individual is in the domestic sphere, especially within the family. The individual citizen is periodically called upon to vote for a leader, but once that task is complete the citizen retires to the private arena to exercise responsibilities within the family as a parent. The private sphere is the place of moral training, but a state is required to police the public domain. In radical Lutheranism, because the individual is ontologically evil, powerful institutions (church, state, and family) are required to train and regulate Man, who has through a misdeed been excluded from the Garden and forced to labour to live. State and family are necessary evils to regulate men. The family is a mechanism for regulating sexual activity as an unfortunate prelude to reproduction. The state regulates the human capacity for violence in the interests of public safety.

The second conclusion is that this theory does not recognize the importance or validity of voluntary associations. Indeed intermediary groups between the individual and state could weaken the undivided authority of the leader. The only intermediary institution which could be recognized was the Party, which in its turn expressed the will of the leader. In Nazi Germany, church groups, working-class organizations and community groups were regarded with suspicion or outright hostility. The Party was the legitimate outlet for youth groups, regional associations and educational institutions, because there was an organic relationship between the Führer, the Party and the state. While we have referred to this position as a fascist theory of individual–state relationships, we fully recognize the irony that it also describes Stalinism. In the Soviet Union, the growth of the Communist Party under the leadership of Stalin meant the destruction of intermediary groups and voluntary associations, because these elements of civil society were eventually absorbed into the Party. Sociologists like Karl Wittfogel recognized a close historical connection between the traditional pattern of Oriental Despotism, as described in Karl Marx's Asiatic Mode of Production, and the growth of Stalinism; both systems were illustrations of 'total power' (Wittfogel, 1957). The quest to rebuild civil society in post-communist Europe and Russia has involved for democratic reformers an attempt to recreate voluntary associations which might stand between the individual and the state.

(b) Liberalism: individual and market

Classical liberalism also recognized the centrality of the individual to political thought, but placed the individual in the market as the arena within which true freedom and individuality could be realized. There are of course many versions of this coupling of individual and market. In his influential study of 'possessive individualism', C. B. Macpherson (1962) provides an economic interpretation of Hobbesian contract theory. With the growth of private property and capitalism, there is a clash of interests between owners and workers over the benefits of production and exchange. Capitalism encourages the growth of a particular type of individualism, namely possessive individualism. It is also a very unstable society, because there is the constant possibility of conflict over economic interest which threatens the economic conditions for profitability. Hobbes' original social contract theory was an early attempt to work out how social conflict could be avoided in a society, where in the market there was an inevitable contradiction between (emerging) classes, namely between the bourgeoisie and the proletariat. Hobbes can be reinterpreted from this vantage point as arguing that the state of nature (class warfare) can be managed through a social contract, whereby the state will secure social peace.

In this tradition, individual freedoms and liberties are functions of the market-place. The growth of exchange relationships and the money market were the preconditions for notions of the individual, contract and rights (Goldmann, 1973). Freedom of exchange, assembly and speech are individual rights which emerge out of the requirements of a free and unregulated market. There is thus a parallel between market requirements for uninterrupted trade and political notions about the liberties of association. The right to buy a commodity requires consumer sovereignty and in liberal theory the individual is seen as a sovereign (over his own private world) (Abercrombie, Hill and Turner, 1986). Marxist critics have challenged liberalism on exactly these grounds of the necessary link between political individualism and private property. It is claimed by its critics that liberalism disguises the inequalities of the market-place behind an ideology of free individuals and exchange. Critics claim that effective individual freedom can only be exercised by persons with property, and that the exploitative relations of production results in an alienation of the worker that rules out the effective pursuit of individual happiness. Sociologists (Parsons, 1937) have also demonstrated that utilitarianism cannot provide an adequate account of the Hobbesian dilemma of social order, because rational individuals will use force and fraud to achieve their ends. In short, what is to prevent utilitarian individuals resorting to criminal activity to satisfy their wants in the market? The dilemma for liberalism is that, when markets are deregulated, egoistic actions by free individuals will, other things being equal, increase inequality and thus magnify conflicts of interests. Individuals will, if they are rational, seek to secure a monopolistic advantage, which has the negative effect of destroying pure market conditions. There is also the threat that criminal activities will prove to be a rational response to scarcities. Given a global demand for drugs, free markets will encourage (or at least not discourage) illegal organization of production and distribution. Given an individual demand for longevity, markets will emerge to satisfy consumer demand through the sale of body parts, if not whole bodies.

Liberalism, like fascism, has a notion that the individual is driven by selfish and hedonistic desires. While fascism responds to this issue by the creation of a powerful state (and state apparatus such as the Party), liberalism believes that the market can solve difficulties in social relationships, by allowing the market to determine value. For radical liberals, the only answer to the question 'what is the value of X?' is 'Let the market decide!' Given a need for kidney transplants, liberals would argue that the value of a kidney is what an individual might pay for one in an open, global market. The logic of the situation is of course to drive down the price of a kidney by encouraging a sick person in Europe to purchase the kidney of a well but poor person in India. A radical liberal committed to free markets following the philosophy of Bentham's felicific principle would argue that such an exchange increases happiness, because the sick person gets better and the poor person gets richer. A corollary is that state intervention in this exchange relationship will reduce happiness, because the state as a third party can never be sensitive to local or specific needs. State planning of kidney production could only end in misery.

Two consequences follow from this argument. The first is that classical liberalism has a rather 'thin' theory of the individual. It is not interested in individuality and creativity, but in a robust vision of the individual driven by need to exchange in the market place. Classical liberalism was not out of principle interested in the education or cultivation of the individual. Its original vision was that of Defoe in his account of the adventures of Robinson Crusoe – the isolated individual already equipped with a language and psychology. In this theory, society is only a collection of isolated individuals, whose interrelationships are purely economic. Robinson Crusoe had a weak sense of obligation towards other human beings. Man Friday had value only in so far as he satisfied Crusoe's needs. The second consequence is that liberalism has no necessary theory of voluntary associations or intermediary groups. Liberalism has no necessary vision of the market-place structured by associations or intermediary groups. It was on these grounds that Emile Durkheim (1957) attacked Spencerian individualism in *Professional Ethics and Civic Morals*. Durkheim's whole sociology can be read as an attack on utilitarian individualism, because he did not believe that the division of labour was increasing happiness, he rejected the hedonistic interpretation of motivation, and argued that society produces individuals and not the other way round. As we will see in Chapter 3, Durkheim made an important contribution to the theory of voluntary associations as necessary linkages between individual and society.

There are two corresponding problems for classical liberalism. J. S. Mill himself came to the conclusion that, as a matter of fact, the utilitarianism of his father and Bentham did not increase his personal happiness. Because utilitarianism did not have a strong sense of the difference between material and spiritual happiness, it could not differentiate between poetry and a large plate of potatoes. Indeed Bentham once said that 'pushpin is as good as poetry' – that is, you cannot decide what the value of a potato and poetry is outside market exchange. Secondly, it had a very thin vision of society as merely a floating network of events of exchange in the market-place. Because force and fraud are always rational responses to market scarcity, liberalism has no consistent response to the problem of non-legal and illegal manipulation of the market. In fact it produced a powerful regulatory response to crime through Bentham's notion of the Panoptic – a cost-effective scheme of prison reform whereby a single guard can control a large body of prison inmates. As Michel Foucault (1975) has argued, panoptic regulation became a fundamental principle of coercive regulation in liberal capitalism. Behind the unstable quasi-social relationships of the market between sovereign individuals, there is the backcloth of micro-surveillance and control. Contemporary debates about the benefits or otherwise of legalizing drug use in the case of heroin reproduce many of these classical dilemmas. The pristine liberal instinct is to treat heroin as simply a commodity for which there is strong demand, and therefore its price is artificially inflated by government restrictions on supply. Liberalization of the market would improve the quality of heroin on the streets and undermine rackets and the black market.

(c) Social democracy: state and community

We shall next consider those theories which are particularly concerned with the relationship between the state and the community sector.

Again there are a variety of such theoretical positions, but here we shall discuss social democracy and associative democracy. In the Scandinavian[1] model of welfare, for example, there is a clear notion that the state should be heavily involved in the planning and regulation of welfare. These models of the welfare state involved a top-down structure of coordination and provision of the community rather than the individual. Such social democratic models of welfare have, however, been differentiated from centralized communism by the fact that independent political parties continued to exist and function in the Scandinavian social democracies, and community groups were neither suppressed nor wholly incorporated into the state. Although the church in Sweden was very closely connected to the state, it remained a separate and distinctive institution.

We may nevertheless notice two rather important issues about the role of community in the Scandinavian social democratic model. First, precisely because the state has played a leading and dominant role in the organization of welfare (which can be traced back as least as far as the last century (Lundstrom and Wijkstrom, 1997: 252)) it is not entirely clear how important voluntary associations are in civil society. There has been some debate in the sociological literature on the existence and extent of the third sector. As we will see in Chapter 3, some sociologists (Boli, 1991) have criticiszed the view that Sweden has a robust third sector on the grounds that Swedish voluntary associations are so dependent on the state that they cannot be regarded as independent; while others claim that these conclusions are the result of the inappropriate application of non-Swedish models of non-profit systems (Lundstrom and Wijkstrom, 1997: 237–8). What we might call the 'strong theory' of social democracy tends to deny the importance of voluntary associations in the community, because it regards the state as the proper provider of welfare benefits. The strong version recognizes the fact that only a centralized system can achieve a universalistic norm of egalitarian provision.

The second and related issue is that, as a result, social democratic theory tends to have an undifferentiated view of 'the community'. Thus, in Scandinavian political culture, 'community' is not necessarily a differentiated collection of community groups, institutions, associations and social movements. It is very closely connected with an emotional and solidaristic notion of *gemeinschaft*; community-based organizations are sentimental groups which function as substitutes for local extended families. In short, the community, which is an emotional social unity, absorbs separate groups and associations (including interest groups and others from the tradition of popular mass movements), and thus provides individuals with a powerful sense of social membership. Social democracy worked by orchestrating the social relations between the state and these *gemeinschaftlich* groups. These communal ties in contemporary Sweden have in recent years been challenged by migration and multicultural pressures on the one hand, and by economic decline and globalization on the other. The assassination of the Swedish Prime Minister, Olaf Palme, in 1986 was in many ways a watershed event and a pointer to the social changes which have begun to push against and transformed the traditional foundations of Swedish social democracy.

However, Sweden has in our view retained a sense of nation-as-community which is quite unlike that in the United Kingdom. This issue is illustrated by, for example, the problems of integrating Muslim communities and Islamic institutions into the emotive or sentimental national community, where the communal bonds have a distinctively religious flavour (Kamali, 1997). The Swedish community is much closer to Durkheim's notion of 'mechanical solidarity' (Durkheim, 1947), because it is traditionally at least an undifferentiated and unitary community. Therefore, in the Scandinavian case, there is a sense in which, while there is a clear separation between community and state, there is no political space for genuine pluralism. Both 'individual' and 'group' are thoroughly absorbed into national community, the leadership of which is the state.

Associative democracy theory offers a pluralistic alternative to social democracy. It has a distinctively English tradition, and an influential contribution to a pluralistic version of this democratic theory has been presented by Paul Q. Hirst, who has in *The Pluralist Theory of the State* (1993) and *Representative Democracy and its Limits* (1990) developed early democratic theories from the work of G. D. H. Cole, J. N. Figgis and H. J. Laski. These elements have been more fully expressed as a theory of associative democracy in *Associative Democracy: New Forms of Economic and Social Governance* (Hirst, 1994) and *From Statism to Pluralism: Democracy, Civil Society and Global Politics* (Hirst, 1997). In Britain, the interest in pluralist associations in the post-war period grew out of a recognition of the importance of intermediary groups in combating the growth of electoral dictatorship. For Hirst, the health of a modern democracy depends on the presence of a plurality of self-governing associations, voluntary associations and communal groups. These groups and associations are clearly outside the state. In addition, these groups are important in the functioning of a principle of subsidiary, by which leadership operates at the lowest possible level of communal organization. Hirst recognizes that there must be deliberate political initiatives by the state to support such groups, for example through economic subsidies and a favourable legal environment aimed at decentralizing welfare and public services but at the same time maintaining common minimum standards and entitlements. The state is important in providing an enabling environment within which a vigorous civil society can recover from the negative consequences of Thatcherite policies of economic liberalization.

The associative democracy debate in Britain had its intellectual and political location in the problems presented by an 'electoral dictatorship', which emerged during the Thatcher years when there appeared to be no effective political opposition to the social and economic policies of a determined leader with a precarious majority in the Commons. Thatcher's critics believed that the normal processes of parliamentary democracy could not contain or caution an ideologically driven cabinet, and pluralism was seen to be important to protect the community from an elected government which was committed to a range of controversial policies such as 'rolling back the state' and market liberalization. Associative democracy (also referred to by Hirst as associationalism) was conceptualized as a political response to an erosion of the institutional framework of strong opposition. It was elaborated to include stronger notions of participation, but it was initially a defensive response. Hirst's associative democracy thesis is a self-consciously 'piecemeal' attempt to rethink the current problems of social democracy and to offer policy solutions. Intrinsic to this project is the juxtaposition of the divergent tendencies inherent in state and market, the favouring of either resulting in a different path. On the one hand it can be read as a kind of state-bounded associationalism (as we have done above), and on the other, through the granting of serious consideration to market-like mechanisms of distribution, as leading ultimately to a situation of social market associationalism.

In this discussion of the theory of associative democracy, we would argue that it is particularly important to remain sensitive to significant historical and cultural differences between societies. These differences can be illustrated by a comparison of the Swedish and English notions of 'community'. In Great Britain, the idea of a national community has always been fragmented by a divided kingdom and thus the United Kingdom has been primarily held together by monarchy as expressed through parliamentary institutions. Within the framework of a constitution which has always represented an historical compromise, the national society has not been integrated around such symbolic systems as a national religion. In cultural terms, the various components of the kingdom have remained separate and distinct. In Scotland, for example, the Presbyterian Church's annual meetings have historically functioned as a quasi-parliamentary association. Furthermore, 'community' has often functioned as the solidaristic end of social class relationships, providing class with a local and thus communal dimension. The classic sociological studies of economic class in Britain have recognized this critical cultural dimension of the class structure: for instance, *Coal is Our Life* or *The Uses of Literacy* (Hoggart, 1957), or *The Making of the English Working Class* (Thompson, 1963). 'Class consciousness' in British social history has always in reality been 'community consciousness'. Unlike Scandinavian communities, England has been a pluralist society in being constituted by an ensemble of different, separate and often conflictual communities. These communities have often been regional, local and class based. They have been combative associations to protect workers or regions or religious denominations from the state. Indeed the whole conception of community in the English critical tradition has stressed the importance of sustaining the autonomy of community against a capitalist state, and this survival depends upon preserving local class cultures. The apex of this critical tradition was *Culture and Society (1780–1950)* (Williams, 1963).

Alongside these cultural differences, there are important historical contrasts between Britain and Sweden in terms of class formation. While Britain in many respects remains the classic illustration of the formation of a capitalist society based on conflicting classes (Dahrendorf, 1959), capitalism in Sweden was developed by small paternalistic enterprises in which the social and cultural cleavage between owners and workers was muted by both physical proximity and social ties. Social citizenship in Britain, as T. H. Marshall's theory (1965) postulates, can only be understood against a background of class conflict and political compromise. In Sweden, citizenship was not fundamentally connected to either class conflict or warfare.

There are various difficulties with Hirst's version of associative democracy read as state-bounded associationalism, which we return to in Chapter 2. The first issue concerns the relationship between the state and plural communities. Whereas social democratic theory presupposes a unified community, the British notion of plural communities assumes a relatively high level of communal competition and conflict. As Max Weber recognized, there will be a degree of social closure in competitive situations where there is scarcity. The question then becomes how these communities can be regulated to achieve communal outcomes. It is the role of the state to insure a secure legal framework within which there can be socially beneficial competition for resources rather than social conflict. The more voluntary associations become dependent on the state through tax benefits, cash payments or administrative services, the less they function as independent forces in civil society. In Britain, it is clear that the voluntary sector is very dependent on government support (Kendall and Knapp, 1996). This criticism has been argued forcefully by those political theorists who entertain the doubt that state power can be diminished by a greater reliance on voluntary associations. Against Hirst, there is the view that 'the attempt to enhance the role of voluntary associations does not result in a diminution of the authority of the state; it merely relocates it' (Runciman, 1997: 264). The second problem is that Hirstian pluralism does not necessarily have an adequate account of the economics of welfare. A competition between communities and associations for welfare benefits might promote a spiral of rising claims and expectations resulting in inflationary demands on governments. This struggle between communal groups produces sectional competition, which encourages political parties to promise welfare measures which they cannot easily honour once in power; the result is a mixture of inflationary and ineffective social policies, and disillusioned and alienated electorates (Turner, 1989). Pluralism may be a solution to certain difficulties in parliamentary democracy, but it is not necessarily a solution to the economic and demographic issues which are behind the search for better economic solutions to welfare provision in industrial democracies. Thirdly, there are inherent problems in the construction of what we might call associationalism-in-one-country. Though Hirst argues that globalization is an overplayed concept (Hirst, 1996), the actual effects that global economic forces would have on the proposed quasi-markets of associationalism remain a hypothetical but troubling question. Lastly, there is little in the way of contemporary empirical examples within these schemata. Indeed, of those we are given, the example of Italian governance provided by Hirst appears over the period of the 1990s to undermine the overall conception (Hirst, 1997).

(d) Social market associationalism: market and community

In both Australia and Britain, political ideology and financial necessity have conditioned the quest for alternative methods of funding welfare. The Thatcher and Major governments were obviously committed ideologically to reducing what they regarded as welfare dependency in order to stimulate the economy by reducing personal taxation and state expenditure (O'Brien and Penna, 1998). The 'Nanny state' was seen to be part of a Labour legacy of welfare bureaucracy and high taxation. A similar ideological position has been taken in Australia by the Howard government in the post-Keating liberalization of the economic environment. These governments have assumed that broadly speaking market strategies can be applied to welfare provision in order to achieve economies. These changes to welfare expenditure in Australia have occurred against the background of a declining economy, a falling dollar, weak exports, a greying population and global uncertainty. In the light of fundamental and continuing workplace and global economic changes, upon which the approaches of statism and then corporatism have foundered, claims made by the government that Australia cannot afford to continue with traditional welfare policies which require significant government expenditure have a certain immediacy and commonsense validity. Following a conventional political strategy, the new Liberal government in Australia could point to the size of the national debt and the growing imbalance between imports and exports as evidence of Labor mismanagement and the need for economies in public expenditure.

Of course, the main problem with constraining public expenditure on welfare, health and education is that the marketization of welfare delivery must, other things being constant, increase social inequality. Electoral alienation will eventually force a government to modify its overt commitment to economic rationalism in order to secure its re-election. Despite the classic contradictions of the 'legitimation crisis' (Habermas, 1976), markets can potentially play an important and positive role in society and in the delivery of welfare in particular, provided there are a variety of protective and supportive mechanisms in place to offset the inevitable trend towards greater social inequality and alienation. It is here that voluntary associations can play an important role. Obviously voluntary welfare groups can in principle supplement or even replace government functions in service delivery, and in that sense voluntary associations can step in to fill the gap left created by deregulation and privatization. The emphasis here is on building a cooperatively based 'social market associationalism' which stresses elements of market mechanism flexibility and choice (but without the basis in profit). In so doing, we seek to highlight the market trajectory of associationalism as opposed to the state trajectory. The arguments against the role of voluntary associations in this area are of course obvious. Voluntary associations cannot guarantee equality of service provision and, where such associations are dependent on unpaid (female) labour, voluntary workers will be exploited. Voluntary associations can also become the 'casualty wards' of the welfare state for individuals who cannot afford private care and cannot access public services. In this capacity, voluntary associations would disguise the inadequacies of government policy, by providing some minimal support for marginalized and deprived social groups. They would indirectly contribute to the legitimization of social inequality in capitalist societies and also protect governments from appropriate political criticism (Roelofs, 1995).

While the negative consequences of profit-centred marketization are well known, traditional welfare agencies have tended to become remote and bureaucratic, accused often of being insensitive to client needs. It is here that the more flexible mechanisms of markets could have a useful role to play in welfare distribution provided that sufficient checks and balances were in place to prevent or offset negative tendencies. Whereas bureaucracies will deliver according to predetermined plans, markets ideally adjust to shifting needs and tend to impose certain disciplines by the usual demand and supply regulators. Failure to honour contractual obligations will reduce trust and confidence, thereby encouraging clients to shift to other suppliers.

Within this ideal typical framework (and as Hirst points out), versions of 'civic' or 'social' markets become a necessary precondition for associative democracy, encouraging the development of subsidiarity and sensitivity to local needs and preferences. Markets would not necessarily destroy communities, provided there is a legal regulatory framework which would provide certain minimal guarantees about equality of provision for minority or dependent groups. However, our view of the importance of voluntary associations is political and social, rather than economic and financial. From a political and sociological point of view, our interest in such intermediary groups is driven by a concern for their potential contribution to the vitality of civil society, to the development of democratic institutions, and to the fostering of compassion, altruism and civic virtue. Voluntary associations can provide opportunities for the growth of active citizenship and civil participation. Voluntary associations can function as schools of democracy, because they offer an experience of or potential for training in the basic procedures of democratic governance. The classic example from British social history is the role of Methodist lay preaching and Bible classes which provided working men with training in literacy, public speaking, and lay leadership (Semmel, 1973). Some degree of 'civic' or social marketization and deregulation of provision would be compatible with active citizenship and community involvement. This pattern of delivery, which would require partnerships between government, community and the market, would be an alternative to top-down bureaucratic welfare on the one hand, and different from a neo-liberal model of possessive individualism on the other.

Australia, citizenship and associationalism

Most of the empirical examples in our discussion of the typology of citizenship and political regimes have been taken from Europe and North America. Before turning to our conclusion, we introduce a brief discussion of how Australia fits into our model. The point of these comments is to note obviously that Australia has been characterized by changing relationships between state, individual, market and community. The major historical peculiarity of Australia as a nation state was that the existence of the state preceded the creation of a civil society. In the early decades of colonization between 1788 and 1821, Australia was settled through the imperialistic intervention of the British state by convicts. With the loss of its American colonies, British governments looked towards south-east Asia and then Australia as a solution to their prison problems. Australia is the classic case of a society within which the individual was regarded as dangerous and corrupt, and thus in need of correction and reform. Colonial Australia was a Benthamite experiment in which, through the moral intervention of the state, a panoptic transformation of individuals became possible (Collins, 1985). Women were seen to have a major role to play in the moral regulation of a frontier society (Summers, 1975). In this early period, the main function of the state was to guarantee the supply of cheap labour.

Australia was quickly transformed into a capitalist white society through the Wakefield scheme and settlement by free men, who came to Australia to mine for gold, create sheep stations and settle the land (McMichael, 1984). Population expansion followed the discovery of gold fields in Victoria in the 1850s, but the settlement of the land eventually came to depend on squatters. The society was to be transformed through possessive individualism to create a free market in primary commodities. Despite the egalitarian flavour of pastoralist slogans ('Every man a vote, a rifle and a farm'), the Eureka stockade was an important illustration of growing individualism and hostility to state taxation rather than the foundations of a socialist revolt against the British state. Australia developed all the principal characteristics of dependent settler capitalism, with striking parallels with Argentina (Duncan and Fogarty, 1984). The state has remained crucial to economic growth, despite the criticisms of neo-liberal politicians. The aridity of the climate, dependence on migration, internal communication problems and the tyranny of distance have meant that the economy continues to depend on state intervention. Australian capitalism has been, through much of the twentieth century, a regulated economy by comparison with the United States. In Australia, industrial disputes, conflicts and wage settlement took place within the legal framework of national and compulsory arbitration. However, with the decline of British influence, Australia has moved closer to the United States as a capitalist system with an increasing emphasis on removing import taxes and controls, reducing farming subsidies, deregulating the banking and financial systems, forcing universities to raise more revenue and selling off public utilities.

With the growth of multiculturalism following the close of the white Australia policy with mass migration between 1948 and 1983, the voluntary sector played a major part in the assimilation of migrant communities. Although the state has been the dominant institution in Australian history, civil society has grown around the diversity of secular and religious associations catering to ethnic identity and migrant needs. With these transformations of the basis of Australian society, there has been an evolution of the concept of citizen to become a more inclusive concept (Davidson, 1997). However, the constitution has yet to accept the basic principle of one vote and one value, and the aboriginal community in particular is in effect excluded from 'the national family'. While migrant voluntary associations have played an important part in cultural and economic assimilation, they have also been manipulated by the political parties in the interests of electoral politics.

In conclusion, Australian society initially was created by the state, which played an essential role during the early stages of colonization. Economic growth has produced a dominant tradition of individualism and, more recently, of free enterprise. Although the primary legal and governmental framework of Australia is taken from English common law traditions, agrarian settlement created a sense of community which was to some extent defined by opposition to aboriginal occupancy of the land. The notion of community in Australia is partly defined by class communities, by ethnic pluralism and by a racial notion of Otherness which embraces both Asian and Aboriginal peoples. Because the state in recent years has been rolled back from education, economy, housing and welfare, the voluntary association sector has been expanding to fill the gap. How effective and significant that development has been in the late twentieth century is the topic of this book.

Conclusion: welfare, rhetorics and scenarios

While we remain optimistic that voluntary associations can play a crucial role in fostering active citizenship and consolidating civil society, we also recognize countervailing tendencies which will contain the emancipatory potential of these associations. We can expect the global economic pressures on national states to continue over the next decade as the financial crises of Asia, Russia and Latin America slow the growth of the global economy. Voluntary associations are likely to continue to function in economic environments which place significant demands for enhanced performance on a range of social institutions.

Within this mix of welfare rhetorics, existing frameworks, and mechanisms, it is possible to generalize and to pose seven scenarios, each of which would have different consequences for voluntary associations:

1. Competitive contracturalism

Here we would see the persistence of the current fashion for contracturalism compelling voluntary associations to operate under the sphere of the state like commercial agencies and their management to behave more like entrepreneurs.

2. Marginalization

The pressures and principles (especially the idea of 'user pays') inherent in competitive contracturalism regimes may not be compatible with the communitarian, altruistic and voluntaristic ethos of the sector. Voluntary associations which fail to find a path through this may find that they are merely the residual agencies for marginal groups – the deprived and forgotten populations of the elderly, the disabled and the unemployed. If the large mass of voluntary associations were affected thus, we would be looking at a scenario of the marginalization of the sector.

3. Bifurcation

While some voluntary associations are marginalized under competitive contracturalism, others adapt and survive, effectively splitting the sector in two with both parts travelling in different directions – one to the periphery and the other to the centre of social and economic planning.

4. Marketization

Further removal of state responsibilities for welfare cast voluntary associations into competitive profit-based market situations. Those associations that can adapt, find a niche, and remain profitable, survive; whereas others are replaced by market-driven enterprises attracted by the potential for profits in welfare fields such as childcare and aged care.

5. Statism

The development or reinstatement of centralized state planning and control of welfare. This would almost certainly require changed and/or higher taxation regimes. The role of voluntary associations would be reduced and become 'reactive' in providing for needs unmet or unrecognized by the bureaucratic systems of administration.

6. State-bounded associationalism

A move towards associative democracy where state control over welfare administration remains relatively high. Voluntary associations would become more central in the delivery of welfare operating in quasi-markets largely controlled by the state.

7. Social market associationalism

A form of associative democracy in which 'civil' markets develop to become the primary mechanism of welfare distribution. An 'enabling' state grants voluntary associations high levels of autonomy to develop the most effective forms of needs assessment and administration.

The following chapters address in more detail some of the issues raised here. In Chapter 9 we return to the idea of welfare futures in the light of the whole discussion and make more structured suggestions about the likely developments of welfare and the roles to be played by voluntary associations.

Note

1   Though Swedish examples are used here, the Scandinavian model is based upon the development of post-1945 welfare systems in Denmark, Norway and Sweden. Arguably, this model of a social democratic welfare state can be extended to a Nordic model with the inclusion of Finland and Iceland.

2
Civil Society and Citizenship

Introduction: theories of capitalist crisis

Throughout the 1960s and 1970s, there was a widespread assumption in the social sciences that industrial capitalism, both as an economic system and as a civilization, was in a deep and irreversible crisis. Social critics such as James O'Connor (1973), Jürgen Habermas (1976) and Claus Offe (1976) claimed that there was a fiscal crisis in capitalism resulting from the irreconcilable tensions between the capitalist need for economic accumulation and the political constraints of liberal democracy, especially as democratic claims on the state were expressed through the provision of welfare services. In response to the problems of legitimacy, there were political pressures on democratic governments, which produced large and inflexible welfare bureaucracies, which were seen to be inefficient and unresponsive to client needs. In order to contain the fiscal crisis, the state constantly expanded to resolve the economic difficulties of faltering economies and to constrain what Daniel Bell (1976) called, in his notion of the public household, 'the revolution of rising entitlements'. Habermas's view of the 'legitimation crisis' (Habermas, 1976) of the state, while paying some recognition to the importance of culture, had an obviously economistic flavour. Given the competition between capitalist enterprises, the tendency of the rate of profit to fall created an economic crisis within which the state exercised the role of policeman. The paradox was that state interventions in the economy necessarily undermined the long-term capacity of private capitalist enterprises to increase profitability, because taxation was a burden on both production and consumption. There was an inevitable tendency to extend public ownership, because capitalists were reluctant to invest in large infrastructure projects (such as building sewerage systems) where profit margins were low. The result was an increasingly bureaucratized social world which was highly regulated, and an economy which was seen to be sluggish and geriatric. Bell's notion of 'the cultural contradictions of capitalism' placed a greater emphasis on the tensions between hedonistic consumerism in which the desire to consume was transformed into a right or entitlement, and the ascetic requirements of capitalist discipline in the workplace.

By the late 1970s, a wide variety of social commentators had identified the welfare state as a burden on the continuous growth of a vibrant industrial democracy. From the perspective of Althusserian Marxism, the welfare state was part of the so-called 'ideological state apparatus' which helped to secure the political hegemony of the dominant class through various concessions to the demands of the working class (Althusser, 1984). Sociology in this period became obsessed by the problem of the existence of a 'dominant ideology' (Abercrombie, Hill and Turner, 1980), because it was assumed that the survival of capitalism in a period of fiscal crisis required a coherent and common ideology. Other conservative critics, from liberalism to the far right, attacked the centralized welfare state, because it undermined the independence and autonomy of the individual. Robert Nozick (1974) provided a controversial rereading of liberal theory to defend individual liberties on the basis of individual property rights. Nozick's defence of individual sovereignty required a minimalistic state to provide safeguards for individual freedoms. This neo-liberal promotion of the market-place as the engine of private freedoms was in some respects a return to the doctrine of J. S. Mill in which capitalism makes the individual sovereign (Abercrombie, Hill and Turner, 1986).

In the United States, a group of social scientists associated with *The Public Interest*, which was launched in the mid-1960s by Daniel Bell and Irving Kristol, came to argue that the welfare state actually undermined the capacity of marginalized groups to respond effectively to social change. Of course, the United States had never had a comprehensive welfare state funded out of universal, compulsory taxation, and socialism had never emerged as a mass political movement. A classical welfare democracy had never been accepted as an objective of social policy. Social modifications of the free market came under attack from sociologists like Nathan Glazer, who attempted to show that welfare benefits and tax thresholds for young black single parents, typically female, prevented them from entering the labour market and forced them into a lifetime of dependency. Followers of Leo Strauss, especially the so-called East Coast Straussians who include Allan Bloom and

Thomas Prangle, saw liberalism itself as the enemy of moral society and a strong state (Drury, 1988; Orr, 1995). Strauss's criticism of American liberalism as a modern version of the Weimar Republic was taken up by Chief Justice Clarence Thomas and Newt Gingrich to redesign the republican perspective on American society. For Strauss, mass democracy created a society in which moral and responsible leadership became difficult, if not impossible. Mass democratic society engendered the sociopolitical conditions which, through weak and ineffective leadership, allowed Hitler and the National Socialists to gain control of Germany.

There was therefore in the late 1970s an ironic convergence of right-wing and left-wing criticism of the welfare system, which embraced liberal capitalism, mass democracy and bureaucratic welfare. For right-wing economists, the welfare state threatened the profitability of industry; for left-wing social critics, welfare capitalism was a contradiction in terms, which could not radically transform the basic conditions of capitalist production systems and at the same time subordinated the working class under a paternalistic, disciplinary bureaucracy. Welfare capitalism was basically a strategy of political reformism, which could radically transform the fundamental problems of capitalism as a system of exploitation.

Since the publication of Habermas's *Legitimation Crisis* in Germany in 1973, there have been three major developments which have transformed this debate and its associated politics. The first was an unanticipated conversion of governments (of almost all political persuasions) to free market principles, or 'Reagonomics' as it came to be known. In Britain, the Thatcher years witnessed a concerted attempt to roll back the state, contain expenditure on welfare and promote a new culture of enterprise. The welfare system was criticized as an albatross around the neck of the entrepreneurs who were the real wealth creators in the system. In New Zealand, there were radical experiments in economic reform and social policy, which removed the subsidies which historically had been the bedrock of agricultural production and economic wealth. In Australia, the ineluctable encroachment of economic rationalists into the ranks of the Canberra public service bureaucracy guaranteed the triumph of market principles in all branches of government and administration. By the 1980s, governments were reluctant to undertake large expenditures on public utilities where these required considerable investment and higher taxation. It became increasingly difficult for governments to win popular elections on the basis of a political platform requiring increases in taxation to improve 'inefficient' public goods like sewerage works or gas facilities. The solution, adopted with gusto by the Kennett government of Victoria, was to sell off ageing public utilities at relatively low cost to multinationals who are able to increase costs to customers and to rationalize supply outside the confines of democratic accountability.

Obviously this neo-liberal and managerialist revolution covered many different, and frequently contradictory, developments, but in broad terms these political and policy changes included in the 1980s a significant departure from the economic policies of social Keynesianism, including a governmental commitment to the target of full employment and state-driven investment as an instrument for managing recession, especially large-scale and permanent unemployment. It also involved the privatization of state utilities, reduction in centralized welfare provision and the removal of trade restrictions such as import duties and quotas. There was also an attempt to create internal markets or quasi-markets to discipline welfare services and increase the efficiency of public utilities. It required the growth of contractualism as a mechanism of public regulation, and a profound deregulation of society by the removal of state support for controls such as food inspection.

There are clearly tensions in these developments, because the emphasis on managerialism (such as the imposition of auditing schemes and accounting techniques to ensure contractual responsibilities) is not necessarily compatible with, for example the Thatcherite emphasis on rolling back the state and the liberation of market destructiveness. The Thatcher government's decision to sell off council houses was not an act of economic rationalism; it was largely ideological and its economic benefits were short term. The appeal of managerialism is tied up with notions of increased autonomy and initiative, efficiency, enterprise and accountability. It secures legitimacy by the rhetoric of subsidiarity and responsiveness to client needs. But managerialism also exists in an auditing environment, which requires detailed regulation and control of operations and functions.

These contradictions between market freedom and social regulation are nicely represented in the popularity of two influential sociological publications whose titles describe the two poles of these contradictory developments, namely *Risk Society* (Beck, 1992) and *The Audit Society* (Power, 1998). By the late 1980s, the Schumpeterian vision of the death of entrepreneurship at the hands of the tax state had been replaced in most societies by the promise of endless consumerism based on low personal taxation, the credit card, the enterprise culture, privatized welfare and market efficiency. It appeared that the 'Nanny State', which protected us from cradle to grave, had given way to what in retrospect we might call 'cowboy capitalism', whose frontier was the ever-expanding world of personal credit and electronic shopping. The concept of risk society attempts to grasp the social consequences of a deregulated social environment where the dangers of global pollution from unregulated market forces are a necessary feature of the process of modernization. At the same time, because risk has been globalized, governments and corporations attempt to insure themselves against over-exposure by new mechanisms of social control, including auditing, managerial accountability, corporate citizenship, quality control and devolved responsibility (as a version of subsidiarity). Both risk and regulation are fundamental, but contradictory, aspects of contemporary social structure.

The second transformation has been the collapse of organized communism, the fall of the Soviet system and the rapid transformation of Eastern Europe into a hinterland of the German economy. Basically the speed of this transformation took everybody by surprise, and ironically probably only Talcott Parsons, in some relatively obscure articles on communism and democracy in the early 1960s, anticipated some of these political developments (Robertson and Turner, 1995). The implosion of the Soviet empire around 1989–92 produced a new triumphalist literature in the West, as expressed by writers like Francis Fukuyama (1992) in *The End of History and the Last Man*. Obviously this triumphalism was somewhat short lived, because it was immediately evident that, without the presence of the Soviet army, much of the political stability of eastern Europe would soon be eroded. The collapse of Yugoslavia, tensions in Czechoslovakia, ethnic conflicts in Russia, and the continuing religious and ethnic conflicts in Afghanistan demonstrated the fragility of the post-communist global order. The tragic processes of 'ethnic cleansing' underlined the problems of securing political security in the euphoric world of liberal capitalism. West Germany's attempt to embrace East Germany produced a significant increase in youth unemployment as the archaic industrial base of communism became obsolete under competitive economic pressure from the West. One consequence has been an increase in ethnic tensions as unemployed youth embraced the fascist politics of the extreme right. In eastern Europe and Russia, fundamentalist Islam has also grown in response to the collapse of the communist party system, where Islam appears to present the only alternative to Western capitalism. In addition, by 1998 the risks of global capitalism had become evident in the Asian meltdown, the financial crisis in the world banking systems, and the consequence political tensions in Indonesia, South Korea and Malaysia. By 1998, New Zealand, where deregulation had been imposed most radically in the 1980s, declared itself to be techni-cally in recession.

The third major change to contemporary society has therefore been globalization. Of course, the capitalist economy has been a world econ-omy since at least the second half of the seventeenth century, and we are familiar with the notion of multinational corporations as major agents within the internationalization of trade. However, we can see globaliza-tion as a stage beyond internationalization, because it involves the emer-gence of corporations which have no specific national base, and financial and economic arrangements which have no specifically national charac-teristics. Furthermore, contemporary globalization requires the contain-ment, if not erosion, of national political sovereignty. Industrial pro-duction, commercial and insurance arrangements, and the mobility of labour through various forms of migration do not require, and may be inhibited by, national regulation by local governments. Globalization in these terms has resulted in considerable instability in global markets as the financial, trading and productive systems become deregulated. We can see for example that since the late 1970s global financial markets are increasingly out of control and current financial speculation in Asian and Australian money markets has no functional relationship to the cap-italist needs for trade and production. Following Beck's notion of risk society, global tourism, global transport and global consumerism con-tinue to undermine national economies and nation-states. As we have argued, the result has been increasing racial tension in the former East Germany, in rural France, in the youth cultures of Japan and in Australia, because labour movements appear to threaten nationalistic conceptions of citizenship. The political problems of globalized cowboy capitalism have resulted culturally in a strange mixture of global cultures which are synthetic and simulated, and local cultures which are highly resistant to global incorporation. Globalization involves the destruction of local cul-tures, the reproduction of local cultures through the heritage industry and the emergence of hybrid forms of cultural synthesis. 'Globalization' attempts to express these three processes in a single concept.

In retrospect, we can now perceive that these world-wide transforma-tions were a consequence of a crisis of monopoly capitalism, but they produced a much more profound crisis, namely a crisis of civil society. Deregulation, restructuring and managerialism are obviously strategies to revive economic growth, to increase profitability and to restore busi-ness confidence, but they produce difficulties in civil society (such as youth unemployment, white-collar crimes, and an erosion of civil values) for which economic rationalism has no obvious solutions. For example, the International Monetary Fund appears to have only one strategy to manage economic crises in Indonesia, Russia or Thailand, which is to reduce inflation by cutting back state involvement in industrial investment, to remove subsidies, to deregulate local markets and to limit the protection of local currencies. The long-term economic benefits of IMF policies are highly controversial, but the main problem with free-market economics is that it often has no effective social policies.

The assumption that the free market will ultimately solve social questions has not changed since Adam Smith claimed that the hidden hand of history would restore a balance to civil society (Seligman, 1992). The arguments against utilitarian economic rationalism are well known (Holton and Turner, 1986, 1989). For example, the globalization of trade has unfortunately also resulted in a globalization of crime, especially in narcotics, pornography and prostitution. Opium production is a perfectly rational economic response to economic hardship on the part of marginalized peasantry in Columbia and Thailand. The new digital economy, while expanding employment opportunities for a new elite of symbolic analysts (Reich, 1993), may not produce any stimulation in the labour market for poorly educated, working-class youths; and at the other end of the generational cycle the deregulation of retirement and changes to superannuation have reinforced the reality of geriatric poverty. Intergenerational responsibilities are a basic component of justice, but these social changes are likely to produce considerable intergenerational conflict over scarce resources (Turner, 1998). The social difficulty of egoistic rationalism is primarily that the economy does not produce any basis by which the Hobbesian problem of the war of all against all can be solved.

The Fordist economy of the post-war period was based on the following assumptions: full employment (at least for the adult male population), factory production systems and work discipline, the notion of a life-long career, early retirement on a pension and a subsidized funeral, and a taxation system which supported welfare and retirement without a significant redistribution of resources. The Fordist economy provided the economic basis of welfare or social citizenship: the right to vote, secondary education, health care and unemployment benefits. By contrast, the post-Fordist economy does not require mass employment and does not guarantee continuous career prospects, or a coherent life cycle. It fragments the labour force into a skilled stratum (especially in the information and communication systems) and a large, casually employed, unskilled manual workforce. The economy also presents severe problems for the state in satisfying traditional assumptions about retirement, health insurance and superannuation. There is a sense in which the disappearance of a traditional life course (often described as the 'seven ages of man') corresponds to its postmodernization (Turner, 1994). The social danger is that the casualization of employment combined with frequent periods of real or semi-unemployment will produce a population which, in the words of Karl Marx, is not only pauperized but also alienated in the sense that they will be no longer be able to articulate either their demands or their aspirations through local or national political institutions. Post-Fordism also creates the conditions for a significant underclass of marginalized and undereducated young people. Whereas resentment and alienation in the 1960s produced a sequence of social movements which attempted to bring about social change, the 1990s have seen relatively little coherent mass political action.

Citizenship and civil society

The contemporary interest in a revival of voluntary associations and the third-sector economy as an alternative to economic individualism has to be seen in the context of global economic and political changes, that is, in terms of the social crisis of post-Fordism. Social citizenship has (re)emerged in the 1990s as an important social response to the social and political difficulties created by the legacy of Reagonomics in the 1970s and global deregulation in the 1980s. Citizenship is part of a broad response to the crisis of civil society in the post-communist societies and to the social risks of the Western economies. There are in fact basically four interconnected intellectual and social responses to the crisis of civil society. There has been the revival of academic and political interest in social citizenship. There is the attempt to restore the institutions of civil society, especially in Eastern Europe. In North America in particular, there is the political and social theory of communitarianism with its attack on liberalism and the privatized individual. Finally, there has been a revival of interest in voluntary associations as part of a broader notion of associative democracy. All four responses share a common criticism of the negative outcome of egoistic individualism.

Citizenship can be sociologically understood as an attempt to civilize capitalism, but the concept of citizenship has undergone significant change and evolution in recent years. In fact, the modern debate about citizenship has gone through three phases (Rees and Bulmer, 1996). The first wave was associated with the idealism of T. H. Green, developed by L. T. Hobhouse, and was influential in the period 1880 to 1914.

The second wave was important in the period from 1945 to the 1960s, and was connected specifically with the work of T. H. Marshall. The third wave has been important from the 1980s to the present, and has involved a variety of criticisms and applications of the Marshallian framework. The current wave of citizenship theory is the product of a variety of social forces: European integration, the decline or erosion of the welfare state, the politics of gay liberation, concern for the environment, the conflict between aboriginal rights and the social rights of national frameworks of citizenship, and finally the challenge of new medical technologies (especially reproductive technologies to the traditional characteristics of parenting). We can summarize the issue behind these diverse social forces in terms of the politics of identity and difference. Conventional forms of citizenship identity were housed within the system of nation-states; these identities were assumed to have a universalistic character. Ethnic diversity, multiculturalism and the postmodernization of cultures have challenged these nationalistic assumptions, placing a greater emphasis on tolerance of difference and diversity.

Secondly, with the collapse of communism there has been a growing recognition that, while communism (at least in its early phase) promoted significant improvements in many welfare services, the dominance of the party machine had the consequence of crushing civil society. Because party intellectuals regarded institutions that existed outside the state with hostility, many social institutions (such as churches, ethnic associations and leisure groups) went underground or out of existence. The party came to regulate, absorb and finally destroy pre-existing patterns of civil society. In a peculiar fashion, civil society was somewhat privatized as oppositional groups circulated literature in clandestine operations. The domestic kitchen often became a site for political meetings or more harmless practices of communal activity such as poetry reading. Paradoxically, bourgeois values – individualism, liberalism, humour and private forms of education and cultivation – were cherished because they existed outside the party ideology and framework. The fall of communism has resulted in a restoration of voluntary-sector activity. Similar processes of reconstruction of civil society out of the domestic domain have been taking place in Hungary and Poland. Perhaps the most influential theoretical study in this field of political analysis has been Jean Cohen and Andrew Arato (eds), *Civil Society and Political Theory* (1992).

Thirdly, in the West in response to privatization and commodification, there has been growing interest in communitarian philosophy as a framework for overcoming the limitations and problems of individualistic liberalism. The sources of communitarianism are diverse – from the post-Catholic defence of communal virtue by Alasdair MacIntyre in *After Virtue* (1981) to the moralistic sociology of Amitai Etzioni in *The Spirit of Community* (1993). Broadly speaking, communitarianism seeks to rebuild the communal basis of society as an antidote to the alienation which is perceived to be an inevitable outcome of the secular impact of the market and market ideologies. In sociology, one important source of this vision of modern capitalism came from the publication of *Habits of the Heart* (Bellah et al., 1985) which, through a survey of attitudes, discovered a profound distrust of public institutions, especially political institutions. The book attempted to rediscover the underlying themes of Alexis de Tocqueville's *Democracy in America* of 1845 in order to rebuild a viable political community in the United States (Tocqueville, 1969).

Finally, there has been a growing interest in the role of voluntary associations, both for their contribution to the economy and for their ability to sustain patterns of active citizenship. As we will show in more detail in Chapter 3, this social sector of voluntary associations is often described as the non-profit third sector. This sector has the following characteristics. It is formally constituted and organizationally separate from the state. It is furthermore non-profit-seeking, self-governing and voluntary (Salamon and Anheier, 1997). The attention that has been given in recent years to voluntary associations is also a product of various re-evaluations of the role of charity and altruism in modern society. The decline of Victorian assumptions about charity and the poor has revitalized interest in the importance of obligation. Two important volumes in this debate have come from the sociologist Robert Wuthnow: *Acts of Compassion* (1991) and *Poor Richard's Principle* (1996).

There is obviously a certain convergence between these separate issues around citizenship, civil society, communitarianism and voluntarism. We wish to suggest that the linking theme here is a sustained, and partly traditional, criticism of egoistic individualism. This theme of the negative or unintended consequences of the emphasis on possessive individualism, which can be traced back to Hobbes' theory of social contract and property (Macpherson, 1981), provides the background or domain assumptions behind recent theories of voluntary associations, or more broadly behind the debate over associative democracy.

Citizenship and democracy

Here we attempt to develop the citizenship perspective of T. H. Marshall to make a stronger conceptual linkage between research on citizenship and contemporary analysis of voluntary associations. The linking concept is active citizenship. Marshall developed a theory of post-war societies through an analysis of the relationships between social class, welfare and citizenship. The aim of this chapter is both to provide a composite picture of his ideas and some fundamental criticisms of his approach. To start with, one may define citizenship as a collection of rights and obligations that give individuals a formal legal identity, and these legal rights and obligations are put together as sets of social institutions. From a sociological point of view when we are conceptualizing citizenship, we are interested in those institutions in society that embody or give expression to the formal rights and obligations of individuals as members of a political community, and one of the key dimensions of citizenship is access to scarce resources.

Citizenship gives individuals and groups access to resources in society. These legal rights and obligations, once they are institutionalized as formal status positions, give people formal entitlements to scarce resources in society, basically economic resources such as social security, health-care entitlements, retirement packages, or taxation concessions, but also including access to culturally desirable resources (within a traditional liberal framework) such as rights to speak your own language in the public arena or rights relating to religious freedoms. These resources therefore include both the traditional economic resources of housing, health, income, employment and so forth, and also cultural resources such as education, religion and language. These rights to cultural resources can be conceptualized within the paradigm of cultural capital via the sociological theories of Pierre Bourdieu, especially in *Distinction* (1984). There are also political resources, which are related to access to sources of power in society, rights to vote, rights to participate politically and so forth. In summary, it may be conceptually parsimonious to think of three types of resource: economic, cultural and political.

The first thing to emphasize about citizenship is that it controls access to the scarce resources of society, and hence this allocative function is the basis of a profound conflict in modern societies over citizenship membership criteria. The process of and conditions for naturalization tell us a great deal about the character of democracy in society. Take, for example, in recent British political history, the anxiety about recognizing full citizenship rights for Hong Kong Chinese. In Australia, limiting migration is also related to an attempt to control access to resources by controlling migration and naturalization. Who does or does not get citizenship clearly indicates the prevailing formal criteria of inclusion/exclusion within a political community. We attempt to analyse this issue subsequently under the heading of solidarity and scarcity.

The next aspect of citizenship is that it confers a particular cultural identity on people. Debates about citizenship normally involve debates about cultural membership and cultural identity – what it is to be an Australian, and what it is to be a member of contemporary Australian society. When migrant groups become naturalized in Australia, there is a great interest about how they are going to be incorporated into existing Australian identities. The issue of multiculturalism raises not only questions about resources but obviously about the nature of identity. When politicians and others speak about 'good Australians' they are thinking about whether it is the case that newcomers have the kind of civic virtues that we regard as appropriate behaviour for Australians. When in popular discourse we speak about things being 'un-Australian', we often mean that certain sorts of behaviours are not compatible with of our image of what constitute good Australian behaviours. Whenever political scientists, philosophers or others analyse citizenship, they are not only studying access to scarce economic, political and cultural resources, they are also concerned about moral behaviour and questions of identity. For example, in formal political philosophy, the notion of republican citizenship contains a clear idea of the civic virtues, which are regarded as necessary for the functioning of a democracy.

The final component of this model of citizenship is the idea of a political community as the basis of citizenship. This political community is typically the nation-state. When you become a citizen, you not only enter into a set of institutions that confer upon you rights and obligations, acquire an identity and civic virtues, but you also become a member or part of a political community with a particular history. In order to have citizenship you have to be, at least in most modern societies, a *bona fide* member of a political community. Generally speaking, it is rather unusual for people to acquire citizenship if they are not simultaneously members of a political community, that is, a nation-state. One should notice here an important difference between human rights and citizenship. Human rights are typically conferred upon people as humans irrespective of whether they are Australian, British, Chinese, Indonesian or whatever, but because human rights legislation has been accepted by the nations of the world, people can claim human rights even where they are stateless people or dispossessed refugees. Generally speaking, citizenship is a set of rights and obligations that correspond to membership of a nation-state. Citizenship identities and citizenship cultures are national identities and national cultures.

The next section of this chapter deals with the theme of the tensions between solidarity and scarcity. From a sociological perspective, citizenship provides modern society with an important ingredient of solidarity. This argument concerns the idea of citizenship as social solidarity: namely that citizenship is an answer to the question, 'how is society possible, given the significant differences that exist between different social groups and different communities within the nation-state?' To some extent, one could argue that most modern societies have passed through a long period of secularization in which there has been a major decline in general religious values, at least if we are talking about Western Christian societies or societies which have a legacy of Christianity. If we regard Australia as a predominantly secular society in the sense that most of our major public debates are neither couched in the language of religion nor resolved by religious institutions, then we argue that citizenship functions or plays the role of a secular religion. With the decline of formal religion, citizenship provides us with a common national culture, set of identities, and value system. What holds societies like Australia together is a common citizenship as a foundational basis in a multicultural environment. Australian multiculturalism is successful because it is based on a successful policy of expanding citizenship participation. A common foundation of citizenship gives different ethnic groups access to scarce resources and makes their cultural diversity possible in modern Australia. Citizenship provides a form of solidarity, if you like a kind of social glue, that holds societies together which are divided by social class, by gender, by ethnicity and by age groups. The solidarity of the political community of modern societies is provided by citizenship, which works as a form of civic religion. This 'sociological argument' about the educative functions of citizenship is taken directly from J. J. Rousseau's account of the social contract (Trachtenberg, 1993).

We note in this chapter that one can conceptualize all human societies as organized along two contradictory principles. On the one hand, solidarity as a principle of social organization, and on the other hand the principle of scarcity. All human societies, in order to exist, have to find some common basis, some form of solidarity, which will not overcome but at least cope with the problems of difference, diversity and conflict. All human societies must have some basis in solidarity in order to exist, but all human societies, precisely because they are human societies, are also characterized by scarcity. What do we mean by scarcity? It exists because the resources of society can never be wholly distributed in an egalitarian fashion to everybody; there are fundamental scarcities of an economic, cultural and political nature. Scarcity is a very difficult notion to define. It is the basis of all economic theory; economics is about the management of scarce resources, but it is wrong to think that scarcity exists only in primitive or simple societies. One could imagine a hunter-gatherer society where access to food was limited by the actual difficulties of hunting wild animals and gathering natural produce. But scarcity is a fundamental element of the most advanced and prosperous societies. This argument is brilliantly analysed in Nicholas Xenos's *Scarcity and Modernity* (1989). Scarcity in wealthy societies is a function of the growth of expectations about assets, wealth and success. In Australia, where the Holden Kingswood car has been relatively available to all low-income families, Rolls Royce, BMW or Porsche cars have an obvious scarcity value. Scarcity is a function as much of prosperity and wealth as it is of poverty. It is manifest in social inequality, and the typical forms of social inequality that we experience in modern societies are, obviously, differences of social class or access to wealth. However, scarcity also follows the contours of gender, age and ethnicity.

In this exposition we return to the work of Marshall, who in *Class, Citizenship and Social Development* (1965) took citizenship and class as fundamental but contradictory features of modern capitalist societies. Referring primarily to the United Kingdom, he claimed that in the seventeenth and eighteenth centuries legal rights were developed in relation to the jury system, the right to a trial, the right to a fair hearing, and access to legal resources. In the seventeenth and eighteenth centuries, there was a growth of legal rights as the first stage of elementary citizenship, and these legal rights were institutionalized primarily in the jury system. In the eighteenth and nineteenth centuries, there was a growth in political rights which eventually resolved themselves into parliamentary institutions. Finally, in the nineteenth and twentieth centuries, citizenship expanded further to include social rights institutionalized in the welfare state. Marshall then went on to argue that citizenship mitigates against the inequalities created in the market-place. To put that proposition more directly, citizenship tends to resolve or minimize the antagonisms between social classes, which are characteristic of the rise of capitalist economies and the capitalist market-place. Although in the late nineteenth century many European societies went through a significant period of capitalist economic development resulting in class division and class conflict, the latter did not spill over into major revolutionary confrontations.

Marshall argued that citizenship reduced the level of class struggle and class antagonism, because it achieved a partial redistribution of the economic resources which had become available as a consequence of economic growth. Through retirement schemes, social security schemes, family benefits, general education and the welfare state, class conflict is contained. While inequality remains a fundamental feature of modern industrial capitalist societies, it is mitigated or regulated by the growth of citizenship entitlements. Marshall argued in effect that citizenship redistributes some of the scarce resources of a capitalist society in order to lessen the revolutionary conflict between classes by creating a common form of solidarity in a political community. The sociology of citizenship has therefore to locate the issue of citizenship within a wider framework of the political debate over reformism (Turner, 1984).

Finally, Marshall went on to argue in *The Right to Welfare and other Essays* (1981) that modern industrialist capitalist societies should be called 'hyphenated societies' because we refer to them as democratic-welfare capitalist societies or societies which have some sort of democratic redistribution of wealth through the institutions of citizenship. Such a society combines some element of democratic egalitarianism and inequality of capitalist relations in the capitalist market-place and the capitalist economy. Marshall laid the foundation for much subsequent writing and analysis of the role of citizenship in contemporary societies.

In the next section of the chapter we raise some critical objections to Marshall's work. The first criticism is that his notion of citizenship could be said to be incomplete. For example, many writers argue that in the twentieth century there was the growth of various forms of economic citizenship in the form of workers' participation and workers' councils, economic democracy or industrial democracy. In many societies, often influenced by Sweden, there were various attempts to create citizenship in the workplace. One of the criticisms of Marshall is that if you do not have basic economic citizenship, then the other rights (legal, political and social welfare rights) tend to be relatively unimportant; for example, citizenship is only half developed if people do not have some control over their work situation. If there is a highly restricted redistribution of shares and profits and if there are no institutions relating to workers' democracy or workers' councils, then citizenship is limited. In many European economies, led partly by Sweden, there were various attempts to set up workers' discussion groups, provide for workers' participation, and create consultative relations which gave expression for some people to the idea of economic citizenship.

Feminists have pointed out that citizenship discourse, as far back as Aristotle's conception of rational discourse and public participation in the Greek polis, which excluded women, is silent on matters of the gendering of citizenship rights. Citizenship rights for women have always fallen behind the rights of men. In particular, social entitlements have been tied in with economic contributions to the community through participation in the paid workforce. For example, (mainly male) 'breadwinners' have the right to welfare entitlements when they become unemployed, although often only for as long as they keep looking for paid work. Breadwinners are deemed worthier of social rights than dependants, such as housewives, because of their formal contribution to the economy as paid workers and contributors to social insurance schemes. Because the contribution of women to society is often as unpaid domestic worker, or child-rearer rather than as paid breadwinner, women are not regarded as significant contributors to the economy or full citizens.

Other writers suggested that Marshall's model was also incomplete because one can speak about the development in the twentieth century of cultural rights. For example, many societies in the nineteenth century developed various language policies that made speaking minority languages illegal or at least socially criticized in public places. To give you one instance, in Britain in the nineteenth century various attempts were made to prevent school children speaking Gaelic in north-western Scotland. In Holland there was a similar decline in minority languages, namely Fresian. In various societies the growth of citizenship in the nineteenth century brought attempts to regulate and control what languages could be spoken publicly, and some writers have argued that with the growth of multiculturalism in the twentieth century there is a greater willingness to tolerate different languages in the public arena. In many European societies, legislation has been brought in to permit or to promote the use of minority languages. In Canada there is a bilingual policy which ensures that French is available at least in the eastern provinces. In Finland there is a bilingual policy which ensures that Swedish is available in the south-western coastal regions and that all official documents are available in both Swedish and Finnish. There is a greater public tolerance of cultural difference. Another illustration would be the great explosion of universities in the middle of the twentieth century, which may be regarded as an extension of citizenship rights into the educational sphere. A mass higher education system is an example of cultural democracy.

The second problem with Marshall's treatment of citizenship is that he regarded the community basis of citizenship as homogenous. That is, in his account of citizenship, it is taken for granted that modern societies are homogenous in ethnic, cultural and other terms. Marshall did not address the issue of ethnic diversity and had no specific interest in linguistic, religious and cultural diversity. The only divisions that he recognizes in the community are social class divisions. The whole point of his theory is directed to the assumption that the only diversity in the community arises from social classes, and that you overcome that class diversity by creating a common basis of citizenship. It is very obvious in the twentieth century that the great majority of societies are heterogeneous; they are multicultural and highly diverse. As a result partly of twentieth-century labour mobility and general post-war migration, most societies are like Australia: they have multiple ethnic communities and a whole series of religious and cultural divisions. The crucial issue is that twentieth-century governments have to come to terms with the legacy of white-settler societies, colonialism and Aboriginal claims to land rights and sovereignty. Most societies, including European societies, have an aboriginal community that lies somewhere outside the official political community. In northern Scandinavia there is the Sami community, which was there long before the Norwegian, Swedish, Finnish or Russian states were created; and in North America there are, obviously, many native communities that occupied the land long before the white settlers arrived. In the forests of South America there are Aboriginal communities that are not part of the nation-state and which exist outside of citizenship. In New Zealand and Australia there are major political problems about Maori, Torres Strait Islander and Australian Aboriginal citizenship. What sort of rights or citizenship status are they likely to have or want? Voluntary associations have played a major part in articulating the specific interests of ethnic minorities in a political context where (national) citizenship often enforces social solidarity, which excludes or ignores ethnic difference.

Marshall's European view of citizenship had nothing to say about ethnic diversity, but it also quite significantly had nothing to say about one of the major problems of modern society: how do you incorporate Aboriginal communities that occupy the land prior to white settlement? It is interesting that most white settlers had a view that the land was empty. There has been a long debate in Australia, where original constitutional arrangements assumed that Australia was an empty land. On reading Alexis de Tocqueville's *Democracy in America*, one discovers that settlers in America also assumed that somehow the North American nomadic communities were not actually there. De Tocqueville said that because native Americans did not create property, they were not actually present in North America. There is a similar view on the settlement of Israel, according to which the early constitution of Israel assumes an empty space. One of the problems about the idea of citizenship is whether it can somehow deal with the question, not only of ethnic diversity, but also of Aboriginal issues. Another way of expressing that is to say that Marshall took identity for granted; it is somehow totally unproblematic for his view of society. In Australia, for example, there are many people who have dual citizenship and in a sense they have a dual identity. If we look at the history of Chinese Aboriginal people in Queensland, these were Aboriginal people who had intermarried with Chinese settlers in Queensland. This group is a good example of the complexity of identity in a multicultural society. Chinese Aboriginal people were often not accepted in the Aboriginal community where they were regarded as Chinese and not accepted in the white Queensland community because they are regarded as Aboriginal, and not accepted within a pure Chinese community because they do not look Chinese.

Another issue in Marshall's theory is that it assumes that these rights are cumulative. Because he assumes that the rights of citizenship are cumulative, he assumes that once you have legal rights and have won the political battles of parliamentary democracy, and once you have won your social welfare rights, then you do not lose those rights. Marshall assumes that each of these stages is a successful accumulation of citizenship. This is a very optimistic picture of the historical evolution of rights. One of the important debates emerging in Australia really is whether previous rights can be sustained in a society, which is more and more dominated by the needs of the market-place. In a market driven society, young people find it very difficult to enter the labour market and get access to resources because of the nature of the modern economy. If one considers calling full employment an entitlement, it could well be that such social rights are obliterated or at least weakened as a consequence of more market driven policies. Marshall had an optimistic view of history in which these rights stay with you and citizenship is like an upward and onward march of democracy. It seems quite clear that one can identify many societies that have reasonably good social and economic rights but might not have legal and political rights.

The final criticism of Marshall is that his theory has a very one-dimensional view of citizenship. In the contemporary literature there is a debate about active versus passive citizenship, summarized in the model below. This criticism, set out in *Citizenship and Social Theory* (Turner, 1993), says that there are different types of citizenships, some more passive and some more active. This involves an historical model. Some types of citizenship may be revolutionary: if you think of the French Revolution, it was a form of citizenship which was grasped from below by popular struggle and by popular social movements. In the French Revolution there was a very clear sense of the public arena as a place where citizens could act as political agents and secure new social rights. This model of citizenship is trying to distinguish active or revolutionary citizenship, which you might say is the product of social struggles like the French Revolution and which involved a very strong sense of the public arena. By contrast, consider the use of a plebiscite as a simple method of electing leaders. You simply organize an election, and once the leader is in power, he or she can do whatever they like because they do not have to confer with their supporters. A plebiscite is simply a way of installing a type of leadership which is not immediately answerable to its mandators. What we suggest is that the French Revolution created a very active sense of citizenship in a European revolutionary tradition, and by contrast Germany had a passive notion of citizenship. If one considers Weber's analysis of German politics, one finds that he advocated the importance of what he called plebiscitary democracy, that is, a democracy based upon strong leadership and passive forms of citizenship. In Germany Lutheranism created a weak sense of the public arena; it said that good citizens were people who behaved well at home. Lutheranism, in defining the public space in moral terms, created a sense of the public arena as a dangerous and negative place. By contrast, the revolutionary struggle to create America as an independent and new nation produced a constitution with a strong sense of democracy from below. American democracy has been weakened by the emphasis on the private in liberalism, which says that people should have freedom of speech and freedom of association. However, American democracy has a rather weak sense of the public domain and a profound interest in the morality of politicians as individuals. England is a top-down democracy in which, because of the monarchical settlement, one finds a patriarchal idea of parliament and the Queen. The Lockean contract, which has operated in Britain since the end of the seventeenth century, creates a weak sense of the public arena and a passive model of the citizen. Anglicanism provided a criterion of public events which was less privatized than the Lutheran version, and the revolutionary settlement of 1688 provided a parliamentary system which was top-down but institutionalized positive models of citizenship. What we want to suggest finally is a historical view of this process.

Citizenship emerges with the city-state and creates an idea of the denizen. With the development of the nation-states, there evolved a primitive notion of citizenship based upon political rights. This form was followed by the welfare state where we have social citizenship based upon social rights. In this historical model, it is possible to antic-ipate the growth of global capitalism, the partial erosion of national sovereignty and the development of entitlements in an international and later global system. There is already an emerging notion of human rights. As the world economy becomes more and more globalized, more and more workers will travel in search of employment and there will be greater conflict in the labour market about access to global resources. The nation state is being eroded by global market trends so that in Australia we find more and more of the economy is owned by international corporations. It may be that the traditional or Marshallian form of citizenship cannot express or does not correspond to the idea of an increasingly global market.

This model of the history of citizenship can either have an optimistic or pessimistic conclusion. The optimistic one is that through the United Nations, through agreements about human rights, we can man-age the problem of interstate violence, terrorism and conflict. The other model is that in fact we do not have cumulative citizenship, what we have is a breakdown of cumulative citizenship. We have not so much secure nation-states providing citizenship for their members as we have a growing war of mega-cities and mega-economies against each other. The pessimistic view of the future is that societies like China will break down into bellicose mega-cities, that international economic links will undermine traditional notions of citizenship and that the future will be a much more insecure and uncertain kind of environ-ment. Whatever happens, the idea of citizenship is a very central aspect of the modern debate about democracy in places like Australia. It is cru-cial to the analysis of how we will manage the international conflict over scarce resources within an increasingly global economy. In this study of the rhetorics of welfare, we take the position that voluntary associations can provide an important link between the individual and the state without the negative consequences of welfare bureaucratiza-tion or marketization. In a period of globalized institutions, voluntary associations offer a local response to community needs and regional conditions. The discussion of voluntary associations will occupy our study in Chapter 3, but at this stage we need to indicate some broad features of that analysis in the context of citizenship and welfare.

Intermediary groups and active citizenship

'Intermediary groups', which in this chapter we employ as a short-hand expression to cover a variety of voluntary associations, have been a topic of considerable interest to social and political theorists for at least one and a half centuries. The importance of intermediary groups which stand between the individual and the state was recognized by Alexis de Tocqueville in his observations on the dangers of the radical doctrine of equality in America in *Democracy in America* (1835–40), where he argued that voluntary associations were crucial in protecting dissent and diversity in a democratic system where mass opinion could exercise despotic powers over the individual (Dahl, 1989). However, the most influential theory of intermediary groups was developed by Emile Durkheim in *Professional Ethics and Civic Morals* (1957), a critique of utilitarian individualism. Durkheim identified four spheres of values – domestic, civil, economic and political. Professional ethics were seen to be necessary to regulate the economic sphere; civic morals, the political sphere. The economic sphere had become chaotic and thus professional groups or associations were necessary to regulate the sphere of economic transactions if individual egoism was to be contained. Intermediary groups mediate between individual and state. They provide moral training. They regulate the market and control anomie. They provide solidarity and counter possessive individualism (utilitarianism and hedonism).

Both Durkheim and de Tocqueville have been influential in modern theories of plural society. The contemporary debate about plural society has been significantly influenced by writers like Paul Q. Hirst who has revived early democratic theories of associationism from the work of G. D. H. Cole, J. N. Figgis and H. J. Laski, for whom intermediary groups were important in combating the growth of electoral dictatorship. Three works by Hirst have been influential: *Representative Democracy and its Limits* (1990), *The Pluralist Theory of the State* (1993) and *Associative Democracy: New Forms of Economic and Social Governance* (1994). Hirst identifies the following key elements in associational democracy. There are a plurality of self-governing associations, voluntary associations and communal groups, which lie outside the state. There is the development of a principle of subsidiarity, by which leadership and welfare responses operate at the lowest possible level of community organization. There has also to be a conscious cultivation of pluralism in culture and social objectives. However, for this plurality of associations to exist, there must be a legal framework, which regulates their behaviour.

Hirst argues that associative democracy is necessary to promote pluralism and to regulate the powers of a democratically elected majority. Thus, interest in voluntary association or intermediary groups has varied considerably, but from a political and sociological point of view concern for intermediary groups is driven by a concern for their contribution to the maintenance of civil society, to the development of democratic institutions, to the fostering of altruism and civic virtue. In particular, voluntary associations provide a training ground for active citizenship and civil participation. They are what we might call schools of democracy, because they offer an experience of or potential for training in the basic procedures of democratic and communal governance.

The most powerful criticisms of associative democracy have, however, been considered by Joshua Cohen and Joel Rogers in their *Associations and Democracy* (1995). These problems include the fact that, with the proliferation of organized groups, their destructive 'rent-seeking behaviour' can have a very negative effect on government and civil society as they seek to win the favour of the powers of government to confer such rents. There is also the classical political problem of division, fragmentation and intrigue between groups, a phenomenon which the James Madison Papers (key to the debates during the growth of American Constitutionalism) referred to as the mischief of faction. Thus powerful state mechanisms, or at the very least a series of comprehensive legal arrangements, are required to regulate the existence and activities of intermediary groups, many of which may be quasi-legal or even criminal. Obvious examples include the role of right-wing militia groups in North America, sub-legal gun clubs in Australia or the Mafia in Italy. Generally speaking, the literature on voluntary associations and civil society naively assumes that such associations will operate in a legal manner. There is the further problem to consider: namely, if a plural society were indeed effective, would it be possible to sustain some notion of common good? We suspect that the pluralistic provision of welfare by voluntary associations could not sustain or guarantee universalistic conditions of provision and therefore could not deliver a system which had uniform outcomes. Provision by voluntary associations might be compatible with the quest to maintain equality of opportunity, but equality of condition could not be sustained.

In order to overcome these problems, Cohen and Rogers argue that an associative democracy would have to satisfy at least the following conditions. There would have to be a significant measure of popular sovereignty and there would need to be extensive provision of formal political equality. The state would need to seek a strong measure of distributive equity to offset the particularized consequences of local associations. Citizenship under these circumstances would also need to work towards a high level of civic consciousness, probably through various educational programmes, especially at the primary level. The political success of associative democracy would also have to rest upon a robust economy to deliver a good and consistent level of economic performance in terms of employment and wage levels: economic underperformance, inflation and downturn would very rapidly undermine the necessary conditions for communal tolerance, equality and involvement. Such an economic programme also has to assume a level of state, especially administrative, competence. In recent years, public anxiety about the ethical character of the role of the President in the United States is a good example of the erosion of public confidence in the capacity of political leaders to act effectively and competently. These conditions have been difficult to achieve in most of the advanced industrial societies. For example, high levels of youth unemployment resulting from structural economic changes have undermined civil consciousness, and the free-market experiments of the 1980s produced throughout the 1990s an increase in the levels of social inequality. These effects have not been entirely uniform, and thus when we discuss the role of voluntary associations we need to examine different political and economic systems.

Political regimes and typologies of citizenship

Accounts of voluntary associations have to be set within the context of different political regimes. As we argued in Chapter 1 theories of civil society typically deal with four components – individual and community, state and market. In our typology of modern societies, these dimensions give rise to four possible combinations: fascism, liberalism, social democracy and associative democracy. While these concepts are universal, their specific or local manifestations can take very different cultural forms. We attempt to modify existing approaches to associative democracy as developed by Hirst, Cohen and Rogers through an analysis of these broader political contexts. We shall argue that the theory of associative democracy attempts to defend a particular relationship between the community and the market.

Our research is based firstly on the assumption that welfare programmes need reconceptualization, transformation and restructuring. Secondly, this restructuring should be based on principles that extend the notion of welfare beyond the idea of social amelioration through top-down service delivery. Thirdly, the characteristics and location of third-sector associations make them an appropriate locus for the development of a new welfare paradigm.

Our research shows that there are a variety of frameworks of organization currently operating in voluntary associations in Australia. We explore these frameworks at various points in this book, but basically they include the charity framework, the activist framework, the welfare state industry framework, and the market framework. The result is that workers in the voluntary sector often have to balance and manage contradictory pressures within their organizations. Professionalization and marketization of the voluntary sector will produce a stratification of the labour force between those who provide casual support and those who have permanent careers in the sector. It is inconceivable that Western governments will return to a centralized and unitary welfare state system, and therefore we can expect this sector to expand, and become more professionalized and more dominated by managerialism. The principles of associative democracy appeared to be more readily achieved where the voluntary organization has a strategic plan which incorporates values of participation, where clients and customers are members of the organizing board, where dependence on charity has been radically rejected, where profits are ploughed back into the organization and where civic consciousness is actively promoted.

In conclusion, there are a number of key problems, which the associative-democracy perspective on voluntary associations and the welfare state must face. It is difficult to see how they could provide a universalistic service without considerable bureaucratic provision of a national system. There is no simple answer to or protection from the criminalization of provision and the mischief of faction. It is not clear how a legal framework could be created to control for these developments. Associative democracy would require the development of a variety of 'safety nets' such as a guaranteed minimum wage. Voluntarism cannot easily overcome the historical problems relating, in Australia, for example, to the dispersion of populations and uneven rural provision. Failure to address these political and economic questions would result in a further marginalization of minority populations.

Finally, we argue that charity as a general activity is subject to processes of rationalization. The voluntary sector is being transformed by, in Weber's terms, the rationalization of service and morality. This raises a question as to the professionalization of training, namely is this the end of voluntary service? Perhaps the most positive conclusion is the capacity of voluntary associations to function as 'schools of democracy' and to produce a culture organized around active citizenship.

Conclusions: transformations of the welfare state

At the end of the nineteenth century, the dominant view of society was driven by utilitarian individualism, often in combination with a social Darwinistic vision of the survival of the fittest. Sociologists like Herbert Spencer argued that governments should not interfere in the organic evolution of society, the dynamic principle of which was conflict over scarce resources. Social Darwinism was a potent ideology of capitalism, because it legitimized the absence of the state from the amelioration of poverty and unemployment. It also encouraged individualistic and privatized charity as the moral response of the middle class to the plight of the poor. The main critic of Spencer was Durkheim, who condemned the utilitarian principles of hedonism and individualism, which were causally associated with social breakdown as measured by rising suicide rates. Durkheim argued that the state had a moral role to play in conjunction with professional associations in the regulation of the market and the constraint of egoism.

At the end of the twentieth century, we appear to have an ironic repetition of similar arguments about the conditions of economic growth. Free-market theorists believe that the unrestrained expansion of the economy will produce the individual rewards which are necessary to sustain consumer demand as the basis for sustaining employment. Those individuals who fail to succeed in the market-place will need to seek out alternative arrangements such as charity support. Communitarians believe that society is in a state of crisis because the force of the market is sufficient to destroy family life, alienate young people and create a new 'underclass' of the elderly, migrants and the sick. Perhaps the new element in this otherwise perfect repeat of the Victorian welfare system is the global development of a grey area between the legal economy and a criminal economy. The black market has always been a rational, if criminal, response to economic opportunity, but the modern economy now appears to depend increasingly on gambling, the casino complex, pornography and sexual tourism as important engines. The growth of the third-sector economy, despite its limitations and contradictions, is an important 'intermediary group' between the anarchy of the market and the modern state.

3
On the Concept of Voluntary Association

Introduction

With the relativistic conflict of values resulting from globalization, decolonization and multiculturalism, governments are forced to operate in a social environment which is confused, complex and uncertain. At the end of the last century, western governments could take more or less for granted the existence of a national hierarchy of values. The state existed to support and promote the moral order that was based upon this authoritative hierarchy. While Matthew Arnold in 1869 recognized important differences between the upper, middle and lower classes, *Culture and Anarchy* (Arnold, 1960) could nevertheless argue that culture was the study of perfection and that the role of the state was to support the best aspects of the national culture. He saw no particular reason to take any notice of regional, communal, ethnic and gender differences. The governments of modern societies are faced with pronounced conflicts over values and culture. Neither governments nor intellectuals can automatically or authoritatively pronounce on matters of value. This fact is the real significance of the notion that postmodernity involves scepticism towards 'grand narratives' (Lyotard, 1984). Postmodernity creates an environment in which governments are reluctant to legislate in areas where there is profound and probably incommensurable conflict over values and moral attitudes.

For modern governments, the solution to moral fragmentation is often to rely on economic forces to resolve conflicts of value through market resolution of interests. For example, in the field of art, the cultural value of a work of art is simply its market price. Whether or not pornography is acceptable is determined by its global exchange value. Following the popular adage about the difference between knowing the price and the value of an object or activity, we might say that where there is an irresolvable conflict over values, then market price functions as a proxy for value. Perhaps a typical example is whether museums are valued for their contribution to culture and education. The simple answer is that the cultural value of a museum is measured by whether the public will pay to enter. The value of charity is not resolved through moral debate but pragmatically by asking what percentage of gross domestic product is covered by charity. The importance of voluntarism in such a society is likely to be resolved by what people will pay for it. The moral value of altruism is likely to be expressed in terms of the parameters of rational choice theory rather than in terms of communitarian or democratic values. Voluntary associations, which have been historically closely associated with values relating to compassion, now have to function in a social space that is dominated by pricing mechanisms. We need to see contemporary uncertainty about the relationship between values, markets and morality as an aspect of the debate about politics and ethics. Political pluralism cannot be isolated from cultural pluralism. The communitarian debate has to our mind missed this aspect of the neo-liberal response to moral diversity; its real argument is that, recognizing the absence of moral argument, let the market decide by taking price pragmatically as an indicator of value. This condition of moral uncertainty produces the social and economic environment within which voluntary associations must operate.

Since the 'declaration of the end of history' amidst claims that the chief differences among societies are no longer political, ideological or even institutional and that the questions of ideology and institutions have been settled (Fukuyama, 1992; 1995), theorists have, at the end of the century, taken the opportunity to examine the condition of liberal representative democracy in advanced capitalist societies. A review of the contemporary literature suggests that there is a crisis in representative democracy for which the voluntary sector provides a possible solution. There is a good deal of debate surrounding the terminology regarding the voluntary sector and the organizations contained therein. Sometimes referred to as voluntary organizations, community organizations, non-government, not-for-profit, and non-profit, they are groups established by communities of people with common interests. They operate a wide range of projects and programmes such as housing projects, disability programmes, community health programmes, self-help programmes, environmental programmes and women's services; and include unions, neighbourhood associations and houses, parent–teacher associations, environmental groups, women's associations and so forth. In this chapter, we examine a range of definitions of and theories about this sector in order to establish a better understanding of the relationships between voluntary associations and welfare.

Voluntary associations and social theory

The idea of voluntary associations has played an important part in western political and social theory. They have been seen as an essential component of civil society and as a training ground for active citizenship. In Alexis de Tocqueville's analysis of the democratic revolution in America, there is a major understanding of the role of voluntary associations in preserving and protecting individual belief and conduct from the levelling impact of mass opinion. They played a crucial role in de Tocqueville's definition of civil society (Schmidt, 1995). In Durkheim's discussion of intermediary associations, there is the development of an understanding of the moral role of voluntary associations in regulating hedonistic individualism. In contemporary debate, voluntary associations are often referred to simply as 'citizen organizations' (Najam, 1999). In the American sociological literature, the vitality of voluntary associations, following de Tocqueville, is seen to be a measure of the health of society as a whole (Janoski and Wilson, 1995; Janoski, Musick and Wilson, 1998) or the middle class in particular (Komarovsky, 1946). The level of participation in voluntary associations can thus come to be seen as a condition of the vitality of civil society (Dekker and van den Broek, 1998). Linked to this, voluntary service has been regarded as an aspect of altruism, a system of values which also plays a part in sustaining civil society (Wuthnow, 1991).

Despite the extent of the debate about voluntary associations, there is little agreement about how they might be precisely defined. At is widest, the definition is highly inclusive. For example:

> 'Voluntary altruistic associations' may be defined as those groups which lie partially or completely in the private sphere (civil society), one of whose chief stated aims is to work for the benefit of others or for the common good, without profit.
>
> (Giner and Sarasa, 1996: 140)

More technically, voluntary associations can be said to have at least five characteristics: they are organized (formal), private, non-profit-distributing, self-governing and voluntary (Salamon and Anheier, 1999: 69).

These definitions are clearly useful and have guided our research. We need to note, however, a number of characteristic difficulties with these perspectives. When Salamon and Anheier describe such associations as 'organized', they simply mean that they are institutionalized rather than being simply *ad hoc* configurations which address specific issues and then disappear. This notion of institutionalization does of course cover a huge variation in terms of the formalization of voluntary associations. Our own research also suggests that there are periods of rapid growth and almost certainly periods of high rates of turnover of associations, which come and go with the vicissitudes of community needs and capacities for organization. Many immigrant organizations rise and fall rapidly with the changing circumstances of migration flows, government policies and local arrangements. Other institutions like Guide Dogs for the Blind have large international operations, extensive assets and professional staff. There appears to be an inherent tension in how voluntary associations are organized, because the growth of professional management values may conflict with traditional notions of philanthropy. The functions and composition of the boards of voluntary associations have been critically discussed in the social policy literature, because they are sensitive sites of public debate and concern (Harris, 1994).

Secondly, voluntary associations are defined as private, because they exist between government and market. Salamon and Anheier (1999) also defined voluntary associations as 'civil society organizations'. There are some difficulties with this location of the voluntary sector, because in practice their connections with government are very strong. There are, for example, a variety of funding arrangements in the UK, which indicate the close relationships between government and voluntary organizations, which include direct financial support and tax concessions (Kendall and Knapp, 1996). The national lottery also channels funding into the voluntary sector under the regulation of the government.

Thirdly, traditionally voluntary associations were not expected to function like business organizations and their funding came from philanthropy, bequests and other gifts. Although voluntary associations are still either non-profit or not-for-profit organizations, they are increasingly under pressure from marketization and commodification. In order to raise funding, they are forced to bid for government grants, and so there is pressure for these associations to become more professional. They need to hire staff who are highly qualified, not only to run large and complex organizations, but who are knowledgeable about costing and managing projects. These developments tend to create a gap between the board of managers and the rank and file.

Fourthly, it is assumed that voluntary associations will be self-governing. The pressure to professionalize in order to increase financial resources also therefore creates new problems about responsibility, access and participation. These management issues are somewhat ironic, given the fact that the voluntary sector is regarded as the spearhead of grass-roots democratization. If voluntary associations become large and bureaucratic, they cannot remain sensitive to local or client interests, and they reproduce the worst features of traditional, top-down, welfare bureaucracies.

Finally, in what sense are voluntary associations voluntary? It does not mean in any simple sense that work is unpaid; rather work in such an association is freely chosen. For example, the creation of a voluntary association is normally a voluntary decision to satisfy a particular need, independently of the state or the market. These associations are consequently often described as a community of interest or community of choice. Secondly, the actual activities and programmes of voluntary associations are freely chosen by an open and unconstrained decision-making process. Finally, membership of and participation in such organizations is voluntary, regardless of whether the work is paid or unpaid. The voluntary nature of such organizations is an important criterion for distinguishing between legal and illegal organizations. A local branch of the Mafia can have many of the characteristics of a legal voluntary welfare association. They are 'family' organizations, which are self-governing and private. They are usually for profit, but more significantly they are not voluntary. Membership is typically for life and attempts to quit the organization may lead to violent retribution. Illegal organizations do not have the voluntary entry, voice and exit features which we expect in legal voluntary associations. Without these defining characteristics, voluntary associations cannot play the normative role which democratic theorists expect of such organizations.

The crisis of liberal democracy

Having provided an outline definition of voluntary associations, we can now look more closely at the problems of liberal democracy which voluntary organizations are said to address. According to Giddens (1994), globalization, increased social reflexivity and the transformation of day-to-day life in an increasingly pluralist society are all challenges liberal representative democracies are failing to meet. While it is true that the last decade has seen a political upsurge in democratic reform movements in various parts of the world, especially in China and the Soviet Union, where democratic institutions had either not existed or were weak, the last decade has also seen an 'erosion of belief in the capacity of democratic institutions to intervene in shaping social and economic life and help solve the most pressing problems' (Wright, 1995: 1). Clearly, in liberal democracies there is large-scale alienation from, and/or indifference to, political institutions (Giddens, 1994: 109), and centralized government is increasingly seen as a burden on economic performance by its dependence on high taxation. Accordingly, recent decades have seen governments focus on deregulation, privatization, reduction of social services, and efforts to reduce state expenditure. Therefore, the challenges to government include the enhancement of government accountability to its citizens (for example, in terms of electoral promises) and the involvement of citizens in policy formation and decision-making. The remaking of citizenship will involve a transition from passive citizenship (as illustrated by limited citizen participation in the formal institutions of democracy) to active citizenship through participation in civil society. The traditional problems of ineffectual and unrepresentative political parties and the excessive influence of exclusive, narrowly self-interested organizations on government need redress. The effective exclusion of large sections of society (unorganized labour and welfare recipients) from political influence and an imperfect and fragmented welfare state produce electoral cynicism in the capacity of governments to serve the needs of the electorate (Hirst, 1995: 111; Giddens, 1994: 113–15).

Wright (1995: 2) argues that the democratic ideals of active political involvement, the creation of political consensus through dialogue and participation, the development of responsiveness to changing needs and the construction of effective forms of state politics are not being achieved. Further, Hirst (1994: 5–6) claims they are not likely to be realized by the 'imposition of common rules and standard services on the increasingly diverse and pluralistic objectives of the members of modern society'. He suggests (1994: 5) that while the state has ample capacity to intervene in society, the mechanisms available to determine and respond to the needs of the citizenry are limited. Indeed, it is only the 'threat of failing to be re-elected' that acts as an effective constraint on politicians. Wright (1995: 2) similarly argues that competitive elections of political leadership for legislative and executive office has become the major representation of democracy and is too narrow. And we might add that it is likely to narrow further, as the crisis of trust in political leadeship makes the 'threat of failing to be re-elected' gain ever growing importance.

Related to the current 'failings' of liberal representative democracies to meet democratic ideals is the fact that participation in the public sphere appears to be declining. According to Hirst (1994: 25), the public sphere is in somewhat of a state of crisis as 'modern large-scale democracies and bureaucratic states seem remote, minimize participation, and are ineffective at providing the services citizens require'. In the spirit of Habermas (1989), it could be suggested that the public sphere is now truly dominated by publicity, public relations companies and personnel, and 'spin doctors' teaching political leaders 'how to spin'. In something of a return to the 'representative publicity' (Habermas, 1989: 8) of the middle ages, where 'the ruling nobility and its powers were displayed before the populace' (Dahlgren, 1991: 3), in the late twentieth century there appears to be ever more limited opportunities for citizens to engage in discussion on the state's power (or any other matters of potential importance).

While these theories point to a retreat from political engagement, others, most notably the ideas of Robert Putnam, have pointed to a retreat in civic engagement. Indeed, according to Putnam (1995), civic engagement in the United States (the findings were also correlated across 35 other countries) is in decline and the stores of social capital are greatly reduced. Turnout in national elections, attendance at public meetings, and attendance at political rallies is falling while churches, labour unions, parent–teacher associations, and fraternal organizations all have memberships in decline. The reason for such diminished civic engagement Putnam suggests is that the technological transformation of leisure (television and computers specifically) has made communities wider and shallower.

Finally, globalization as a process is stretching the capabilities of liberal democracy (Giddens, 1994). The radical reorganization of global capital and its associated processes are challenging national sovereignty, political identity and citizenship. Further, the parameters of the debate on the attack on the principles of public welfare are global and specifically linked to the development of a world recession and the radical reorganizations of global capitalism (Turner, 1992; 1993). Ranci (1997: 82–3) suggests that the decline in economic growth followed by a period of stagnation has meant resources have become increasingly scarce and economic inequalities more pronounced, leaving liberal citizenship in crisis. It is these inequalities and the emergence of 'identities that cannot be integrated through the further amplification of social and political rights' that makes citizenship increasingly fragile. According to Ranci the crisis is expressed in yet another version of the duality between the state and the market, and the debate on ways out of the welfare crisis reflects 'the end of a phase of history in which the bond between welfare policies and economic development had made the achievement of social citizenship a realistic objective' (1997: 82).

This literature therefore points to a narrow, limited and inadequate form of democracy, a public sphere that lacks participation and engagement, low stores of social capital where trust, mutuality and norms of reciprocity are absent, a fragile and passive concept of citizenship, increasing economic inequalities at a time when the welfare state is under severe attack and there are few means of determining citizens needs. However, while outlining the current 'malaise' a number of writers are proposing a consideration of voluntary associations or alternatively the 'third sector' as a possible 'cure', suggesting the crisis is not necessarily terminal.

The voluntary sector as a panacea

A review of recent literature focusing on the third sector (and the voluntary associations that exist within it) suggests that many regard it as potentially a place where politics can be democratized, active citizenship strengthened, the public sphere reinvigorated and welfare programmes suited to pluralist needs designed and delivered. Further, it is suggested that a strong third sector can reap significant economic benefits. Indeed, as Dekker and van den Broek (1998: 12) conclude, a 'flourishing civil society has been argued to enhance social cohesion and foster political democracy' and their comparative analysis of thirteen western nations finds empirical evidence to support this claim.

Hirst (1994) believes that voluntary associations have the potential to be the principal organizing force in society providing public welfare and the primary means of democratic governance. Indeed, if government really is part of the problem, then Hirst's proposal should be all the more attractive since its primary aim is to reduce the scale and scope of the affairs administered by the state. This would be achieved through a process of devolution of state functions, authority, and funding to a network of voluntary associations. Hirst claims that such a system, which he outlines in *Associative Democracy* (1994), can ameliorate the process whereby citizen choice is combined with public welfare. Further, that voluntary associations have the capacity for a high level of communicative democracy would allow for widespread consultation, cooperation and collaboration (1994: 6–40).

The ability of voluntary associations to create high levels of communicative democracy is clearly important if they are to reinvigorate the public sphere. In *The Structural Transformation of the Public Sphere*, Habermas (1989) questions what the social conditions are in which the idea of a public sphere (in which 'rational-critical debate about public issues conducted by private persons willing to let arguments and not statuses determine decisions') can prevail? (Calhoun, 1992: 1). As opposed to pre-established forms of power, Giddens (1994: 16) claims late twentieth-century democracy requires a public arena in which controversial issues can be resolved, or at least handled. This he calls dialogic democracy. Hirst's model of associative democracy would appear to have something to offer in achieving these objectives.

It is to the question of democracy that those interested in the idea of voluntary associations inevitably turn. Cohen and Rogers (1995: 1–44) believe that invigorating voluntary associations is a means to deepening and extending the democratic state. Due to the fact that voluntary associations are characterized by organizational autonomy from the state and are therefore potentially more democratic, they are better suited to promoting general welfare than the present institutional arrangements. Cohen and Rogers suggest that voluntary associations have four specific democratic enhancement functions: they provide information to policy-makers; redress political inequalities that exist when politics is materially based; act as schools of democracy and provide alternative governance to markets and public hierarchies that permits society to realize the important benefits of cooperation among citizens.

Putnam (1993: 83–99) makes a similar point, suggesting that voluntary associations are significant contributors to the effectiveness and stability of democratic governance and can lead to significant economic benefits as well. This is due to the internal effects on members who develop habits of cooperation, solidarity and public spiritedness. The external effects include effective social collaboration and effective self-government. Indeed, Putnam's study of communities throughout the regions of Italy provides practical examples of the potential benefits of voluntary associations to community life, and the denser the networks in the community (that is, the vibrancy of associational life), the more likely the citizens will be able to cooperate for mutual benefit. Furthermore, Putnam claims members of associations display more political sophistication, social trust and political participation. Since voluntary associations represent horizontal interaction they can sustain social trust and cooperation in a way that vertical networks cannot, and therefore are essential to the production/reproduction of social capital. Putnam defines social capital as the 'features of social organization, such as trust, norms, and networks, that can improve the efficiency of society by facilitating co-ordinated actions' (1993: 167). It is clear then that Putnam (1993: 87–9) believes associations have the potential to strengthen citizenship, which he claims is marked in a civic community by active participation in public affairs. This also incorporates commitments to equal rights and obligations for all, where the community is bound by horizontal relations of reciprocity and cooperation rather than by vertical relations of authority and dependency. However, for Putnam, citizenship in a civic community amounts to more than simply active, public-spirited and equal citizens. It also includes citizens who are helpful, respectful and trustful towards one another. Civic communities are not conflict free, they are simply more tolerant of their opponents. They also have greater stores of social capital. Ranci (1997), in pointing to a fragile concept of citizenship, believes this form of participation (in voluntary associations) must be entrusted with the task of solving the crisis of legitimating citizenship and welfare systems.

Lyons' (1997) summary of the literature suggests that positive claims regarding non-profit organizations include the following: they are a crucial determinant to political participation; they are more efficient than government provision and can be more sensitive and responsive to the needs of client groups; they are crucial for the reproduction of social capital that underpins effective democratic political systems and strong economies; they provide for a strong civil society that counterweights the tendencies towards domination of the state and market forces.

Counterposing these optimistic accounts and appraisals are those which are not so convinced. Here the suggestion is that the third sector itself might be an illusion, or at the very least not the conduit for positive externalities and sets of social relations.

The voluntary sector and civil society

As we have seen, many accept that the third sector and voluntary associations are core elements of civil society (notwithstanding the debates around the notion of civil society itself), and those focusing on the changes to Eastern Europe and the former Soviet Union over the last decade have often placed primary importance on questions to do with the degree to which civil society is established or can be established in the new and emerging nation-states. The relationship of civil society to the state and the market are also major areas of focus for these writers, together with the relation of the economic, political and social realms to civil society (Cohen and Arato, 1992).

In terms of a more negative stance towards the possibilities of civil society renewal through the medium of voluntary associations, Boli (1991) has questioned whether there is such a thing as a viable voluntary sector in Sweden, since the organizations are so bound to, and dependent on, the state that their independence is crucially compromised – this for a sector that comprises some 200,000 organizations with more than 31 million members in a population of 8.3 million people (Boli, 1992: 240). Despite the high numbers of participants/ members, James (1989: 9) earlier claimed that the Swedish non-profit sector is in fact small and plays only a minor role when regarded as a producer of private and social benefits. Other analysis of the Swedish voluntary sector has challenged the approach of Boli and James (notably Wijkstrom, 1997; Lundstrum and Wijkstrom, 1997). However, questions regarding the independence of the voluntary sector appear all the more relevant if there is a movement to transfer greater responsibilities to voluntary and non-profit organizations.

O'Connell raises similar issues. He suggests that voluntary organizations that receive substantial and long-term government funding can become quasi-governmental entities (O'Connell, 1996). While he does not suggest that these voluntary organizations cannot still be effective representatives of their clients and causes, his point is that 'if government is a very substantial source of an organization's support, its ability to be relied upon as an independent force has to be in question' (O'Connell, 1996: 222–5). O'Connell further claims the independent sector is small when compared to government. That is, non-profit expenditures are approximately 14 per cent of government expenditures in the United States, and only 2 per cent of government expenditures in the UK. While O'Connell argues that these small percentages can be spent in ways that make a difference beyond their relative size, his concern is that if a large part of the non-profit expenditure is redirected to cover programmes and services the government feels it can no longer provide, then the sector grows on the very ground that the state had inhabited, meaning that organizations can lose their capacity to be different from government. Indeed, O'Connell stresses that the small percentage non-profit expenditure represents is hardly worth preserving if it is not utilized for unique extra purposes. He clearly believes that voluntary associations and the voluntary sector allow for innovation, advocacy, criticism and reform, and he warns against processes that prevent them achieving this end. Voluntary organizations

provide wonderful elements of spirit, participation, service, influence, and the freedom to do one's own thing, but if government overloads them with the basic responsibility for public services, undercuts their income, and limits their roles for advocacy and criticism, they fail society, and America will be at another point of national breakdown when people demand government to do it all.

(O'Connell, 1996: 225)

Not surprisingly, a tension between voluntary associations and the market is also identified. According to Dekker and van den Broek (1998: 15), for example, market and state can be regarded as equal threats to voluntary associations.

Defending the voluntary sector would only seem to have relevance if it can deliver some of the lofty claims many of its advocates have made. While research is ever increasing it is not conclusive in its support for voluntary associations and the crucial findings of Robert Putnam outlined above. Indeed, if 'Putnam's book is the crescendo of a tradition of studies of the consequences of social participation for political democracy' (Dekker and van den Broek, 1998: 18), the critiques are clearly as important as the study itself.

In a special issue of *Politics and Society* (1996) three contributors analyze Putnam's *Making Democracy Work*. Goldberg (1996) re-examines the statistical validity of Putnam's findings and produces results very different from those that Putnam delivers. Accepting there is much variation between the two traditional Italies of the north and the south, Goldberg states that for the very reason that 'every southern region scores below all the northern ones, the danger of confounding within-group and between-group variation is especially acute'. As such, the critical test must be whether the variable, which is said to explain between-group variation (between northern and southern regions), can also explain within-group (within the north and within the south) variation. Through a number of examples Goldberg demonstrates that the correlations exhibited between variables within the north and south do not sustain the very strong correlations exhibited between north and south. According to Goldberg's (1996: 7) analysis the judgement of Putnam's proposal that 'civic culture and social capital undergird the creation of effective democratic institutions which in turn contribute to social and economic well-being' is at best 'not proved'.

Sabetti (1996: 19–44) critiques Putnam's explanation of 'differential performance of regional governments in terms of culture', and his claim that 'systematic variance between north and south' occurs due to the medieval legacy of civic norms and networks. According to Sabetti, the limitations of Putnam's study are firstly that the regional experiment was hardly the 'natural' experiment Putnam claims; secondly, that patterns of civic culture do not explain the whole story of regional government performance; and thirdly, that institutions more modern than the medieval ones Putnam considers have shaped civic society and constitute a south different from the one Putnam proposes. Sabetti claims that even the sketches Putnam begins his inquiry with of Bologna and Bari do not quite fit the 'facts on the ground'.

Levi (1996: 45–55) believes Putnam fails in his application and understanding of the concept of path dependency. She notes that historically given structures and experiences must be reproduced to have the same effects they had in the past. Putnam fails to explain this, she argues; and he does not pay sufficient attention to technical and social change. However, Levi's key reservation is regarding Putnam's concept of social capital. She suggests that he offers an incomplete theory of its origins, maintenance, transformation and effects. Indeed, while Putnam's definition has been widely accepted elsewhere, other recent literature has also begun to question the validity of the definition (Newton, 1998), and whether it is consistent with Coleman and Bourdieu, who were the first to use the concept (Edwards and Foley, 1998).

Levi (1996) further claims there is a general romanticism in *Making Democracy Work* regarding the positive effects of civic engagement and the image of community. Indeed, she is doubtful whether associations are up to the task of producing better governance and suggests social trust is more likely to emerge in experiences and institutions outside such associations rather than within them. According to Levi, under certain circumstances state institutions can be a more likely basis for generalized trust. Where some have suggested voluntary associations as the answer to the inclination of modern society towards the Hobbesian view, Levi suggests it is more likely the absence of an effective state that leads to a nasty and brutish society with the 'war of all against all'. Importantly, Levi criticizes Putnam's tendency to assume that the capacity to engage in collective action is always virtuous, and correctly identifies Bosnia and Rwanda as recent examples where collective action was clearly something other than that. In an obvious reference to Putnam's 1995 article 'Bowling Alone: America's Declining Social Capital', Levi alerts the reader to the fact that Timothy McVeigh and his co-conspirators in the Okalahoma City bombing were members of the very bowling leagues whose declining numbers Putnam laments. On the other hand, while these examples appear arresting in their potency, it is important to note that reciprocity and generalized trust (Giddens, 1994) were clearly lacking in the cases used by Levi, and that both of these might be critical to the production/reproduction of social capital. The Putnam debate has to some extent motivated interest in developing measures of social capital for use within voluntary sector research. Onyx and Bullen (1997) argue that social capital is amenable to empirical testing and stress the importance of three main constituent factors: community participation; proactivity (a sense of personal and collective efficacy with the active and willing engagement of citizens within a participative community); and trust. Post-Putnam, we however still await more definitive (empirical) research on the social-capital debate which is capable of moving the ideas along. As it stands, there appears to be no clear evidence of the effectivity of the voluntary sector as a promoter of social capital.

A final comment needs to be made regarding the contribution of civic activism to economic success. In the current climate of economic stagnation (and possible world recession) much has been made of this particular finding of Putnam. For example, Fukuyama (1995), in *Trust*, builds very much on the ideas of generalized trust in claiming that high-trust societies tend to be economically more successful. Yet others argue that Putnam overstated the contribution of civic engagement. Kenworthy (1997: 645–57), for instance, suggests that civic engagement has had little or nothing to do with national economic success in recent decades, and uses data from the 1991 World Values Survey to demonstrate the point. The jury on Putnam therefore remains decidedly out.

Voluntary sector institutions and capitalism

In his 1988 presidential campaign George Bush used the evocative metaphor of 'a thousand points of light' when referring to voluntary associations and their potential to address pressing social conditions. Roelofs (1995) suggests that in the light of Bush, the nonprofit sector can be viewed as a system of power exercised in the interest of the corporate world:

> one reason capitalism doesn't collapse despite its many weaknesses and valiant opposition movements is because of the nonprofit sector.
> (Roelefs, 1995: 16)

Following a traditional Marxist argument, Roelofs claims that the critical question presented by Marx and Engels in *The Communist Manifesto* regarding a section of the bourgeoisie being interested in addressing social grievances in order to secure their own continued existence, has been sorely neglected. The section of the bourgeoisie so identified includes economists, philanthropists, humanitarians, improvers of the social conditions of the working class, organizers of charity, and temperance groups. That is, voluntary associations and particularly those most interested in 'welfare'.

This argument is a transfer to the voluntary sector of the familiar 'critical' approach to the welfare state which argues that it exists to shore-up the status quo, particularly in social and economic spheres. As the welfare state is dismantled ('re-mantled' may be a better term), the voluntary sector assumes the role of a buffer zone. As Bauman comments, this view was probably always too narrow, even in the high tide of centralized welfare (Bauman, 1998: 46). Nevertheless, the question of the autonomy of the voluntary sector bears some examination.

The major claim here from Roelofs is that the few truly independent organizations in the voluntary sector are usually small, poor and obscure, and that most organizations in this sector are 'linked to each other and to the major corporations by their funding, their invested assets, technical assistance, interlocking directories and peak organizations' (Roelofs, 1995: 17).

Roelofs further claims that the non-profit sector serves as a protective layer for capitalism for the following reasons: it facilitates the concentration and distribution of capital for the profit-making sector; non-profits provide goods and services that the market cannot; in the United States at least, advocacy and reform are largely monopolized by foundation-supported non-profits rather than political parties, unions and social movements; the non-governmental and non-partisan status of these organizations generates the idea of altruistic organizations which becomes useful in terms of their international activities; the large foundations have great influence regarding their planning and funding, and in supplying ideas for political change; the foundations serve the purposes of the major players, allowing them to dispose of vast fortunes, initiate social control through philanthropy, and improve public relations. Thus Roelofs claims that these foundations, in terms of their funding, can determine the political and social agenda, even steering organizations with more radical agendas to reasonable and pragmatic goals by pouring money into them, both at home and internationally. For Roelefs, the non-profit sector has too great an influence: 'the US nonprofit has not only funded individual nonprofits of all kinds, but has attempted to create an entire world in its own image' (Roelofs, 1995: 25).

The extent and nature of the automony of the non-profit sector is clearly a crucial question; and in any analysis of the potential determinations of its actions the focus needs to be sharply on, we would argue, both state and market.

Voluntary association – a unique opportunity

We have considered here only part of the recent literature generated on the subjects of the third sector, non-profits, voluntary associations and social capital. This survey is not intended to be exhaustive, but rather an attempt to draw together some major contemporary themes. While the analyses vary greatly, the common thread that runs through most of the work is an uneasiness regarding, in Foucault's words, 'the nature of the present'. Suspicions have arisen regarding the ability of the state and the market to address the challenges outlined in the first section of this chapter, which in some respects increases the pressure on the third sector to be the 'true and proper' solution.

In this study we would want to hold to O'Connell's (1996) position (though perhaps for different reasons than he), that state-initiated moves to increase the responsibility of the third sector and voluntary associations should 'proceed with caution'. It would appear that there are voluntary associations have unique elements that should be preserved irrespective of whether they exist to the degree and with the benefits that Putnam (1993) and those that follow him claim. The ideals of participation, service, influence and the 'freedom to do their own thing', can probably only be met if such associations are not overloaded with responsibility for public services as *de facto* or quasi-state functionaries. Their roles in advocacy and criticism would almost certainly be undermined as well in such a scenario, for their contribution to democratic ideals, subsidiarity and a reinvigorated public sphere is critical.

The threat of the state appears to be matched by the threat of the market, if we are to give credence to the work of Roelefs (1995), Dekker and van den Broek (1998) and others. Indeed, since anything that enhances the market's ability to generate more profit is invariably appropriated by the market, the more relevant question in light of the current environment might be: on what terms can an independent voluntary sector survive, let alone become more influential?

What is clear is that there is a need for more research into the voluntary sector that moves beyond descriptions of various voluntary sectors across the globe (Salamon and Anheier, 1997). Following Dekker and van den Broek (1998), we would argue that before debates regarding associative democracy can truly be engaged, we need more detailed research on the sectors and more appreciation of the ways in which voluntary associations are connected to the processes of social capital formation. Accordingly there is a need for comparative in-depth studies 'of civil societies in municipalities, cities, and regions within nations' (Dekker and van den Broek, 1998: 35–6), as well as between nations. Only through the application of such enquiry can we enhance the debates around citizenship, the public sphere, democracy, social capital and community, and questions regarding the perceived problems of, for example, 'mischief of factions' and 'free-riders'.

Part II
Analysing Voluntary Associations

4
Setting the Boundaries: Established Frameworks of Operation

As indicated in preceding chapters, a key issue addressed in this book is the role of voluntary associations in strengthening civil society. This issue is gaining attention in the burgeoning theoretical discussions of voluntary associations and civil society. However, these discussions have not, in general, been informed by empirical analyses of the operating rationales and organizational forms in voluntary associations. In this chapter we present a typology of four frameworks for investigating the rationales and forms of voluntary associations, and we analyse the major themes in three of these, the activist, charity and welfare state industry frameworks. In the following chapter we analyse the fourth framework which is constructed around the discourses of the market.

The idea of operating rationale refers to values, assumptions and principles underpinning organizational forms, everyday activities, practices and social relations. Operating rationales provide organizational logics and are manifested in specific discourses. Operating rationales, organizational forms and everyday practices, processes and social relations come together to constitute an operating framework. Operating frameworks can be linked to different political regimes. We can link each of these four frameworks to the four basic concepts of social theory discussed in Chapter 2. Each framework engages the concept of community, but in different ways. The activist framework places the idea of community at the centre of its activities. Here the privileged concept of community mediates the relation between the individual, state and market through relations of mutuality and solidarity. The charity framework mediates the relation between the individual and the community through the construction of relations of patronage and dependency between individuals and voluntary associations. The welfare state industry framework is dominated by the state, which sets the conditions for the relations between the state, community and individual. In the market framework the market determines the relations between the individual and the community. We can also relate each of the four frameworks to different types of association. In the activist framework the major principle of association is cooperation. The charity framework association is based on patronage. In the welfare state industry framework, rule-based procedures set the context for association, whereas in the market framework association is structured by the principles of competition.

While the activist, charity and welfare state industry frameworks are well-developed in voluntary associations, the market model has only just begun to make its mark upon the voluntary sector, and it appears to be producing both dangers and opportunities for voluntary associations. However, our position in this book is that regardless of one's normative position in regard to the market framework (and we agree with those who view the application of the logics of the capitalist market to the voluntary sector with some concern), market principles are in the ascendant. An appropriate approach to this ascendancy is to analyse and engage market logics, rather than dismiss them out of hand. It is important to understand that the frameworks are not exclusive and they can operate concurrently. They often overlap in inconsistent and incongruous ways. Voluntary associations might function on the basis of a range of different operating rationales, organizational forms and everyday practices. We discuss these constellations of operating frameworks in Chapter 7.

Our focus in this and the following chapter is the ways in which the frameworks have developed in Australia, although we draw on applications and analyses from outside Australia. We consider the dominant discourses in each framework, some of the key historical factors, the organizational forms and the types of social relationships inhering in each framework, its role in civil society and some of the debates and issues concerning the operation of each framework.

The activist framework

Activist discourses

It is the activist framework that is most commonly invoked in discussions of voluntary associations and civil society. In this framework voluntary associations are organized around the discourses of mutuality, empathy, trust, solidarity and democratic organization oriented to social change. Voluntary associations or organizations operating within an activist framework (in this book we refer to these as activist associations or organizations) can be issue based, in the sense that they are organized around social, cultural and environmental orientations and concerns, such as a forest action group or a human rights organization. They can be member-serving with a mutual aid function, such as a tenants' association or a self-help group. Activist voluntary associations can also be public-serving, by undertaking pressure group functions or offering specific services to the general public, such as legal aid and consumer advocacy, or to special interest groups, such as women victims of torture.

The social change rationale of activist voluntary association is constructed around the importance of community participation or control in social organization and a commitment to social change. This rationale draws on the communitarian emphasis on mutuality, civic virtue, trust and moral obligation, and the activist logic of political mobilization and resistance. Communitarianism is concerned to rebuild communities as a process of reinvigorating civil society against egoistic individualism. Political mobilization provides a way of giving organized expression to solidarity, advocacy and self-determination.

The activist framework privileges the rhetoric of community participation, democratization and empowerment. Participation is required to extend the terrain of democratization and to ensure the self-formation of communities. Empowerment takes place as groups and communities are resourced to take control of their own destinies. The processes of community participation, democratization and empowerment are central to a way of working with communities that has come to be known as community development. Community development methods offer a way of facilitating citizen empowerment through the development of ongoing structures and processes by which communities can identify and address their own issues, needs and problems within their own terms of reference, and mobilize as a group to obtain the resources necessary to meet their needs (Kenny, 1994).

Social change occurs at three levels. First, at the structural level, whereby oppositional and political mobilization strategies shift control of resources and power to the community sector; second, at the ideational level, where citizens come to understand their interdependence and the value of mutuality, reciprocity and compassion; and finally, at the level of skills, where citizens become skilled in participating in articulating concerns, identifying needs and resolving conflicts, and in so doing, become active agents in their own destiny.

Activist voluntary associations have a broad concept of welfare, as embracing a whole range of activities that can enhance well-being, including activities organized around cultural development, international aid, race relations, environmental matters and disability issues. Welfare services are distributed on the basis of mutuality, compassion, equality and social justice. The activist rationale rejects both the charity approach to welfare and welfare state forms of delivery because the methods used in these approaches are paternalistic and disciplinary.

Welfare needs are located in communities, rather than individuals, and are articulated and resourced at the level of community. Community denotes both a form of association and a site. The construction of community as a form of association has dominated communitarian and other forms of normative analyses of the 'good life'. As a site, community is a geographical location or a social space where social relations are formed, reproduced and contested. In the activist framework the boundaries of community are less important than the way in which social relations and power structure relations are shaped. In the meta-discourse of activist voluntary associations, community has been identified as the site for forming identities and fulfilling social needs. Community reinforces the mutuality of social relationships and the social ontology of individuals being constituted and defined by their social attachments. Community is a foil against abstract individualism, rational egoism and the instrumental conception of human relationships (Friedman, 1989). From an activist perspective, communities are self-forming entities, rather than pre-given, completed projects (Everingham, 1998). The development of welfare is inextricably linked to the development of these self-forming communities.

Activist voluntary associations concerned with service delivery are established as a response to specific circumstances and needs, rather than for the purpose of providing universal programmes. Participants are concerned to develop the most effective programmes and campaigns for their identified constituency, rather than operate according to specific standards.

Historical background

The activist tradition in voluntary associations has taken different shapes in different countries. For example, in the United States activist voluntary associations have drawn on the principles of self-reliance and civic virtue which have been central to the development of American culture (de Toqueville, 1968), the community organizing tradition of neighbourhood activism (Alinsky, 1972), the theoretical strands of communitarianism, and the political mobilization approach which has been closely associated with civil rights, feminist and other social movements.

In Britain, activist voluntary associations gained a foothold in the 1970s as community struggles around unemployment, social security and local development issues took shape (Jones and Mayo, 1974). As communities came to be acknowledged as important sites for class struggle (Castells, 1983; Cochrane, 1986) the Left began to articulate a vision of grass-roots activism aimed at establishing local socialism (Boddy and Fudge, 1984; Gyford, 1985; Mackintosh and Wainwright, 1987). In Australia the development of the framework of activist voluntary associations is also placed in the Left tradition. Its ascendancy took place alongside the political and intellectual reinvigoration of the Australian Left in the 1970s. The activist framework of voluntary associations which prevailed in the 1970s focused on the politics of equality and redistribution (Fraser, 1995). During the 1970s and early 1980s a range of new community organizations was established around environmental concerns (Hutton, 1987; Mundey, 1981; Sanders, 1991; Wade, 1991) and green analyses were overlaid on other Left analyses (see Burgmann, 1993; Ife, 1995). By the late 1970s the discourses of identity and difference were also being articulated. These discourses were clearly manifested in activist community organizations concerned with gay and lesbian rights (see Altman, 1979; Burgmann, 1993; Kitchen, 1982).

Throughout this period many of those involved in activist voluntary associations argued that communities were effective sites of struggle, while at the same time they distanced themselves from traditional welfare work at the local level and they eschewed state funding. Their position was influenced by their concern about technocratic style and the disciplinary powers of the state. They emphasized the regulatory and co-optive implications of dependency on state support, the need to reject state funding, and as far as possible, to bypass state regulatory requirements. Members of these groups, including unemployment activists, feminists, environmentalists and gay and lesbian groups, tended to identify with new social movements rather than with welfare programmes (see Burgmann, 1993; Goodall, 1988). In particular, the activist perspective in community organizations gained inspiration from the activist Aboriginal and Torres Strait Islander movements for land rights and self-determination (Burgmann and Lee, 1988; Burgmann, 1993; Foley, 1988; Turner, 1987), and the burgeoning green campaigns, including what came to be known as 'The Green Bans', involving alliances between green campaigners, trade unions and community activists (Burgmann, 1993; Mundey, 1981).

The activist voluntary associations which continued to apply for state funding argued for both the efficacy of community struggles and the importance of not allowing the state to abrogate its responsibility to fund programmes for all its citizens. For these groups, it was possible to work 'in and against the state' (London Edinburgh Weekend Return Group, 1980).

These organizations took hope from government policies backing self-managed and advocacy programmes, including unemployment and welfare rights organizations, women's health programmes and women's refuges, tenants' unions, and projects based on a commitment to self-help and self-determination at the local level as a form of activism (Smith, 1978; West, 1991). They were often influenced by a government policy initiative supporting regional development, known as the Australian Assistance Plan, that was established during the period of the Whitlam Labor Government in the early 1970s (Thorpe, 1985). It was during this period that governments, at both the state and federal level, developed policies and institutional settings that facilitated the establishment of community development strategies for self-determination at the local level. Funding regimes were established that were based on voluntary associations identifying needs and presenting the case to governments for supporting community programmes responding to local needs (Lyons, 1997).

Organizational themes and forms

As discussed above, there are two different discourses influencing the organizational form of activist voluntary associations. The first is concerned with ideas of mutuality, empathy and trust. The second is concerned with political mobilization. These two discourses can have slightly different organizational outcomes. Because mutuality, empathy and trust can be ends in themselves, some activist voluntary associations focus on developing sharing and caring organizational environments and the establishment of full participatory structures. Where the political mobilization discourse dominates, certain types of instrumentally oriented structures become important. These are not the structures of formal instrumental rationality, concerned with developing performance indicators, or instrumentally rational mechanisms for the distribution and delivery of welfare programmes, for example, that have been developed in the framework of managerialism. Political mobilization requires the development of a strategic instrumentalism in the context of political struggle.

Whatever the organizational focus, the activist framework offers a commitment to organizational structures that maximize participant input and control. To facilitate maximum participant input and control, it is necessary to establish non-hierarchical structures and open decision-making processes. Thus activist voluntary associations appear to exude democratic principles. Social relations are characterized by a high degree of symmetry. The solidaristic core of activist voluntary associations means that accountability is both horizontal and reciprocal and involves all participants, including members, workers and, where there are service-provision activities, service users. In a community development framework, all participants should be provided with resources to contribute to the strategic development of their voluntary association. The participatory and democratic rhetoric also means that the power relations between employers and employees are equalized, or even eliminated, as in the case of collectives. For those voluntary associations offering services, the notion of professional expertise is rejected. Participatory processes require that relations between provider and recipient are symmetrical, and they can even be interchangeable, as in the case of self-help organizations. Lines of accountability are primarily to co-members of the organization, which because the distinction between providers and recipients is weakened or non-existent, will include both co-workers and recipients of programmes.

The political mobilization theme in the activist framework brings voluntary associations conceptually close to new social movements. While there may be some overlap between new social movements and activist voluntary associations on one level, some important differences can be discerned. As well as organizing politically around issues, activist voluntary associations develop and provide ongoing services and programmes. They have some degree of formality in their structures and employment practices. A defining characteristic of new social movements is that they exist outside the state, formal institutions and mainstream political processes. Rarely will new social movements seek or receive government funds. In contrast, activist voluntary associations do seek and receive government funds, if not directly for their political activist work, for their service provision.

Activist voluntary associations and civil society

From the civil society perspective there is considerable appeal in the activist framework of voluntary associations. This framework ensures that the realm of politics is extended beyond governments, political parties and experts. It defines politics as a process which stretches from the level of micro-politics, such as the daily experience of ordinary life, to wider questions of resource allocation (Cochrane, 1986) and the self-determination of communities. Activist voluntary associations mediate between the individual, the state and the market on behalf of communities. They have appeal to many in the Left because they provide forums where the interests of working-class, women's and disadvantaged minorities can be articulated. Activist voluntary associations do not claim to serve universal needs or interests. Their interest is in providing a space for the development of oppositional interpretations of interests and needs, where the voices of those who are excluded from the dominant discourses can be listened to. Through their participatory processes, activist voluntary associations can provide organizational forms for the development of individual autonomy, where self-determining moral agents capable of resistance are formed (Franklin, 1998). They are unique in opening up sites for the celebration of difference and micro-political resistance. The operating rationales and organizational forms of activist voluntary associations offer a way of holding back the logics of administrative and economic mechanisms in favour of the logics of social participation and self-empowerment (Cohen and Arato, 1992).

The concept of citizenship informing the activist framework of voluntary associations emphasizes rights rather than obligations and duties. The rights discourse and the rhetoric of empowerment and self-determination imply active citizenship principles at work. The renovation of citizenship in its active form has been absorbed into a range of contemporary Left agendas for voluntary associations. In particular, active citizenship has become part of the repertoire of the search for new progressive agendas seeking the radicalization, deepening and pluralization of democracy (Mouffe, 1992). Yet in Australia voluntary associations concerned with democratic agendas are currently struggling to maintain or even reclaim the democratic rights that have developed over the past twenty years.

Debates and issues

Notwithstanding the general endorsements of activist voluntary associations by those who are committed to strengthening civil society, the activist rationales and operations have been subjected to a significant body of critique and a number of debates have ensued. These debates have been constructed around the issue of whether activist voluntary associations do provide appropriate sites for participatory action oriented to social change. They centre on several concerns.

The first concern is constructed around debates about macro- and micro-strategies for change. Much activist endeavour is still embedded in the left rhetoric of the 1970s, with its grand narratives and commitment to challenging and overthrowing state apparatuses (Althusser, 1984) and dominant ideologies (Abercrombie et al., 1980). In this rhetoric, power struggles are congealed in large-scale confrontations and social change involves mass mobilization and sweeping power shifts. In contrast, there is a view that rejects the search for privileged sites upon which power relations can be challenged. Analyses should focus on how power is exercised through a multiplicity of forms, for example, through dispositions, manoeuvres, tactics and techniques occurring at the micro-levels of society. From this perspective activist voluntary associations are sites for micro-resistance, not large-scale political mobilization. Voluntary associations provide the venues from which to launch symbolic, ideological and micro-structural challenges to the ongoing subjugation that occurs in everyday life.

The second concern focuses on the Left critiques of the community location and orientation of activist voluntary associations. This debate was launched in the 1970s, when Marxist and feminist analyses identified community as an ideological construct. In Britain, for example, a range of writers argued that the concept of community had been hijacked by those in power to obscure class and gender inequalities (Cockburn, 1977; Repo, 1977). In the 1980s the experience of the failure of the 'local socialism' of the Greater London Council was cited as proof of both the impossibility of local socialism and the unsuitability of voluntary associations as a site for prefiguring socialist relations. A more recent version of this debate has been articulated through the critiques of communitarianism. The focus on community is seen as a manifestation of the nostalgia for the mechanical solidarity of *gemeinschaft*, with its unitary social forms and authoritarian social structures.

In Australia, Mowbray (1985) has argued that community participation has become a modern panacea which uses the rhetoric of cooperation and harmonious relations, while obscuring class inequalities and the interests of those in power. Participation is a disguised management technique used to co-opt communities. Through engagement in policy making and negotiation with governments, the disruptive energies of activist voluntary associations are channelled in ways that legitimate the existing system of authority. More recently, Everingham (1998) has argued that despite all the democratic rhetoric of participatory politics, participation has been hollowed out, to be replaced with processes for consultation, advocacy and self-help.

The third concern focuses on the extent to which community life and democratic activities are circumscribed by the solidaristic tendencies and concealed authoritarianism in activist organizations. Much of this debate has been steered by feminist critiques of communitarianism. For example, Friedman (1989) argues that the communitarian concept of community life based on family and neighbourhood provides a troubling paradigm of social relationships and communal life. She points out that communities are not immune to forms of domination and subordination through which individual views can be subdued. Young (1990), critiquing both the nostalgic yearnings for community and the authoritarian tendencies which are found in the solidaristic forms of community participation and activism, argues that the ideal of community privileges unity over difference and sympathy over the recognition of the limits of one's understanding of others from their point of view. Much of the advocacy work of activist voluntary associations, for example, which involves speaking for others, sets up a context in which subaltern voices are filtered through experts, thus reinforcing ideas of dependency. Activist voluntary associations with a strong strategic instrumentalist agenda carry dangers of intellectual and organizational imperialism in the sense that in their passion to achieve change, activist leaders can impose their perceptions upon both other participants and the community. Preoccupation with securing commitment to a cause engenders leadership and organizational styles that prohibit the development of horizontal reciprocity to those not fully committed to the 'faith'. In some activist voluntary associations disagreement and difference are often read as 'breeches of solidarity' (Young, 1990). Strong identity politics can have other effects too. Whilst identity politics and the celebration of difference set the framework for the development of micro-political resistance, they also open the way for the establishment of 'political enclaves' which are characterized by social, intellectual and political closure (Mansbridge, 1996). There are other, more insidious forms of 'enclave politics' that have found homes in activist voluntary associations. These are the anti-civil activist voluntary associations that organize around intolerance, such as anti-gay and racist organizations.

Fourthly, the informal decision-making which has been seen to characterize activist voluntary associations, is not necessarily democratic. Denial of power structures does not eliminate underlying power relations. In fact as Feher and Heller (1983) point out, lack of formal structure can actually mask the relations of unequal power and foreclose the possibility of removing small power groups. An ostensibly open, tolerant structure without rules can enable the most articulate and active people to dominate (Keane, 1988). Democratic participation can also be circumscribed by the way political leadership develops. For example, Alinsky (1972), for all his claims for community self-determination, had his own rules and political programme, and brought in expert organizers from outside the community. When empowerment is something that you do to others or they do to you it loses its reflexive and collective meaning (Baistow, 1994/5).

The final debate concerns the extent to which activist voluntary associations should seek and receive government funds. In the 1970s voluntary associations dominated by the activist framework operated against the backdrop of a popular acceptance of state responsibility for welfare provision. However, activist associations have always been divided in their response to the welfare state. While they agree that their role is to mediate between state and civil society, there is no consensus over questions of state funding. Some organizations have emphasized the co-optive implications of dependency on the capitalist and patriarchal state and eschewed state funds. Others have invoked concepts of state responsibility and citizen rights and argued for acceptance of state funds, even when the price to pay has been increased control by state institutions. Linked to the arguments proffered by the latter camp are a commitment to social rights and decommodification of welfare.

Despite some unrelenting critiques of the efficacy of activist voluntary associations it would be fair to say that the overall assessment of the role of activist voluntary associations in civil society is positive, as will be discussed in Chapter 8, below. While it may be argued that the activities of activist voluntary associations not have resulted in major power shifts in structural terms, or overall success in confronting practices at the level of micro-power, nevertheless, government social agendas have been altered and there have been some important challenges at the level of micro-power. For example, as their self-confidence and sense of personal agency has developed in feminist organizations, women have constructed new politics of resistance (Baldry and Vinson, 1991; West, 1991). Women's voluntary associations have managed to place violence against women on the public policy table (Weeks and Gilmore, 1996). Residents' groups have won battles to stop unsuitable urban development, and environmental groups have campaigned successfully to save wilderness areas (Sanders, 1991). There have also been limited, if not forestalled, achievements for Aboriginal and Torres Strait Islander organizations in their struggles for land rights and self-determination (Burgmann, 1993).

The charity framework

Charity discourses

The charity framework is organized around three thematic discourses. Firstly, virtue, service and compassion; secondly, moral discipline; and finally, discourse constructed around ideas of dependency and patronage. Charity relations fit most comfortably with *gemeinschaft* constructions of community, as a form of association organized around close personal bonds and moral obligations. Both spatial and temporal referents are evident in the constructions of community underpinning charity discourses. The spatial referent is apparent in the idea of small-scale and close relations. The temporal referent surfaces when the *gemeinschaft/gesellschaft* typology is formulated in a nostalgic paradigm and based on a normative characterization of pre-modern forms of social relations as essentially nurturing and virtuous.

The charity framework eschews any structural or collectivist solution to issues of disadvantage, poverty, social justice and inequality, in favour of 'relief from poverty' based on patronage of individuals. Welfare services are distributed on the basis of different mixes of obligation, compassion, individual patronage and moral discipline. Thus the welfare principle underpinning the charity framework is a narrow social amelioration one, concerned with limited social provision dispensed to dependent (and deserving) individuals. The individualist approach to welfare inscribed in the charity framework means that it is the individual who is the locus of the resolution of welfare problems, not communities.

The distinction between deserving and undeserving poor and the discourse of moral discipline, which were at the heart of the charity framework which was established at the beginning of white settlement in Australia, has weakened in contemporary charity-based organizations in Australia, ironically, to be taken up within the welfare state industry framework in the form of media and government led attacks on 'welfare cheats' and 'dole bludgers'. However, the discourses of individual dependency and patronage, public service, private virtue and compassion have remained strong components of the charity framework.

Underpinning the discourses of the charity approach to welfare are social relations based on vertical reciprocity. Vertical reciprocity provides benefits to all parties in the relationship, but in the context of asymmetrical power relations. For example, the giver in a charity relationship might provide material or moral sustenance to the receiver, but the receiver can also bestow moral redemption upon the giver in the very act of receiving charity.

Historical background

Historically, the charity ethos is embedded in a social relation and a value system which begins with the idea of devotion to the welfare of others. This ethos has a presence throughout human history. In Western societies planned giving or philanthropy has bestowed goodness upon the giver and has often offered a path to religious salvation. The principles of charity brought by the white settlers to Australia were developed in Britain at the end of the eighteenth century as the critique of the existing British Poor Law gained momentum. In this critique, community- and church-based philanthropy that had dominated the system of poor relief for centuries was deemed to be indiscriminate, arbitrary and inappropriate to the needs of capitalist work orientation and discipline.

The ascendancy of the belief that poverty was the result of individual moral failure found clear institutional expression in Britain in the new Poor Law of 1834. As industrial capitalism developed, the idea of 'needing protection' came to be connected with moral weakness or inferiority. Those who were dependent were stigmatized and even identified as deviant individuals (Fraser and Gordon, 1994). The new Poor Law was developed around a particular social construction of the categories of poor, dependent and destitute, which were embedded in the distinction between deserving and undeserving poor. The distinction between deserving and undeserving poor rested on normative views of the work ethic, individual responsibility and frugality. The whole discourse of deserving and undeserving poor provided an effective disciplinary regime for the unemployed, and other victims of early industrial capitalism, who 'might otherwise have rebelled against their situation'. During the nineteenth century the moral judgements on industrious habits, destitution frugality and philanthropy were carried to Australia by working-class migrants and the philanthropically minded bourgeoisie, especially women (Beilharz et al., 1992). The idea that the 'well-to-do' had a moral obligation to assist the deserving poor and preventing the vulnerable from becoming idle or immoral led to the establishment of benevolent societies throughout Australia. These benevolent societies have been significant deliverers of welfare throughout the nineteenth and twentieth centuries. As Summers (1975) points out, women have had a central role in benevolent societies, as 'god's police' and providers of welfare, as well as the victims of both poverty and their own weaknesses, who required protection against vagrancy and tendencies towards immoral behaviour.

In the post-Second World War period charity organizations developed new organizational forms and rationales, and they have rejected the distinction between the deserving and undeserving poor, the Christian 'do-gooder' image, and their role in the inculcation of moral discipline, although they have maintained asymmetrical power relations and notions of dependency. In the last few years charity-oriented voluntary associations have established professional modes of operation and employed professionally qualified workers.

Organizational themes and forms

The traditional charity framework is most clearly linked with pre-welfare state regimes, where responsibility for welfare provision lay outside the state, with the family, the church and other benevolent institutions. Thus, institutionally, the charity framework of voluntary associations indicates autonomy from the state. However this framework can exist under regimes of state intervention, where relations between state actors and welfare recipients can be influenced by the charity ethos. For example, the charity ethos is manifested in government funding through what Lyons (1997) calls the 'philanthropist model', where the government acts as a wealthy benefactor.

The major sites of the charity ethos in the contemporary period today are middle to large size voluntary associations that are public serving and have an historical link with a major religion. These organizations have traditionally been involved in providing poor relief as part of their commitment to enhancing religious and public virtue. Many of these voluntary associations have become secularized and now provide relief outside the protocols of religious morality, although they still operate on the basis of patronage. The relations of patronage are embedded in a clear distinction between the provision and consumption of welfare. Asymmetrical relations of power are maintained and reinforced by this framework. It has no interest in the politics of redistribution and no concern with either equality of services or equality of outcomes.

Traditionally, charity organizations have not been bureaucratically or managerially organized, although the imperative to develop professional administration which is affecting much of the voluntary sector is now being embraced by medium and large size charity organizations.

Interestingly, there have been several new institutional applications of ideas of dependency and patronage which are relevant to voluntary associations. Firstly, through the development of what is known in Australia as volunteerism, which involves people giving unpaid time to voluntary associations to help in their activities. While volunteerism has always existed in Australia and most Australians have undertaken unpaid work in the community at some time in their lives, in recent years volunteer work has become more formalized. There is even talk of a new 'volunteer industry'. The benefits of volunteerism include the view that volunteers are closer to clients, thus reducing the distance between providers and recipients (Hadley and Hatch, 1981) and the moral satisfaction that volunteers will gain through helping others (the redemptive appeal). But there are also strong instrumental factors at work. Volunteers take on volunteer work in the hope of gaining experience that will give them some leverage in the job market. From a critical perspective, volunteers are being brought into voluntary associations to undertake tasks for which there is no money for paid work. The use of volunteers can reinforce the view that welfare work is not worthy of pay and welfare recipients have no rights to welfare support (Cochrane, 1986).

The second institutional application of the charity ethos is in the idea of corporate giving, which is sometimes known as corporate sponsorship or corporate citizenship. Corporate sponsorship tends to be a 'second level' charity relationship in so far as the benefit is given to an association or organization as an intermediate body and deliverer of welfare programmes, rather than directly to the welfare recipient. Ostensibly corporate sponsorship is based on altruistic sympathies and citizenship obligations, but also provides moral and positive citizenship standing to the giver and reinforces formal asymmetrical power relations. However, what is interesting about corporate sponsorship is that it does involve some redistribution of resources from wealthy sections of the community to disadvantaged ones, although this occurs within the framework of existing power relations. Critical commentators claim that corporate giving bolsters the argument that the private sector should take responsibility for welfare needs, thus allowing the government to withdraw from state provision of welfare. Others argue that this 'philanthropic capitalism' is no more than a new construction of the labour/capital compromise, which also serves as an effective public relations exercise for corporations.

Charity-oriented voluntary associations and civil society

While there have been some strong and persuasive critiques of the charity framework, it is important to note that it also presents a system of social relations which is not commodified, or rationalized in the sense that it is not rationally instrumental or concerned with goal achievement. The social relations inscribed in the charity framework, while reinforcing asymmetrical power, can be likened to the gift relationship, whereby the gift itself is not as important as the relationship between the giver and receiver (Squires, 1990: 142). The actual giving provides recognition of the value of other people's lives. The act of public giving, such as occurs in much corporate giving and large philanthropic organizations, opens up public space for the articulation of the discourses of compassion and public service. In so far as they are dominated by a concern with public service and compassion beyond formal service-delivery, charity oriented voluntary associations offer a form of vertical reciprocity which is embedded in compassion and empathy rather than professional expertise. As a structural form even vertical reciprocity can shore up some of the networks of mutuality that are important for civil society.

Citizenship is much diminished in the context of charity principles. Charity principles privilege the discourses of dependency, moral obligation and duty, over the discourse of rights, entitlements and mutuality. Welfare recipients are passive citizens who have few unencumbered social rights and limited power for self-determination. Obligations are not constructed as part of a relationship based on mutuality between provider and recipient, but within the context of impersonal institutional requirements, such as moral obligation, as a religious imperative or a disciplinary measure to ensure work motivation.

Debates and issues

From the standpoint of strengthening active citizenship and reinvigorating civil society, there are many weaknesses in the charity framework of voluntary associations. The charity model works with an individualist approach to welfare, locating the cause of disadvantage in individuals alone, ignoring the systemic forces in society. The history of the charity framework is permeated by the distinction between deserving and undeserving poor, patronage and judgements of the moral weaknesses of people who are dependent. The focus of traditional charity organizations has been the morality of private individuals, rather than development of the public arena. Relations of mutuality are structured by vertical reciprocity, rather than the symmetrical power relations of horizontal reciprocity.

In view of the stunted concept of citizenship, the lack of a sense of a public arena and its asymmetrical power structures, the charity framework of voluntary associations lacks empowering and democratic forces. Perhaps the strongest critiques are from those on the Left who argue from socialist and feminist perspectives. For example, Squires (1990) draws our attention to the view that charity relationships freeze inequalities and reinforce stigmas. The dependency relationship is infused with coercive power and constructed in a way which complements the exploitative conditions of the labour market. Feminists have pointed out that the relations of charity are gender coded. While women have always been involved on both sides of the charity relation, as dependants and moral guides, the notions of dependency and patronage are set within the context of patriarchal constructions of power (Bielharz et al., 1992; Fraser and Gordon, 1994; Summers, 1994).

The welfare state industry framework

Welfare state industry discourses

The welfare state industry framework signals the high tide of the modernist welfare state. It based on the incorporation of the principles, values, social relations and organizational forms inscribed in the post-Second World War welfare state. This framework is applicable to voluntary associations concerned with service functions, and particularly public-serving associations, such as organizations providing services for those who are deemed to require authoritarian protection, such as the elderly, young people and people with disabilities. Centralized welfare bureaucracies almost always fund such voluntary associations, and they tend to be identified as semi-autonomous agents of the state.

The operating rationales of the welfare state industry are constructed around two normative premises. The first premise is that it is the role of the state to intervene in civil society and the workings of the market to ensure certainty and stability in people's lives. The second premise is that this intervention should be based on the principles of social rights, social justice, social equality and redistribution. Formal equality is manifested in structural features such as standardized rules and procedures and standardization of programmes; and distributional features, such as entitlements as rights, equality of welfare delivery practice, such as equal treatment of 'clients' needing support, and commitment to the redistributional logic of state transfers of income to disadvantaged groups, such as the unemployed and pensioners.

The imperatives of state intervention and formal equality mean that responsibility for the well-being of citizens does not lie with individuals, families, local communities or private corporations. It is the role of governments to ensure the security and prosperity of all their citizens, through government departments and external government agencies. The welfare state industry framework implies a neutral independent state, general acceptance of the authority inscribed in the state, and a reasonably high degree of trust in state institutions and mechanisms. Government responsibility for the welfare of citizens is expressed in two ways. Firstly, through government management of society at large, which involves interventions such as regulating capital and organizing the production and distribution of goods and services. Secondly, governments are responsible for social amelioration through income transfers and the establishment of social services and protective institutions. The role of voluntary associations is to support and supplement government initiatives and services, and act as agents for government policies and programmes.

Welfare needs inhere in both communities and individuals, and it is the role of welfare professionals to define, respond to, and treat communities and individuals. Within the welfare state industry framework communities, as both sites and forms of association, are already formed. These formed communities are reified, classified (as suitable objects for treatment, for example), and monitored. They 'become transformed into various categories of disadvantage, and the main symptoms of their disadvantage become strategically defined as needs, to be managed through the welfare system' (Everingham, 1998: 38).

It is important to note the centrality of the notion of industry in the discourse of the welfare state industry framework. The industry framework draws attention to the location of welfare work within a specific industry, involving professionalization and industrial rights based on industrial awards. However, as the welfare state industry has developed, there have been different constructions of the idea of professionalism, which we will consider below.

Historical background

As discussed in earlier chapters, the idea that the state should intervene to ensure economic and social prosperity gained momentum towards the end of the nineteenth century as market mechanisms stalled and the harsh social effects of the unfettered market became apparent. At the beginning of the nineteenth century the Fabians were arguing successfully for collectivist solutions to welfare problems, within the framework of rational state administration. The British social insurance scheme, which was developed in the early twentieth century, drew on the model of national social insurance which had been introduced in

Germany in the 1880s. By the 1940s, in the context of the ascendancy of Keynesian economic theory, Beveridge provided a blueprint for the welfare state in Britain in which the state would guarantee welfare support from 'cradle to grave'. From the 1940s until the 1970s the idea of the welfare state, based on the politics of equality and distributive fairness, dominated thinking about how to organize welfare. The Keynesian view of state intervention influenced the expansion of the welfare state in both Britain and Australia in the early post-Second World War years.

However, in Australia the broad mechanisms of the welfare state had been established much earlier in the century. A centralized system of industrial conciliation and arbitration was set up in 1904 to resolve industrial issues, which it did on the principle of workers' needs rather than the interests or capacities of capital. The idea of a (male-based) basic wage constructed around family needs was fixed in 1907. Selective national state provision of age pensions and maternity allowances were in place by 1912 (Bryson, 1992). The emphasis on state intervention to ensure acceptable working conditions and wage levels has led to its description as the 'wage earners' welfare state' (Castles, 1985). The experience of the Great Depression of the 1930s and the new ways of thinking developed at the end of the Second World War entrenched the commitment to state responsibility for the welfare of citizens, which continued until the 1980s.

Yet analyses of the welfare state in Australia have revealed how state responsibility has always been affected by social and political factors. The contemporary Australian welfare state provides residual welfare with modest benefits and entitlements, which are circumscribed by traditional work-ethic norms. Along with the welfare state structures in place in the United States and Canada, Esping-Andersen (1990) has identified the Australian welfare system as a 'liberal' welfare state regime, in which state welfare is stigmatized and there is minimal decommodification and tightly means-tested entitlements. Decommodification occurs when 'citizens can freely, and without potential loss of job, income and general welfare, opt out of work when they consider it necessary' (Esping-Andersen, 1990: 23). Recent attempts by conservative governments to dispense with minimal wages and working conditions have undermined the notion of Australia as the 'wage earner's' welfare state.

As the welfare state industry framework has developed, different bureaucratic principles have come to the fore. Considine (1996) distinguishes between what he calls procedural bureaucracy and corporate bureaucracy. The driving force of the procedural bureaucracy is its focus on standardized rules and preoccupation with due process. Corporate bureaucracies shift the organizational emphasis from adherence to standardized procedures to performance, strategic planning and output. Corporate bureaucracies signalled the shift from rule-driven organizations to mission-driven organizations (Osborne and Gaebler, 1992).

In the procedural bureaucracy the administrative focus of voluntary associations providing programmes for government departments is on ensuring that social policies are pursued through agreed procedures. In the procedural bureaucracy attention to process and inputs is all-important. We can see how this shift has taken effect in voluntary associations. The mechanisms for funding voluntary associations in the procedural bureaucracy model are submissions and government planning (Lyons, 1997). In the submission approach, voluntary associations identify community needs, follow procedures set down by governments, and request funds to develop programmes in response to these needs. In the planning process government officials determine in advance what is needed. Government departments will follow procedures for choosing appropriate voluntary associations to deliver services.

In the late 1980s and 1990s a new funding regime was established. This funding regime began to emphasize efficiency (defined as lowest cost per unit) and output, rather than processes and inputs. Ideas of contractual relations between the state and voluntary associations were introduced. Workers in voluntary associations had to get used to a whole new set of operating logics, constructed through the language and practice of service agreements, programme budgeting and strategic planning based on mission statements and goals. These new operating logics signalled a deepening of the rationalization of welfare. They also opened the way for the establishment of new forms of control and supervision of programmes in the voluntary sector, based on the ideological force of economic rationalism, the language of efficiency and effectiveness and state adaptation of technologies of surveillance, such as auditing principles. These new forms of control sat quite comfortably with the hierarchical structures of authority that dominated welfare bureaucracies. However, they were also overlaid, somewhat uncomfortably, on the practices of welfare professionalism, which had always been at the heart of the relation between the welfare worker and the client. The focus on aggregate output and efficiency, rather than treatment of individual welfare clients, began to undermine notions of skilled care and case work that are central to the role of welfare professionals. But it did more than this. It opened the way for new managerial practices that weakened the autonomy of professional case workers and signalled the erosion of the power of welfare professionals. Central to the new managerial discourse is the idea of the new breed of generic managers with different types of professional expertise to those held by welfare workers. These generic managers required administration skills, but no knowledge, experience or interest in the field of activity in which an organization operated. Central to the new managerial ethos is increased power and autonomy to recruit and shed staff, make decisions and develop strategy. Managerial rewards are structured around individual performance and based on employment contracts. More will be said about the power of the new managerial discourse in the discussion of the market framework in Chapter 5.

While corporatization of welfare state programmes has weakened the actual power of welfare professionals, ideas of professionalism and a community service *industry* remain central to work within the welfare state industry model of voluntary associations. The language of industry does connote both professionalism and an economic contribution to society. In Australia welfare workers are still identified as part of the social and community services industry and many continue to work under the specific Social and Community Services industrial award.

Organizational themes and forms

The organizational logic of the welfare state industry framework is set within the principles of bureaucratic structures and administration. These principles include a hierarchical structure of authority, with clear channels of command and responsibility; a clearly defined division of labour based on functional specialization; tasks distributed as official duties; impersonal relationships; formal rules setting out rights and duties of workers and procedures for dealing with interpersonal relations; recruitment of personnel on the basis of ability and technical knowledge; and promotion on the basis of seniority or merit (Gerth and Mills, 1991).

The institutional autonomy of voluntary associations operating with welfare state industry rationales is circumscribed by the power wielded by centralized welfare bureaucracies. While the extent of bureaucratic control and intervention may vary according to socio-political conjunctures, government policies set the parameters of the activities of voluntary associations.

Asymmetries of both individual and institutional power are inherent in the welfare state industry framework of voluntary associations.

The line-management administrative structure within organizations ensures asymmetries in workers' power. These asymmetries are often constructed through a distinction between policy-making and executive work, which may be manifested in the relation between managers or coordinators and other workers, or committees as management and workers. The way in which the distinction between providers and recipients of welfare services is constructed also ensures unequal power between them. Three factors reinforce this unequal power. Firstly, the construction of the welfare recipient as a failure in the market-place, together with strict entitlement rules, ensures an unequal relationship between the welfare provider and welfare recipient. Secondly, the commitment to a professional workforce, procedural rules and the imperative of impersonal relations reinforces the formal separation between the professional worker and client. Finally, a system of paternalistic or authoritarian protection operates, which can involve a contradictory role for the welfare professional, as both an advocate who 'speaks for' a client, as well as a regulator who disciplines the client.

Social relations within the welfare state industry model are also gendered in terms of both the production and consumption of welfare services. The gender segmentation of the welfare workforce is evident in the dual labour market of well-paid, high status positions dominated by men and a majority of low-paid, unpaid and insecure positions, mainly held by women (see Chapter 7). The feminization of poverty, in which women are over-represented as welfare recipients, is largely the result of the general gendered division of labour in which women's role is seen as dependent wife, child-rearer and unpaid domestic. In welfare relations it is women who are located in the least powerful and positions.

In what seems like a turn to active citizenship, the themes of consultation, client choice and empowerment have been developed within the welfare state industry framework. Interestingly, the emphasis on the effectiveness of welfare programmes has opened the way for the establishment of new consultative processes between welfare recipients and welfare workers, or what Smith and Lipsky (1993) call 'street level bureaucrats'. These 'street level bureaucrats' work with communities to identify and diagnose problems, prescribe courses of action and offer services. The methods of these street level bureaucrats are a departure from the conventional methods employed in the welfare state framework of service delivery and are in line with the methods of community development which were discussed in the activist framework. However there is also criticism of the ideological use of the idea and practice of consultation. This criticism holds that consultation tends to involve no more than a form of communication or a management technique. The communicative function occurs when workers communicate government policies to welfare clients or where there is an exchange of views between workers and clients. Everingham (1998) argues that while consultation ostensibly involves a process of mutual exchange between government and citizens, it is really a one-way communication system used as a legitimation device. Consultation is a management technique used to direct attention away from significant issues of power and control. It is a process which allows clients to give advice on administrative issues that are marginal to government political agendas, and in the case of consultation about the operation of voluntary associations, consultative processes are devices for directing attention away from important decisions about policy matters.

In a move that has opened the way for market practices to be introduced into voluntary associations, the welfare state industry framework has also tentatively adopted ideas of empowerment through client choice and consumer sovereignty. Client choice is facilitated when a professional welfare worker identifies strategic life-style choices for a welfare recipient in the course of professional counselling. Consumer sovereignty is facilitated when workers become accountable to clients for the quality of their services. In both these senses empowerment is constructed in an individualist, rather than a collectivist way. From an activist perspective the processes of empowerment used in the welfare state industry framework, because they are tightly controlled by the state, are flawed (Croft and Beresford, 1989). Nevertheless the acceptance of the language of empowerment weakens the discourse of dependency and the stigmatization of welfare recipients that goes with it.

The welfare state industry framework and civil society
The welfare state industry framework sits ambiguously with civil society. The welfare state was developed around a clear commitment to formal welfare rights and entitlements, which were privileged over moral obligation and informal mutuality. Formal social rights and entitlements are a necessary part of the development of citizenship. Yet as we have seen in preceding discussions, the history of the welfare state also involved the inexorable expansion of the networks of administrative state power into civil society (Keane, 1988; Mishra, 1984; Offe, 1984). The welfare state industry framework operates within the context of the rationalization of services, through formal and impersonal administrative structures and procedures. In this framework, an expert,

professionally trained workforce, best delivers welfare services. Thus citizenship rights have been contained within asymmetrical power relations. It does not help people to identify their own needs. Furthermore, it does not adequately facilitate responses in the satisfaction of needs. It does not open up public space in civil society, in which people could enter voluntarily, to articulate their views and deal with disagreements.

The liberal welfare state regime that has grown in Australia has undercut social citizenship rights in a number of ways. Firstly, low and decreasing levels of decommodification mean that citizenship eligibility for welfare support is increasingly defined in terms of a client's role in the production system, rather than on right or need (Latham, 1998). Welfare rights are tightly controlled through entitlement tests, including preparedness and ability to participate in the labour force. There is growing emphasis on citizens' duty (to obey government rules regarding social security payments, or develop work skills, for example). Secondly, through the process of validation of eligibility for welfare, clients and communities become cases, to be treated and monitored, through the application of bureaucratic rules (Turner, 1986). For example, clients and communities are constructed according to set categories of disadvantage and need. They become special target groups whose needs are to be identified, catalogued and managed through professional welfare workers. Concepts of client/dependent individuals construct welfare recipients as unified and socially problematic identities requiring support, regulation and surveillance. Finally, the separation of provider and client and the asymmetrical power structure in which this separation is embedded, together with the professional standing of workers, ensures that welfare recipients are the passive consumers of welfare, rather than active citizens identifying their own needs and developing programmes in conjunction with welfare providers. The institutionalized asymmetries of power and the construction of the culture of dependency have undermined the possibility of the development of a culture of effective participation in decision-making and problem solving that is essential for active citizenship.

Debates and issues

As discussed in Part I, debates about the crisis of the welfare state were first articulated in the 1960s. By the end of the 1970s many commentators were predicting confidently the immanent end of the welfare state. However, this immanent end has turned out to be somewhat exaggerated. In Europe, the welfare state, although a little battered and modified in some ways, remains a central part of the policy platforms of social democratic governments. Even in English-speaking countries, which have been at the forefront of the attacks upon the welfare state, have not been able to wind down the state structurally. As we will argue in the following chapter, the rhetoric of 'rolling back the state' is a code for new sets of relations between the private sphere and the state rather than whole-scale state withdrawal from intervention into society.

For those supporting the strengthening of the social democratic welfare state the discourses of formal equality and redistribution remain more than just residues in the operational rationales of the welfare state industry framework. They keep social justice issues on political agendas and remind us of the structural features of capitalism that the welfare state was meant to moderate. Yet there remain tensions between different principles of operation in the welfare state framework. First, there is a tension between the principles of social rights and social justice. Where social rights and universalism in welfare provision dominate, such as in the model Nordic welfare state, there are no or minimal eligibility requirements for welfare recipients. Where the principles of social justice mean a focus upon redistribution, and social welfare is constructed as a means to counter individual disadvantage and adversity, residual welfare programmes are dominant and welfare services are carefully targeted. Second, social rights discourse implies a welfare system constructed to meet the different needs of different groups. Indeed, the language of welfare targets suggests that welfare programmes are developed to meet special needs. Yet central to the development of welfare state industry programmes are ideas of equality and standardized services which militate against the establishment of disparate programmes for different groups. Centralized bureaucratic control certainly impedes efforts to develop flexibility in the delivery of programmes. Critics informed by postmodern analyses of the grand narratives of welfare state provision note that the welfare state industry framework has no room for the politics of difference. There are scant elements of pluralism, mutuality and voluntarism in this framework. In operating through state bureaucratic regulations voluntary associations can be hampered in their attempts to respond to diverse needs.

Feminists point out that despite the rhetoric of equity, the welfare state industry framework draws on moralizing constructions of dependency which maintain the gendered framework of the charity framework (Fraser and Gordon, 1994). The new discourses of dependency construct recipients of welfare as clients, needing advice, counselling and therapy, rather than moral guidance (Beilharz et al., 1992). The residues of the moral discourse of charity are not necessarily articulated in the language of deserving and undeserving poor, but in the language of genuineness and fraud (as expressed in the ideas of welfare cheat and dole-bludgers) and in the construction of a hierarchy of 'genuine needs'. To some, influenced by the work of Foucault, the welfare state industry framework is just another form of disciplinary charity. It maintains the asymmetrical relations between provider and recipient, but now using a professional disguise. In the professionalized relation, subjects become more than dependants. Subjects now also become objects of study.

In the context of the erosion of commitment to the welfare state there are many who yearn for the rehabilitation of a strong welfare state, with robust welfare rights. This strong welfare state would ensure decommodified welfare, guarantee a certain level of welfare service and provide full state protection from adversity and the perils of risk and uncertainty. These are understandable yearnings and they sit nicely with the ideas of social rights derived from the work of Marshall. The bureaucratic structure of the welfare state industry framework, with its concern with set procedures and rules, does provide a level of certainty and stability. But the certainty and stability is embedded in paternalistic and often disciplinary welfare programmes. Citizenship rights provided by the welfare state are passive rights. Essentially, what welfare state industry programmes offer is a certain level of material security, not the resources for autonomous action and empowerment. At the heart of the structural form of the welfare state industry framework is an inflexibility which inhibits creativity and self-determination. Ultimately, inflexibility and the goal of establishing certainty are no solutions in a world of risk and uncertainty.

5
Unsettling the Voluntary Sector: the Emerging Market Framework

Introduction

As the critiques of the welfare state gained momentum in the late 1970s, the welfare state industry framework began to be overlaid by a whole new set of operating principles. These principles had no truck with Left concerns about redistribution and equality and other unfulfilled promises of the welfare state because they were articulated in a completely different frame of reference. This frame of reference is known as neo-liberal economics, or in Australia, economic rationalism (Pusey, 1991). From the perspective of neo-liberal economics, the operating rationale that is appropriate to the provision of welfare, and particularly the provision of welfare by voluntary associations, is the capitalist market. In this chapter we consider the various applications of the market framework to voluntary associations. It is important to acknowledge at the outset that market principles have only recently been applied to the operation of voluntary associations and we are still in the process of mapping the dimensions of the market framework. However, we devote a whole chapter to the discussion of the market framework and its complex effects upon the voluntary sector because, as we will argue in the following chapters, the evidence suggests that the relation between the market and the community will be increasingly significant for understanding the operational principles and organizational forms of voluntary associations as they develop in the early twenty-first century.

Market discourses

The market framework differs radically from the other frameworks we have discussed in this book. It dispenses with the interpretation of welfare within the discourses of resistance, compassion, mutuality, social rights or discipline, and replaces these with the discourses of individual self-interest and self-help, private initiative and enterprise, and competition. To make sense of market discourses we need to locate them in the context of the ascendancy of the principles of neo-liberal economic theory. From a neo-liberal perspective, many social, economic, cultural and environmental activities and responsibilities have been wrongly appropriated by the state. Optimal output and efficiencies are not possible when there is state control and management of society's resources and instrumentalities. It is necessary to transfer activities from the state to the private sector, or at least reorient state activities to the logic of the private for-profit sector.

The market approach to welfare provision is impersonal and instrumental. Responding to welfare needs is therefore a strategic and organizational issue, not a moral one. The source of disadvantage, whether it be structural or individual, is irrelevant to the goal of establishing efficient welfare organizations and servicing the needs of individual welfare clients or consumers. Because of the importance of individual needs, there is no politics of equality or interest in standardized or universal welfare programmes.

Historical background

As discussed in the preceding chapter, the immediate post-Second World War period was a time in which the state consolidated large, centralized welfare bureaucracies in response to growing expectations of welfare provision. The setting for the development of market operating rationales began to take shape in the late 1960s and early 1970s, through the compounding forces of increasing demands for welfare services and service improvements, the notion of capitalist crisis and the critiques of the welfare state (Beilharz et al., 1992). By the 1980s the rhetoric of the fiscal crisis of the state and the need to halt welfare demands led to the search for new ways of delivering welfare that would focus on efficiency and output. The organization of welfare programmes within and through the state shifted from a concern with procedural protocols to a corporate orientation (Considine, 1996).

By the late 1980s there was agreement between Left and Right commentators that the welfare state was a profound disappointment. From the perspective of the Left the welfare state had not redistributed wealth and had dampened the oppositional capacities of the working class. Feminists pointed to how the welfare state was constructed along patriarchal lines and was responsible for the feminization of poverty. Right-wing commentators argued that the paternalistic and passive welfare provided by the welfare state leads to ever increasing demands for resources which are finite, and they posed the question of how the state could continue to raise revenue without affecting the growth of capital. At the same time neo-liberal economists emphasized the lack of concern with efficiency as a fatal flaw in the economy of the welfare state. They attacked the self-perpetuating nature of the welfare industry, arguing that welfare needs were fuelled by self-serving professionals in whose interest it was to maintain welfare dependency. Moreover, they argued, because of the lack of welfare workers' concern about utilizing resources wisely and achieving efficient outcomes, the welfare state industry undermines enterprise and initiative.

These critiques of the welfare state fuelled the arguments for the superiority of the market system as a method of organizing and resourcing welfare. The market system offered a mechanism for improving productivity, increasing efficiency, curtailing spiralling welfare expectations and ensuring flexible responses to welfare needs. But it also presented an opportunity to establish a cultural orientation that would ensure the development of private initiative and enterprise as the foundation for the reinvigoration of the capitalist economy.

This new culture could only be established if the state's role in organizing, resourcing and delivering programmes to society was wound down, and in particular, the monopoly of the welfare state eliminated. The 'right to welfare' should be limited and replaced with incentives to shift from dependency within the welfare state to dependency within the labour market. Lee and Raban (1988) note that the arguments in the Right's position on the importance of unleashing personal initiative included the following: unrestrained competition (for jobs and contracts to undertake work, for example), would unleash sufficient entrepreneurial energy to increase productivity and jobs, for the benefit of all; only the market can secure freedom and justice, because people are free to enter and leave the market; and lowering taxation is far more likely to benefit the poor than the welfare state and central planning because it encourages personal incentive. In Australia and other English-speaking countries these rhetorics of the market system are no longer just imperatives espoused by the Right. They are invoked by governments of all political persuasions.

Market operation

For the purposes of analysing the idea of markets in voluntary associations it is useful to distinguish between two forms of market operation. In the first form the emphasis is on construction of the market as a place where there is a maximum number of choices (Walzer, 1992). This market is free in the sense that individuals and groups are free, to enter or not, into any particular exchange. To ensure choice there must be options available for all those who enter the market. For example, in a free labour market, there must be the choice to enter a particular market or not, for both employees and employers. In an intellectual market-place academics are free to enter into a market in order to exchange ideas. In the case of member-serving voluntary associations, the market principle requires that there is a plurality of voluntary associations and potential members, and thus options, for both members choosing a voluntary association, and a voluntary association in accepting and rejecting members. The distribution of services is driven by entrepreneurial mechanisms (Mune, 1989). In this situation voluntary associations want members and prospective members want to be part of a voluntary association. In the case of public-serving voluntary associations with providers and consumers of welfare programmes, there must be a choice for consumers, and the providers (voluntary associations) must attract consumers, but providers can also choose which consumer group they wish to provide programmes for. This form of market operation is not based on or driven by a profit motive. We have indicated this form of market in the preceding chapters when we have used the term social or civil market. Because it does not operate according to capitalist market mechanisms we will refer to this form of market as a social market from now on.

An example of a social market can be found in a cooperative programme which has come to be known as LETS. The acronym LETS stands for Local Employment and Trading System. First established in Canada, LETS enables community members to exchange any goods and services through an established trading system that does not require money. LETS is based on the idea of barter, but it is not premised on simple exchange and it is more flexible. A traditional barter system requires equivalence of value between the goods and services exchanged. Under LETS, if it is agreed that the value of the goods and services to be exchanged is not equal, then free trading begins and LETS points are then accredited to one party on a LETS register. The enthusiastic supporters of LETS emphasize the way in which the programme is constructed around the principle of choices and encourages mutuality. They argue that it demonstrates how every member of a community has a contribution to make, and it has the potential to be developed more fully as a (quasi-market) mechanism for free exchange. The second form of market operation is the dominant one. It is constructed around the concept of a capitalist market of buyers and sellers engaging in for-profit activities. In this capitalist market framework prices for goods and services are established on the basis of supply and demand. Prices of goods and services rise or fall when the buyer's demand for them rises or falls or the seller's supply of them decreases or increases. Because of the forces of supply and demand, and competition for buyers, the market mechanism is seen to be an efficient way of producing and distributing goods and services. The distributional logic of the capitalist market is based on entrepreneurial skills, money, power and individual self-determination.

Both social and capitalist market forms are formally invoked in the market framework used in the voluntary sector, although the rhetoric of the capitalist form is by far the most prominent. Notwithstanding this, we suggest that elements of the social market have probably always existed to some extent in voluntary associations. It is just that they have not been recognized as such. In practice, the adoption of market principles in voluntary associations has been quite selective. As we will argue below, it is more appropriate to identify the market system in operation in the voluntary sector as a quasi-market framework.

Governments, particularly those in the English-speaking world, have argued increasingly that capitalist market mechanisms should be introduced into welfare programmes in order to cut costs and check spiralling welfare wants. In the strongest case, either for-profit or not-for-profit voluntary associations on the basis of user-pays should provide welfare programmes. A user-pays system maintains the sovereignty of the consumer, and therefore improves the quality of the service. Competition for clients between providers ensures efficient production. That is, competing voluntary associations will keep the cost of their services down in order to attract clients. Clients will not be over-serviced or have spiralling wants because the cost keeps the demands in check.

The application of market discourse to the voluntary welfare sector

A key problem with the idea of offering welfare services on the basis of user-pays is that welfare clients require welfare support exactly because they do not have the financial resources to purchase services through the private market. It was because poor people did not have the resources to provide for themselves that they were provided with non-commodified welfare, first in the form of charity and then through the welfare state. Even where the poor do have some welfare income, such as unemployment benefits and pensions, this income is kept low deliberately, and does not make for a lucrative source of profit for private companies.

There are other problems with the application of market principles to voluntary associations. At the centre of the market model is the assumption of self-interested actors, oriented to the maximization of their own welfare through their rational choices. These self-interested individuals, as buyers and sellers of services, operate in the context of a plurality of choices. However, assuming self-interested utility maximizers and plurality of choices is problematic. Firstly, in the case of the welfare sector, the motivation for engagement in the sector is not necessarily, and often not at all, self-interest. The motivation of welfare providers might be civic commitment, compassion or mutuality, as discussed in our analysis of the activist and charity frameworks. Secondly, not all individuals and groups operating in the welfare market have a choice in regard to whether they enter the market-place or not, and if they do have this choice, they might not have a choice in regard to welfare programmes that they can be involved in, as consumers or producers. Finally, the conception of market principles that is invoked in the application of market discourse to voluntary associations assumes an ideal market. Even the corporate for-profit sector is characterized by market failure, through monopoly capital and knowledge, for example, which undermine the possibilities for a 'pure market'. The difficulties in establishing a 'pure' or 'free' market, which already exists in the for-profit sector, are exacerbated in the voluntary not-for-profit sector. Given the difficulties of developing a welfare system operated according to either social or capitalist market principles, the market framework established by governments in the welfare sector is really a quasi-market system. This quasi-market system draws selectively on the principles of both the social and capitalist market forms, and it provides an operating process through which private entrepreneurial activity can be developed.

Organizational themes and forms

The establishment of a culture of private initiative and enterprise requires a reordering of social and political relations in line with a neo-liberal economic framework, and the establishment of a new mode of welfare governance. This new mode of welfare governance has a number of features. Firstly, as far as possible government bureaucracy will be minimized and activities will be shifted from the state to the private sector. Secondly, programme design and funding criteria will be restructured to emphasize outputs rather than process and inputs, and to ensure clear lines of responsibility and accountability. Thirdly, consumer choice and client power should be fostered. Fourthly, a 'business-like' approach should be implemented through new managerial techniques, such as performance-based pay and productivity incentives. Finally, competitive behaviour and (quasi) market operations should be developed (Alford and O'Neil, 1994). These features are organized around two legitimating themes, devolution and marketization.

Devolution is based on the principle of subsidiarity. It occurs when activities, processes and responsibility are passed from high levels of power to lower ones, where there is more flexibility and a greater degree of responsiveness to consumer need. There are different forms of devolution. First, there is full-scale devolution when ownership and control of a state instrumentality is sold to a private company. This form of devolution is generally known as privatization. It occurs when a state utility, such as a power utility, is sold to a private company. The second form occurs when resourcing and service delivery responsibility for an activity is transferred from the state to the community or the family, such as shifting responsibility for elderly care from state funded and operated nursing homes to families and unfunded voluntary associations. The final form of devolution, and the dominant form in the welfare sector, occurs when the state remains the funding body and retains full policy control, but shifts the service delivery and day-to-day responsibility to a voluntary association, a for-profit company, or even another government department. This form of devolution involves the establishment of a contractual relationship between the government (as purchaser of the service or programme activities) and the provider of activities. This separation is often known as the purchaser/provider split. Following the influential work of Osborne and Gaebler (1992) this contractual relationship is also identified as the steering/rowing distinction. For Osborne and Gaebler the solution to the problem of inefficient, inflexible and unresponsive governments is not to dispose of government, but to reinvent it. They argue that the work of governments must be restructured so that overall policy and strategic control remain with what they identify as mission driven governments, and service delivery functions are transferred to the private sector. Mission driven governments, as steerers, will develop policies and purchase services. They will 'shop around for the most effective and efficient service providers' (Osborne and Gaebler, 1992: 35).

The second theme is marketization. According to those who support the introduction of the market framework to the welfare sector, the introduction of market logic provides the resolution to the increasing and unsustainable costs of the welfare state and the inefficiency of state welfare delivery systems. Marketization has been championed because it instils enterprise culture and the principle of competition. In Australia, following the National Competition Policy Review, or what has come to be known as the Hilmer Inquiry (Hilmer, 1993), 'competition' has become a key mechanism for economic growth. In turn, economic growth has become the panacea for society's ills. Policies and regulations have been introduced to maximize competition within and between public utilities for contracts, and between Australian and overseas companies, for example. A market mechanism is at work when governments sell state instrumentalities to the highest bidder and that bidder sells the goods and services in a competitive market-place, or when a process of competitive tendering for government contracts is introduced. In regard to welfare programmes, the establishment of an ethos of competition signals a shift from the funding regimes based on the charity approach of 'government as philanthropist' and the welfare state industry approach based on submission and planning models, to competitive tendering and even user-pays funding models (Lyons, 1997).

The establishment of the contractual and competitive tendering model for funding welfare programmes has come with significant changes in thinking about the appropriate roles and responsibilities of the state and voluntary associations. As indicated above, this thinking has led to the identification of a new form of state known as the contract state (Alford and O'Neill, 1994). The contract state is based on a particular configuration of the relation between the state and voluntary associations. While the general idea of the state outsourcing some of its activities on the basis of contracts is not new, deepened commitment to contracturalism and competitive tendering as a mechanism for changing the relation between the state and voluntary associations and inculcating competitive and enterprising attitudes and behaviours is.

The contractual framework has been embraced most comprehensively in the State of Victoria. It was in Victoria in the first half of the 1990s, under the Kennett Liberal/National Coalition Government, that the themes of the contract state in Australia were first laid out and implemented. These themes include reduction in the size of the public service, by focusing on the 'core functions' of government, such as policy, resource allocation, standard-setting, monitoring and evaluation; the devolution of service delivery functions to separate agencies, including 'outsourcing' activities to private contractors, that have some autonomy in the ways in which they deploy resources; the establishment of contractual relationships between the government purchasers of services and other government or private providers; a preference for market mechanisms, involving competition for government contracts; an organizational focus on output, responsibility and accountability for results; and public sector adoption of an entrepreneurial management style drawn from the private for-profit sector (Alford and O'Neil, 1994). The private for-profit sector is the privileged site of entrepreneurial management style because it fosters attitudes and values that promote hard work, competition, motivation, self-reliance, flexibility, boldness, daring, innovation and success (see Fairclough, 1992; Keat, 1991).

Alford et al. (1994) point out that the contractual framework actually covers different types of contracts. These are employment contracts, covering agreements between employer and employee on such matters as work tasks, performance outcomes and performance indicators; intra-public-sector service contracts between separate sections of the public service, involving agreements between one section as purchaser of the service and one section as provider of the service; public–private service contracts between public sector organizations (as purchasers of the service) and private for-profit or non-profit organizations (as providers of the service); and finally contracts between welfare recipients and service-providers, where service-providers have a disciplinary role of ensuring that contractual obligations by recipients, such as attending literacy classes, are met.

As indicated above, the central component in the contractual-oriented state is the separation of the activities of funding, policy development, regulating, standard-setting, monitoring and evaluation, from the activities of providing a service. According to supporters of the contract state model, the private sector is the best site for the providing of services and development of a society's resources. The role of the state is to steer the activities of the private sector. According to this view, it is the responsibility of the rowers (those directly operating the programmes) to find ways to ensure that they provide a quality service. Thus the government, as purchasers of the service, have the responsibility of developing policies which will steer the activities (see Osborne and Gaebler, 1993). Quasi-marketization occurs as private providers compete for state contracts to provide services.

Why is this process of contracting by government identified as a quasi-market system? The reason is that the market relation between the contract state and providers of services is a limited one. While both the government and the tenderer for the contract are free to enter, or not, into the bidding and contract arrangement, the government has a choice of contractors, but the contractors have only one purchaser of their service. The government therefore has a monopoly position in regard to picking and choosing the lowest tenderer. The corrective to this monopoly is said to lie in the political process. If governments tender to agencies providing poor services, governments will hear about this through the ballot box. The involvement of the political process undermines the possibility of the free play of an independent market system. In addition, unless there is a direct system of consumer sovereignty, through a user-pays mechanism (which could be facilitated by the establishment of a living wage based on a Guaranteed Minimum Income Scheme, for example), or an indirect system of consumer sovereignty, through government provision of vouchers to welfare clients who could exchange their vouchers for services, then consumers are not the purchasers of services (Lyons, 1997). Governments purchase on behalf of clients or consumers. While there might be some choice for consumers in welfare services, their consumer sovereignty is generally circumscribed by the inability to sample the programmes or demand recompense for poor service. In fact, constructed as they are as individual welfare dependants, lacking power, resources and status, and given the asymmetrical power relations between welfare consumer and the government, welfare recipients are reluctant to complain about unsatisfactory programmes.

From the point of view of those whose primary aim is establishing enterprise culture and decreasing the cost of welfare services, it is not of central importance that the new ways of delivering welfare programmes are fully marketized. For the purpose of generating a culture of private initiative and providing efficient and accountable programmes it is enough to have the actual delivery of welfare programmes shifted from the state to the private sector and to confirm the principles of competition for government funding.

In Britain the arguments for instilling an enterprising culture in the popular consciousness can be traced back to the election of the Thatcher Conservative government in 1979. The establishment of an enterprise culture was driven by some key Thatcherite objectives. These included a commitment to individual incentive, freeing private enterprise from government interference, the development of policies to weaken the power of public sector unions, and a concern to enhance managerial skills and resourcefulness. These objectives underpinned the push to expand what came to be known as popular capitalism. Popular capitalism is characterized by popular ownership of privatized enterprises, consumer sovereignty, team-based organizational structures, and a flexible, non-union workforce (Saunders and Harris, 1994). The commitment to enterprise has continued in Britain under the Blair Labour government.

In Australia, securing an enterprise culture is championed as a necessary part of the positioning of Australian capitalism to make it viable in an increasingly competitive international arena. The push for the establishment of enterprise culture has taken different forms in different parts of Australia. Firstly, for some groups the key to fostering an enterprise culture is cutting government red tape and control. For example, the small business lobby has argued for less and less government regulation of their activities. Commitment to cutting red tape and control is embodied in the discourse of deregulation. Deregulation involves removing bureaucratic restrictions on private enterprise and withdrawing government controls on financial markets, labour markets and the activities of corporations. Commitment to deregulation provides the macroeconomic setting in which devolution can take form.

Secondly, for others, including the growing band of management consultants, the best way of establishing enterprise culture is to introduce certain types of management practices that have come to be known as the new managerialism. While there is some debate about the different types of managerialism and the implications of new managerialism (see Considine and Painter, 1997), there are some central themes. New managerialism involves the strengthening of managerial leadership, autonomy and initiative; streamlining decision-making and increasing flexibility in employment practices; the introduction of individual performance initiatives and rewards; a focus on output and outcomes; weakening or eliminating the power of unions; and a commitment to 'best practice' services and 'best quality' products.

The internal organizational structures of voluntary associations operating within the market framework are increasingly drawing on the discourse of new managerialism. New managerialism is concerned with output and outcomes, goal-directed behaviour and a commitment to managerial leadership, autonomy and initiative. While some kind of hierarchical structure is required for the establishment of managerial leadership, this structure is not organized around the bureaucratic imperatives of procedures and rules, but around finding ways to resolve problems and expedite decisions. New managerialism has meant that in place of stability and certainty for the workforce, there has been an increasing emphasis on flexibility in working conditions and work practices, with workplace contracts replacing industrial awards.

There is a third approach to enterprise culture that is based on a commitment to the establishment of facilitating, empowering workplaces. In this type of workplace hierarchy is eliminated, to be replaced by multi-skilled workers, operating through teams, who not only undertake the everyday tasks required, but also identify and solve problems (Gee and Lankshear, 1995; Osborne and Gaebler, 1992; Reich, 1993; Scott and Jaffe, 1991). It is only in a collaborative environment that the creative talents of individual workers can be unleashed. Only certain aspects of this approach to enterprise culture are found in Australia, such as multi-skilling and team-based organization, and when multi-skilling and teamwork are found, they are circumscribed by the hierarchical focus of new managerialism.

The market framework signals some profound changes in social relations within voluntary associations. The objective of enterprise culture is to introduce an ethos that emphasises a concern with resources, results and efficiency. This ethos requires clearly focused, instrumentally based interactions, rather than social relations based on political solidarity, civic virtue or dependency. New managerialism sets up different kinds of relationships between workers in voluntary associations and between workers and welfare recipients, based on clear lines of authority and the separation of policy and strategic activities and programme delivery. The contracting regime sets up different types of associations between voluntary associations, welfare recipients and the state. Thus, in the place of mutual social relations based on horizontal reciprocity, which feature in the activist framework, and the relations of service and vertical reciprocity in the charity and welfare state industry frameworks, comes a narrow contractual reciprocity based on a deeply individualistic and instrumentalist approach to social relations. For all the claims of free-market exchange, this reciprocity is vertical in the sense that the state has monopoly control of funding and the terms of the contract. The ability of voluntary associations to negotiate contracts rests on their political power and cultural capital.

There is an interesting packaging of community in the market framework. The associational and normative meanings of community remain residual, to be invoked in policies praising the virtues of volunteerism, for example. Community becomes a reified site, to be modernized, professionalized and even marketed. For example, 'community' has significant purchase as a set of images which can be transformed into marketable products for the purpose of securing government and other funding.

Asymmetries of power are inscribed in the very organization of the contract state and new managerialism. While there has been much discussion of the need for increased transparency in programmes and funding and mutual accountability between all participants in contracting arrangements, in practice transparency is limited. In contractual arrangements subject to 'commercial in confidence' clauses, transparency is diminished and accountability is one-way – from voluntary associations to governments. Governments might invoke a rhetorical notion of accountability to the tax-paying public, through the electoral system, but they have no commitment to downward accountability to voluntary associations or welfare recipients for their executive decisions (Muetzelfeldt, 1994). As discussed above, new managerialism usually means that workers' activities are set within the context of hierarchical management structures and managerial autonomy. For the purposes of increasing organizational efficiency managers are given performance targets and are rewarded personally when they manage to increase the productivity of their workers.

The capitalist market framework brings with it new constructions of 'professional' which also affect the social relations within voluntary associations. The emphasis on management skills has opened the way for employment of generic managers, requiring, not education or experience in social service work, but business and organizational skills, which may be gained through management experience or through professional management courses. Professionalization in this context refers to the employment of people with these management skills to positions of authority. A form of deprofessionalization also occurs, as qualifications in social service work are deemed unnecessary for employment in voluntary associations. This form of deprofessionalization leads to a reopening of jobs to people without formal social service qualifications, particularly at the bottom end of the occupational hierarchy. Ostensibly this means an opening up of employment for volunteers, organic workers and grass-roots activists. However, in practice, it can mean the establishment of new career paths for people with business experience who have no interest in the caring and solidaristic themes of voluntary associations. The introduction of individual work contracts and performance-based pay that go with the idea of enterprise culture not only erodes the industrial working conditions and security of workers, but also undermines solidarity in the way in which it constructs workers as self-interested individuals.

There are different ways of constructing the relationship between welfare recipients and providers in the market framework. The market system opens the way for the establishment of new power relations. Firstly, the commodification of welfare that occurs in a user-pays system can empower welfare recipients if they have the financial resources to pay for welfare services and if they have a choice of welfare providers. Consumer power is also maintained when welfare recipients are issued with vouchers that can be honoured at a range of voluntary associations.

However, in the quasi-market system that operates in voluntary associations in contemporary society, the market features of a plurality of purchasers and providers of welfare services are missing. As discussed above, in the delivery of welfare services the contract state does not have the usual contractual features of purchaser/consumer and provider/seller, because three parties are involved: the purchaser, which is government, the provider, in our case a voluntary association, that sells its services and programmes, and the consumer or welfare client. The government is generally the only possible purchaser of the services offered by the voluntary association. In controlling the terms and conditions of the contract or tender, the government also sets service goals and quality. Thus the power relation between government funding departments and voluntary associations is heavily skewed in favour of government.

The competitive contracting regime has involved the reordering of the priorities of service-oriented voluntary associations from a concern with social rights and distributive justice to a focus upon the discipline of competition as the method used to ensure efficient programme delivery. Moreover, with welfare income cutbacks and harsher eligibility conditions, welfare recipients have little purchasing power. For all the rhetoric of consumer or client sovereignty, welfare recipients are only quasi-consumers. They just do not have the knowledge, fiscal power or resources that could really empower them to demand 'quality' services.

The market framework, welfare and civil society

In contrast to passive welfare citizenship, where responsibility for identifying and responding to needs lies in the hands of external experts, the market framework shifts this responsibility to individual consumers and participants in voluntary associations. Individuals become active citizens when they attain consumer sovereignty.

What happens to citizenship under marketization? In this section we will consider some of the constructions of citizenship in the market framework. First, there is a clearly articulated argument that marketization can provide a balanced approach to citizenship through its facilitation of active citizenship and its equal emphasis on both the rights and obligations of citizens. This argument begins with the critique of the welfare state model. The welfare state industry model has been dominated by rights discourse. This emphasis on rights has led to an unbalanced conception of citizenship in which the state is obliged to satisfy the rights of welfare clients, but welfare clients have no obligations to the state. The implication of the welfare state approach to rights is that a one-way, passive concept of citizenship is constructed, which pre-empts the development of active citizenship, through which individuals would take an active role in the satisfaction of their own welfare needs. The market framework also champions obligations as well as rights of citizens. That is, welfare recipients are carriers of both obligations and rights. They have an obligation to contribute to society, through taking initiative, seeking employment, and doing voluntary work, for example; but they also have rights as consumers of welfare. Marketization, in emphasizing the importance of individuals accepting their obligations to society, taking responsibility for their own affairs and developing personal enterprise, provides an important corrective to the 'ever-demanding' passive citizenship. This can be an appealing argument. However, when we consider the extent to which all citizens are resourced to develop their active citizenship, then the claim that markets are sites for the development of active citizenship in weakened considerably. In particular, the capitalist quasi-market system that dominates the operation of marketized voluntary associations, is essentially one of unequal power and resources, which severely limits the active citizenship of both voluntary associations and welfare recipients. To really be in a position to facilitate active citizenship, voluntary associations and welfare recipients would need to have real social market choices and equalized material and intellectual resources to enable them to access markets. In the market model, active citizenship is developed when individuals take personal responsibility for their lives through their own initiative and enterprise.

Yet success in the market-place requires cultural and fiscal capital, and for those who lack these forms of capital, self-determination is a shallow promise. As we will argue in Chapter 8, the capitalist market framework actually undercuts the possibilities for the development of social capital and non-contractual reciprocity in a number of ways. Indeed, marketization constitutes relations between humans as commodity relations rather than sharing, reciprocal relations. The privileging of contractual relations over relations of mutuality weakens other dimensions of civil society, such as trust, cooperation and solidarity (Cox, 1995; Muetzelfeldt, 1994). Moreover, in the capitalist market framework active citizenship refers to individuals taking responsibility for their own development. This conception of active citizenship precludes collective political action to resource disadvantaged groups so that there can be collective self-determination.

Second, critics of marketization have analysed the narrow social ontology that lies at the heart of the market framework. This social ontology is constructed around the idea of self-interested utility-maximizing individuals. On one hand this social ontology secures the emphasis on individual freedom and choice in welfare provision and undermines the paralysing forces of centralized bureaucracies. For example, the idea of voluntary associations being 'communities of choice' is underpinned by the conception of self-interested individuals (Hirst, 1994). The fostering of authentic individual self-interest is necessary to prevent the 'mischief of faction', in which public power is captured by cartels of groups who set agendas on the basis of their collective control. On the other hand, from the civil society perspective the social ontology of self-interested individualism is extremely problematic. It involves an evacuation of civic discourse, as ideas of the public good are reduced to private transactions between individuals, to be evaluated in terms of what can be quantified economically (Tam, 1998: 5). These private transactions are bled of sociability and mutuality (Muetzeldfeldt, 1994). In its preoccupation with rational action, the market framework allows no room for altruism, empathy and compassion as forces in human behaviour. Moreover, the claim that self-interest, and particularly material self-interest, motivates people is unproven empirically. Alford and Consodine (1994) cite research indicating that solidaristic and public commitment are the important motivations of public sector workers, rather than material self-interest.

As well as evacuating civic discourse, the social ontology of self-interested individualism denies social contextual features of human behaviour and life-chances. It assumes that self-interested individuals have within them the power to control their life-destinies. Those who do not exercise their own power deserve to be victims. This view not only favours materially self-interested, resourceful individuals, it also denies the systemic social inequalities that permeate human existence. Tam (1998: 130) in a communitarian critique of market individualism argues that:

> Capricious fortune may endow some of us with better initial conditions than others to live a fulfilling life, but it can just as easily throw us into tragic circumstances. It is the deep-seated feeling that we need to care for others, just as we need others to care for us, that

lies at the heart of human solidarity. When this feeling is dismissed as unworthy of competitive market heroes, it threatens to undermine the possibility of communal existence.

In the market framework self-interested individuals gain resources through competitive processes. These competitive processes exist not only at the level of individual competition for resources, jobs and power, for example, but also at the organizational level, where organizations such as voluntary associations compete for contracts. As discussed above, the contracting regime, and particularly the competitive tendering process, involves a complete reorientation of the way voluntary associations relate to the state, each other and the participants in their programmes. Competition undercuts collaboration, solidarity and mutuality. The type of reciprocity that dominates contractual relations is simultaneous reciprocity, rather than generalized reciprocity. Simultaneous reciprocity is an exchange that occurs simultaneously and instrumentally. In contrast, generalized reciprocity is based on a general commitment to other human beings in the context of a belief that someone, sometime, will repay the activity.

Debates and issues

As we have seen, the introduction of the operating rationales and organizational forms of the market framework has already had profound effects upon the voluntary sector. While we acknowledge that market organizational forms are still unfolding, we have identified some of the features of the market framework and these might indicate certain trajectories. We will take up our analysis of market trajectories in Chapter 9. In this final section of Chapter 5 we consider some of the correctives to other frameworks, discussed above, that the market approach may offer, and we identify some of the key problems in applying the market framework to voluntary associations.

In the first part of this book we discussed the far-reaching changes that are taking place in contemporary life. We noted the difficulties of analysing and responding to contemporary societies. In particular, we considered the uncertain, risky and complex social environment. Arguably, the market framework can respond to many of the new problems and issues that permeate contemporary societies, which have been ignored in other operating frameworks. This is because there are certain features of the market framework that makes it appropriate to this social environment.

Let us consider threes of the key arguments here. Firstly, the market framework confronts the problem of scarcity and it does have mechanisms for dealing with the problem of rising demands and entitlements in the context of economic scarcity. These mechanisms involve both operational logics and forms of organization and governance. The operational rationale of the market framework is built on the terrain in which 'State social service provision is rationed and 'targeted' (residualized), cash-limited through financial regulations, and considerable portions of services have to be purchased from the private and voluntary sectors' (O'Brien and Penna, 1998: 157). Enterprise culture, which is a central component of the market framework, is not just about developing personal initiative. It also involves the application of 'commercial discipline' upon the public sector. Commercial discipline is concerned with costs. It requires a focus on the price of welfare services, and welfare programming is based on income, rather than need, or even outcome. The distribution of resources is decided through entrepreneurial and problem-solving performance, rather than through precedent or priorities based on need or dependency.

Secondly, the market framework engages the politics of risk society. Under the welfare state industry, responsibility for risk management is congealed in the state. The way in which the welfare state tends to respond to risk is either to deny its existence or to seek certainty through reinforcing bureaucratic inflexibility. In contrast, the way in which the market framework responds to risk is to engage risk and even experiment with organizational risk taking. For example, risk management is not just a matter of clever strategic planning. It involves an understanding of the reflexive nature of social existence, and the promotion of flexibility, innovation and creativity. The discourses of the market, through their emphases on enterprise culture, pluralism and choice, provide a discursive framework for deliberating risk.

Finally, there is a view that once the processes of marketization are embraced fully, both institutional and individual asymmetries of power will be redressed. When the full market mechanism is put in place, voluntary associations will be equipped to respond quickly to changing economic and social conditions and to respond effectively to the needs of clients. Voluntary associations will be empowered to choose their own funding sources, and develop, choose and operate their own programmes. Once welfare recipients are constructed as consumers, they will have the power to enter or not enter the welfare market-place and to choose whatever service they want. The devolution of responsibility to direct service providers for the delivery of programmes will guarantee responsiveness to consumer needs and good quality programmes.

There are both persuasive and questionable aspects in these three arguments. The market framework certainly does engage the issues of scarcity and risk. Its response to these issues is essentially strategic, based on its preoccupation with flexibility, responsiveness and efficiency, and does cut through some of the obstacles in the search for new ways of dealing with questions of welfare. There is evidence that workers in marketized voluntary associations are becoming more flexible and strategic in orientation and welfare programmes are becoming more focused, tighter in their operations and more business-like (Hooper, 1998). The entrepreneurial market approach can force voluntary associations to do some hard thinking about their roles and tasks. Whether this is a good thing, of course, is debated. It means that the large competitive voluntary associations are in a better position to prepare successful submissions and tenders than the small, more informal community organizations. But it also means that the soft underbelly of voluntary associations that was particularly evident in the charity and activist frameworks, the caring, sharing and largely 'unbusiness-like' approach to welfare needs, is being eroded.

As indicated above, underpinning the commitment to market mechanisms is a faith in the possibility of a pure market, operating freely, through the activities of self-interested individuals, and with power located in the operation of the market, rather than in authoritarian bodies such as the state, or in market cartels, such as multinational corporations. What is required to ensure the establishment of this pure market form is the creation of enterprise culture and the strengthening of new managerialism. Faith in the pure market, the creation of enterprise culture and the strengthening of new managerialism are all problematic from the perspective of voluntary associations. We have already argued above that the type of market dominating the voluntary sector is a capitalist quasi-market. We will consider the possible trajectories of this capitalist quasi-market in Chapter 9. But it is clear that this type of market is a long way from a pure market. Moreover, even in the high-powered world of large for-profit corporations, there are no pure capitalist markets.

The overall analyses of the concept of enterprise culture and the development of new workplace environments are mixed. There is support for the development of transparent processes in government and an economic and social environment that encourages and facilitates creativity, innovation, autonomy and productivity. The argument that Australian workers need to embrace an ethos of hard work and competition has gained considerable support amongst the population and in both the main political parties, particularly in the context of the claim that Australian workers must become more internationally competitive.

Yet the harsh effects of these changes have not been completely hidden by the lexicon of new managerialism and the so-called empowering 'enchanted workplace'. The promise of autonomy and encouragement of creative, team-based solutions to problems is not matched by changes to structures and power relations that make participation genuinely possible (Pateman, 1970). Empowerment and creativity are instrumental tools to improve organizational performance in so far as workers are encouraged to 'own problems' and develop creative solutions. Empowerment is therefore not a mechanism for ensuring active citizenship (Everingham, 1998). The enchanted workplace remains at best a benevolent dream, and at worst a trick to seduce workers into taking more and more responsibility for increasing their productivity while giving them no real power over decision-making. Downsizing and rationalization might sound quite neutral. Critics of the new workplace environment argue that they are not. They mean increased profits for share-holders in large public companies and performance bonuses for chief executives, while at the same time they spell out unemployment for 'downsized' workers, more work, and uncertainty for remaining workers, and often poorer services for customers. Similarly, 'outsourcing' of work in government departments means the 'insourced' work within government departments disappears, as do many of the workers.

This critical perspective has also been expressed in the view that the new managerialism has meant less control and autonomy for workers (Buchanan, 1995). Certainly, there is no evidence that workers are more trusting of managers or feel more comfortable or empowered in the multi-skilled workplace. Rees (1995), for example, draws out the links between new managerialism, bullying and greed. To the extent that new managerialism means tighter control by top management (Buchanan, 1995), results in an increase in stress and anxiety, and engenders a senses of powerlessness and low morale amongst employees (Rees, 1995), the new enterprise and workplace cultures can be seen as industrial strategies which strengthen the class structure.

The commitment to narrow instrumentalism and autocratic structures underpinning this work environment is extremely problematic for those committed to the development of democratic processes. For example, under new managerialist strategies collective organizational structures are rendered obsolete and community control inefficient. In Victoria, for example, many committees of management comprising local community representatives and participants in programmes have been described as unprofessional and 'unbusiness-like' by government funding bodies, and have been replaced with government appointees or even abolished altogether. In the competitive tendering environment the key criteria of the success of voluntary associations are not the ability to solve social problems, develop mutuality and social trust, involve grass-roots communities, or even satisfy welfare clients. Success is defined on the basis of the ability to produce professional 'business-like' submissions and minimize programme costs.

Finally, as discussed above, a key theme of the organization of the market is devolution of power and decision-making from the government to the non-government sectors. The way in which the processes of devolution have actually developed in the market framework has been the source of a great deal of debate and criticism. Under neo-liberal policy regimes, devolution can refer to a withdrawal of government intervention or control of an activity, or it can mean new administrative arrangements for developing and providing services. There is popular support for the idea of governments relinquishing control of areas that they have taken control of. In particular, the idea of freeing the economy and society from state control has considerable appeal. However, once we begin to unpack the logics and practices in the rhetoric of devolution, we find some significant discrepancies. The most obvious discrepancy is revealed in an analysis of the rhetoric of devolution and the actual sites and processes of devolution. Take, for example, the rhetoric of deregulation. Deregulation implies the withdrawal of restrictions and other forms of government intervention. It promises increased autonomy for the non-government sectors, including voluntary associations.

Yet in Australia deregulation is most clearly manifested in the context of economic deregulation, where government restrictions on foreign trade, capital transactions, property development, safety standards and working conditions are minimized or even eliminated. Critics argue that this form of deregulation means a strengthening of the role of the state as an agent of capital and the re-establishment of the 'unfettered market'. For example, the concept of 'freeing up the labour market' is an invitation to eliminate collective bargaining, reduce pay, and worsen working conditions. The powers of many government and business watchdog bodies have been eroded. Ironically, at the same time as the economic sphere is being deregulated, social and democratic spheres are being re-regulated. We have witnessed increased state control and restrictions in the areas of public education and local government. Governments have increased restrictions upon eligibility for social security support, and especially unemployment benefits, through mechanisms such as 'work for the dole'. From the perspective of voluntary associations there is no evidence of a decrease in government restrictions and bureaucratic regulations resulting from the devolution of responsibility for programmes to the non-government sector. Moreover, new contracting regimes can bring with them increased transaction costs due to the expanded administration required for tenders, submissions and monitoring (see Davis, 1997; Neville, 1999). It would seem, then, that the process of deregulation has been highly selective.

What issues are involved in administrative devolution through the state relinquishing its role as deliverer of services and programmes? As discussed above, administrative devolution involves an arrangement whereby governments retain overall command of projects, including policy directions (the steering process) and overall fiscal management. The task of administering and delivering the programmes within policy guidelines and fiscal constraints (the rowing process) is the responsibility of those directly operating the programmes, whether public sector workers, private contractors, community volunteers or families.

A major concern about this form of devolution is the extent to which power and decision-making are transferred from government to the non-government sectors. For those who critique this steering/rowing administrative arrangement, this new form of welfare governance actually provides new methods of state control. The rhetoric of devolution conceals the development of a new form of disciplinary state power, which is exercised through new funding mechanisms based on contracts, and competitive tendering and new monitoring techniques based on auditing principles and performance appraisal. Moreover, for all the promises of diminishing state intervention, markets need a strong interventionist state to protect them and corporations (against labour collectivities, for example). If we consider all the issues in the application of the market framework to voluntary associations, there is an argument that perhaps the idea that the welfare sector can be marketized is misplaced, for the configuration of market rationales and structures which operates in the voluntary sector comprises quasi-markets at most, but may be after all just a new form of state control in disguise.

To conclude this chapter, then, it is clear that the application of the market framework to voluntary associations poses some important questions and dilemmas. These questions and dilemmas will be investigated further in Chapter 8, where we consider how the market framework affects the development of the public sphere and social capital, and in the concluding chapter where we consider the possible trajectories for welfare programmes in the voluntary sector and return to the key question addressed in this book: whether active citizenship can survive the marketization of welfare provision through the medium of voluntary associations.

6
Approaches to the Study of Voluntary Associations

Today we appear to be in the middle of an extraordinary explosion of associational activity as new forms of organised citizen action are taking shape and expanding their role in widely disparate parts of the world.

(Salamon and Anheier, 1996: xiii)

Voluntary action is notoriously difficult to quantify, definitions of voluntary organisations are contested, and the boundaries of the sector cannot be drawn with confidence.

(Smith et al., 1995: 2)

Introduction

So far in this book we have focused on the theoretical and conceptual bases of voluntary association. We now turn to look specifically at some of the emerging literature based on empirical research into the scope and operation of voluntary associational sectors around the world, before considering our own research into the voluntary welfare sector in Australia.

The growth of empirically based literature on sectors of voluntary association has been argued to both reflect the world-wide growth of the sector itself and to act as a corrective to previously dominant discourses which ignored or minimized non-state, non-market activity (Salamon and Anheier, 1997: 2). Such research is, however, faced with a range of problems. First, there is the issue of definition – what exactly constitutes the organizational basis for voluntary association? Related to this is the question of the aggregation of such associations into a 'sector'. Is this process to be inclusive or exclusive and on what bases? Secondly, by what means do we identify organizations which have, by and large, existed without comprehensive 'official' listings and established registers? Thirdly, defining the scope and shape of a sector often says little or nothing about the day-to-day work and operation of constituent organizations.

We identify three general approaches to these questions which are characteristic of work in this area: the classificatory, the operational and the structural. Of these, the classificatory contributes to the greater part of the empirically based literature.

The classificatory approach aims to answer questions about what the sector is and what it looks like. It turns on the vexed question of definition. What we see here is very much an inclusive stance towards the voluntary sector in which the criteria of inclusion are drawn so widely that the sector is seen to comprise organizations and groups from the largest and most highly organized educational or health enterprise through to the smallest self-help group. Probably the best example of this is the Johns Hopkins Comparative Nonprofit Sector Project which is discussed below. Claims that we need to recognize the importance of a part of social life which was previously undervalued or ignored, are clearly advanced by means of this approach. Conversely, the resulting breadth of the constructed sectors can be regarded as problematic in terms of arguments about whether such apparently disparate organizations should properly be regarded as belonging to one sector. This is not so much a problem that arises from questions of positive definition (what a non-profit or voluntary organization is) but from negative typing (what the sector is not). As Marshall points out, a residual view of the voluntary sector defines it as what it is not (non-government, non-profit and so on) and tends therefore never to say what it is (Marshall, 1996: 45). The residual classification must then be further typed to separate out the accumulated mass of associations. Depending upon the level of detail chosen by the research, classifications at this level can be in the region of six-fold divisions (charities, social reform, self-help, community service, collective service and social movements – Dalton et al., 1996: 67), rising to the order of twelve-fold (Marshall, 1996), or even achieve a systems-approach appearance with 110 in the case of the Johns Hopkins project's 'international classification of non-profit organizations (ICNPO)' (Kendall and Knapp, 1996: 269–73; Salamon and Anheier, 1977: 67–77). The problems inherent in the classificatory approach have led some to advocate the use of a multiple approach which recognizes sectors of voluntary associations rather than one sector (Marshall, 1996: 52) and others to abandon the notion of sector altogether (Evers, 1995). Despite its problems, the careful and methodical work of the classificatory approach can be a necessary and useful step in the empirical investigation of voluntary associations. The operational approach emphasizes questions of how voluntary associations are constituted as organizations and operate to achieve their goals. Here classification is more conceptually driven. This can, for example, be aimed at understanding the results of organizational actions within a wider societal context. Lyons (1997) develops the argument that a distinction between the operations of member-serving and public-serving non-profit organizations is necessary in order to chart the possible effects of the generation of social capital. Alternatively, it is used in studies which seek to understand voluntary associations contextualized within the structures of wider processes such as 'effectiveness' (Knapp, 1996), organizational change (Galaskiewicz and Bielefeld, 1998) and norms and values (Gerard, 1983). This approach is useful in allowing insights into the ways that the voluntary sector works, together with the possible consequences. It also acts as a corrective to the highly aggregated nature of the classificatory approach.

The structural approach is characterized by a more generalized and sustained theoretical stance which sets the voluntary sector firmly within a societal analysis. While much work of this nature is not empirically based (see Chapter 3 for examples), those studies that do combine theoretical and empirical work have the potential to combine the strengths of the other two approaches. Dekker and van den Broek (1998) utilize a hypothetico-deductive approach to test propositions about the possible negative consequences of modernization and individualization on the strength of civil society and social capital.

The comparative non-profit sector project

The most sustained attempts at national studies can be seen in the development of the Johns Hopkins Comparative Nonprofit Sector Project into the 'voluntary' and non-profit sectors (Anheier and Seibel, 1997; Archambault, 1997; Barbetta, 1997; Kendall and Knapp, 1996; Kuti, 1996; Lundström and Wijkström, 1998; Salamon, 1997 and Yamamoto, 1998). National sectors studied and/or defined began with the United States and have since ranged across all continents. The project, like the sectors it defines, is large and growing.

The project grew out of dissatisfaction with dominant approaches to social welfare (in its most inclusive sense) structured by a binary conception of state and market. Its specific origins lay in the late 1980s, a time in which the certainties of various dualities began to be severely questioned. As other traditional societal outlines lost their clarity of definition, the project sought to give body and substance to the 'nonprofit' sector at an international level. This corrective empirical exercise aimed to 'chart the [sector's] scope, role, and operations' (Salamon and Anheier, 1996: 7). As such, the project is influenced strongly by the classificatory approach outlined above.

The work has produced useful and interesting research in a significantly under-researched area. The aim of this brief discussion is to consider the assumptions and main findings and note the inherent strengths and weaknesses in the design of the work as a whole. As such, this section informs the development of the research reported later in this chapter and in the next chapter.

The project's origins were set firmly within an economic framework, its genesis resulting from a 1988 philanthropic conference which agreed that the non-profit and voluntary sector needed to be put 'permanently on the economic map of the world' (Salamon and Anheier, 1996: 7). This context set the scene for the project's concentration on size and cost as the twin yardsticks of research into the non-profit sector.

Integral to the work is the assumption that national sectors are unitary enough to be classified as a unit and goal of analysis and able furthermore to be compared internationally. Given the general lack of knowledge of these areas at the time of the project's inception, the assumptions made are understandable but inevitably tend to present an overly unitary sectoral view at a high level of aggregation.

Faced with seemingly endless diversity within the range of organizations which can possibly make up a sector of voluntary or non-profit associations, research must set definitional limits. Clearly, this work of defining what constitutes a non-profit organization is central in determining what is found. Within the general approach we have identified above as classificatory, a 'structural–operational' definition was developed by the Johns Hopkins project which specifies five criteria which must be met by a non-profit organization: that it be organized/formal; private (non-government); self-governing; non-profit distributing; and voluntary in the sense that voluntary participation must be present to 'some meaningful degree' (Salamon and Anheier, 1996: 33–4). It is worth noting Marshall's (1996) point about residual classification once more, as all five can easily be read as negative typing – not informal; non-government; not subsidiary; non-profit distributing; and not compulsory. Their definition excludes political and religious organizations to make the project research manageable (thereby adding two additional negative criteria), but still includes an enormous range of organizational fields comprising: culture and recreation; education and research; health; social services; environment; development and housing; law, advocacy and politics; philanthropy and voluntarism; international; professional and business.

Consistent with the plan to measure economic impacts, the studies tend to employ one of two methodological mapping approaches: first, the use of existing statistics, especially employment surveys, in order to generalize to a national level (for example, Anheier and Seibel, 1997; Archambault, 1997; Salamon, 1997); second, a modular approach using government statistics, auspice body lists, registers (such as the Charity Commission register in the UK) and sample surveys (for example, Kendall and Knapp, 1996: 101–6; Lundström and Wijkström, 1998: 268–9). The general findings are that:

- In every country studied, the non-profit sector is argued to be a significant force both economically and, by implication, socially (Salamon and Anheier, 1996: 23–31). Data are presented showing the impact of the non-profit sector in terms of outputs, employment and expenditures. Thus, across 7 countries the project found that one in every 20 jobs and one in every 8 service jobs are accounted for by the sector (Salamon and Anheier, 1996: xviii). There is also engaged an 'added dimension' of volunteer labour in the order of 7 per cent more than the sectors' paid workforce. In addition, the sectors are shown to be rapidly expanding, at least in France, Germany and the United States, where comparative measures were possible (Salamon and Anheier, 1996: 28).
- There are variations between countries studied, with the sector in the United States being the largest (in total and relative to population).
- Not surprisingly given the broad classification scheme, the sectors are shown to be highly diverse, though education and research, health, social services and culture and recreation appear to dominate.
- Public and private sector monies and fees are found to be more important than 'private giving.'

In Chapter 1 we discussed some differences between Sweden and the UK in terms of the development of different welfare state paths. Both countries have been studied within the Johns Hopkins project (Kendall and Knapp, 1996; Lundström and Wijkström, 1998). In line with the general findings of the project, both studies found large and diverse sectors but both had problems in applying the definitions and set methods of the project, which required some adaptations (Kendall and Knapp, 1996: 16–24; Lundström and Wijkström, 1998: 46–51). Sweden was found to have a non-profit sector dominated by culture and recreation (22 per cent of sector expenditures), labour/business (21 per cent) and education and research (13 per cent), while being low on philanthropy (3 per cent), health care (3 per cent) and social services (7 per cent) (Lundström and Wijkström, 1998: 140). The UK was characterized by a high proportion of organizations in the areas of education and research (43 per cent), culture and recreation (21 per cent) and social services (12 per cent) (Kendall and Knapp, 1996: 113).

Such descriptive outlines and comparisons form the basis of the wider project and relate to its classificatory approach. What these studies achieve is the broad picture of the often disparate sectors brought together for the first time. The data are illuminating in terms of the size, range and scope of the voluntary sector. Indeed, general points made in Chapter 1 are in line with the findings of the Swedish and UK studies. Swedish voluntary associations were found to play a lesser role in traditional areas of welfare (social services and health, for example) than their UK equivalents where British state involvement has been less comprehensive than its Swedish equivalent. Whereas the UK sector has long-established links to charities, this is far from the case in Sweden, where charity holds highly negative connotations (Kendall and Knapp, 1996: 40–6; Lundström and Wijkström, 1998: 65–77).

Wider conclusions of the project as a whole are rather limited and strongly tied to the economic basis of the research. The application of theory to the highly aggregated data is channelled through the dimensions of sectoral expenditure and size, which are used in a four-fold typology of nonprofit development by Salamon and Anheier (discussed in Burger et al., 1997: 25). High levels of government spending on social welfare and a large non-profit sector are taken to characterize the 'corporatist' model, whereas with a small non-profit sector the 'social democratic' model results. Low levels of government expenditures and a large sector are termed the 'liberal model' and with a small sector the 'statist' model. The classification, dependent as it is on the measurement of two levels (size and cost), is reminiscent of Therborn's (1983) early analysis of welfare states which tends to concentrate on absolute levels of social entitlements and commitment to full employment. The criticism of Therborn's model can also be applied to Salamon and Anheier's in that both classifications can be argued to underplay the importance and role of wider sets of social relations: 'Comparing welfare states on scales of more or less or, indeed, of better or worse, will yield highly misleading results' (Esping-Andersen, 1990: 29). The theoretical development from the non-profit sector project may therefore be too blunt an instrument and in fact does not appear to explain the situation described in the Swedish project, where the data show a high number of non-profits together with high government expenditure. It is questionable whether Sweden is a case of the 'corporatist' model (see also the discussion of conflict and interdependency theory applied to Sweden in Lundström and Wijkström, 1998: 239–41).

While the Johns Hopkins Comparative Nonprofit Project has advanced our knowledge it leaves many questions open. The archaeological approach – measuring by traces left behind – cannot (nor was it meant to) give us a picture of the sector in operation. We therefore also need studies that can provide focus on the processes involved in how voluntary associations operate and through what kinds of frameworks.

Sighting the iceberg: outlines of the Australian voluntary welfare sector

In addition to [non-profit organizations that employ people] there are many hundreds of thousands of small organisations. The non-profit sector is somewhat like an iceberg: only a small part of it is above water and measurable; it must be recognised though that this is balanced by a much larger number of nonprofits that are not so clearly seen, nor so readily measured.

(Lyons and Hocking, 1998: 2)

In the context of the prevailing socio-economic climate of the 1990s, there are a number of normative and theoretical issues within the recent Australian literature on the voluntary sector and its contributions to social capital and democratic processes (see for example, Cox, 1995; Hewitt, 1997; Lyons, 1997; Melville and Nyland, 1997; Morgan, 1996; Onyx and Bullen, 1997; Riddell, 1997; Robinson, 1997). What is noticeable about these discussions is that with some exceptions (such as the work by Melville and Nyland, 1997; Onyx and Bullen, 1997 and Robinson, 1997), there is a general lack of studies providing current empirical data on the practices and processes in voluntary welfare organizations. While there has been some classificatory research probing the scope and size of the not-for-profit, non-government community sector, research into the dimensions, activities and operations of voluntary associations is still largely in the pioneering stage (Bailey, 1977; Brown et al., 1990; Brown et al., 1994; Lyons, 1994; Lyons and Hocking,

1998; Lyons and Pocklington, 1992; Milligan et al., 1984; Pocklington et al., 1995). There remains a significant lack of data on the dimensions, activities and operations of voluntary associations in Australia. In particular, little empirical material is available that could throw light on the question of whether the characteristics and location of voluntary associations make them appropriate loci for the development of active and pluralist welfare. To further address issues identified in previous chapters as being important for an understanding of voluntary associations, a research project was developed. It was designed to examine both the outline of the sector in Australia and the perspectives of people who worked in and for organizations, and through this to understand better the sector's range of roles and potentials. The project aimed to outline the extent and nature of the sector, trace points of convergence and difference between organizations and address issues of pluralism and subsidiarity. In this way we hoped to combine classificatory, operational and structural approaches to the study of the sector.

To begin to chart the Australian voluntary welfare sector both above and below the level of immediate 'visibility', the study developed a three-stage, inductively based design:

- construction of a sample national database of voluntary welfare associations;[1]
- focus group discussions ($n = 14$) with voluntary welfare sector workers and participants ($n = 202$) across Australia (these data are analysed in Chapter 7);
- administration of a random sample survey ($n = 495$) of Australian voluntary welfare associations.

As Lyons and Hocking highlight in the above quotation, part of the explanation for the relative paucity of empirical studies into voluntary associations in Australia lies in the sector's relative and uneven 'invisibility' within available statistical records. This is especially the case for data aggregated at state or national levels.

We have seen that the Johns Hopkins studies use either existing statistics, especially employment surveys, in order to generalize to a national level (Anheier and Seibel, 1997; Archambault, 1997; Salamon, 1997); or a modular approach using government statistics, auspice body lists, registers (such as the Charity Commission register in the UK) and sample surveys (Kendall and Knapp 1996: 101–6; Lundström and Wijkström, 1998: 268–9). Both approaches were problematic for our research. Existing Australian employment and workplace surveys would provide at best partial measures of third-sector welfare organizations, and while a modular approach would provide a better indication, the national basis of the records would mean that it would be partly or wholly aggregated above the level of detail required to identify individual organizations (Lyons and Pocklington, 1992; Pocklington et al., 1995).

As our research needed to map the national sector and conduct representative empirical work within it, another approach was required. The research therefore developed a more inductive procedure similar to that of Milligan, Hardwick and Graycar (Milligan et al., 1984), beginning with the construction of a database of community welfare organizations in Australia. A multi-stage sampling procedure was developed to draw a random sample of 100 statistical local areas across Australia. The present study used statistical local areas, which provide national coverage and achieve smaller and less diverse units. The database was constructed between October 1993 and September 1994 using secondary sources for 100 Australian Bureau of Statistics (ABS) statistical areas.[2]

At the first stage, the ABS statistical local areas (comprising 1,298 populated areas) were stratified on the basis of population distribution (stratum 1 by State and Territory and stratum 2 by Capital City and remaining populations). Second, a cluster of 100 statistical local areas (Castles, 1991: 40) was drawn randomly to achieve a proportionate sample.

Secondary sources were then used to construct a census of third-sector welfare organizations in each of the 100 areas. These sources included: federal, state and local government listings relating to each area; auspices body lists; Telstra white and yellow pages; business directories; community information and educational materials. As pointed out by Pocklington et al. (1995), a multi-source approach to listing is necessary to overcome the inherent shortcomings in any one source. Where list information was inadequate to address issues of definitional importance, such as the organization's focus, governance or auspice arrangements, telephone checks with the organization were made.

We have discussed issues of definition in regard to voluntary associations above. For our research, we required a formal set of criteria to delimit the focus of our enquiry. In definitional terms, we chose to adopt a classification of voluntary associations somewhat narrower than the 'structural/operational definition' used by the Johns Hopkins Comparative Nonprofit Project (Salamon and Anheier, 1996: 14–15), though key features are common to both. In particular, we limited the research focus to 'welfare' organizations in order to make the project manageable; and at the same time to concentrate on perhaps the key area in terms of the discussions in earlier chapters, to do with the changing nature of the welfare state and possible moves towards alternatives (see the discussions in Part I above).

Our research defined voluntary welfare associations as meeting the following criteria:

Formal

In the creation of our database, an organization's presence on a listing (government, local council, auspice body, telephone directory and so on) was taken as evidence of their formal existence. Like the Johns Hopkins project, purely *ad hoc*, temporary and informal groupings were excluded.

Non-government and self-governing

Separate from government in some institutional way. That is, not created by or subject to government direction. Thus, government grants and monies may be used by non-government organizations so long as that arrangement does not formally cede either long-term or day-to-day governance and decision-making to government. Thereby self-governing with a measure of autonomous control over policy and procedures.

Non-profit or not-for-profit

Specifically, not for *private* profit in that organizational procedures must ensure that any operating profits are utilized within the organization in a collective sense for the benefit or growth of the organization and not for an individual or group within it.

Welfare

A primary focus on welfare. This includes:

- Service provision (for example, childcare, advice, education, accommodation, health care, crisis care);
- Mutual support (for example, self-help, health and education);
- Advocacy (for example, rights groups, pressure groups). (See also Kendall and Knapp, 1996: 67–8.)

In terms of the ICNPO classification, we focused on social services; health; environment; development and housing; and law advocacy and politics.

Voluntary

Salamon and Anheier (1996: 14–15) state the need for a 'meaningful degree of voluntary participation'. Burger et al. (1997: 20–1) note the problems in a rigorous application of this principle, particularly in circumstances of high levels of professionalization, such as in the Netherlands, and they concentrate on the 'voluntariness' of membership and contributions to the organization. We used an inclusive approach to voluntariness which can be satisfied either by the presence of voluntary contributions of all kinds to an organization, through membership (freely joined), or through the capacity to freely exit. We did not automatically exclude organizations that were specifically religious or political; however, for this research, the organization (or self-managed part or affiliated programme) must be engaged primarily

Table 6.1 Organizational function, focus and national estimates, and 1994 data

Function of organization	% in sample[a]	National (sample *n*=7233)	Range estimate[b]
Support/social organization	48	45,064	34,962–55,166[c]
Neighbourhood house	28	26,288	20,395–32,180
Childcare centre	12	11,266	8,741–13,792
Action/rights group	5	4,694	3,642–5,747
Self-help	5	4,694	3,642–5,747
Crisis/counselling[d]	2	1,878	1,457–2,299
Estimation of population total 100% (community welfare organizations)	93,884	72,838–114,930[e]	
Primary area of organization focus (top 6)			
Health	15	14,083	10,926–17,240[c]
Disability	13	12,205	9,469–14,941
Poverty	13	12,205	9,469–14,941
Youth	12	11,266	8,741–13,792
Women	11	10,327	8,012–12,642
Elderly	10	9,389	7,284–11,493

Notes:
[a] Random stratified sample of 100 ABS statistical local areas (SLA).
[b] Total SLA/sample in SLA × (total n. organizations in sample = 1278/100 × (7233).
[c] Range estimates for function and focus areas based on proportion of sample applied to estimations of total population range. NB: restricted to non-ranged high/low estimates for clarity of presentation.
[d] Includes category of 'refuge' for these calculations.
[e] Based on calculation of the bound of error at the 95% confidence level for the estimation of the total population from a cluster sample (Scheaffer et al., 1985: 206). The bound on the error of estimation for this example is: +/− 21,046.

in welfare. Thus, while churches, trade unions and sporting clubs are not included *per se*, specific welfare programmes with a distinct organizational form auspiced by or organized through such bodies are included. The resulting database comprises 7,233 organizations and allows an estimation of the extent and composition of the sector in Australia. Inferring from this we estimate that there were 93,884 community welfare organizations in Australia in 1993/4 (range = 72,838 to 114,930). The main categories of organizational function and focus are listed in Table 6.1. We agree with Kendall and Knapp (1996: 67) that almost all organizations are multi-functional to some degree, but we have, like them, chosen to focus on the organizations' primary function for the purposes of this classification.

As Table 6.1 shows, Australian community welfare organizations dominantly function as support/social organizations (48 per cent), neighbourhood houses (28 per cent)[3] and childcare centres (12 per cent). Almost three-quarters of the organizations have a primary focus on health (15 per cent), disability (13 per cent), poverty (13 per cent), youth (12 per cent), women (11 per cent) or elderly/aged (10 per cent).

These figures show the Australian voluntary welfare sector to be substantial. Comparisons with previous studies (though limited in number) suggest that while the sector was stable between the mid-1970s and early 1980s, there had been rapid growth by 1994. Table 6.2 compares estimates of the size of the sector for the years 1976, 1981 and 1994.

On the basis of these estimates, the sector grew by over 56,000 organizations in the 18 years to 1994 – an increase of 150 per cent or an average annual rate of growth of 11.5 per cent between 1981 and 1994. This achieves a measure of substantiation when we consider that between 1989–90 and 1995–6, Commonwealth of Australia expenditures on welfare services to 'non-government community services organizations' (including for-profit and not-for-profit organizations) achieved an average annual rate of growth of 16.4 per cent (Australian Bureau of Statistics, 1997a: 24). It must be noted, however, that while

Table 6.2 Australian national estimates of the 'non-government welfare sector'

Study	Year	National estimate of non-government welfare organizations	Range estimate
Bailey (1977)	1976	37,500	15,000–60,000
Milligan et al. (1984)	1981	36,967	25,000–48,000
Present study	1994	93,884	72,838–114,930

Table 6.3 Distribution of organizations in database and survey by state and territory

Australian state/territory	Database organizations (%)	Survey (see next ch.) organizations (%)	Australian population 1991 (%)
NSW	34.9	36.6	34
VIC	23.7	26.7	25
QLD	10.3	9.3	18
WA	8.2	9.7	9
SA	13.4	13.7	8
TAS	5.2	4	3
ACT	3.1	_a	2
NT	1.2	_b	1
Total	100	100	100
	(n = 7,233)	(n = 495)	(n = 16,850,540)

Notes:
[a] ACT, NT not included in survey owing to small absolute numbers.

increases in government expenditure indicate an expanding sector, this may not necessarily translate into greater numbers of organizations.

Therefore, while there are some problems with direct comparison between the studies considered in Table 6.2 due to the different bases of the sampling and questions of definitional difference, the scale of the increase suggests that, at the very least, real positive growth occurred during the period 1976 to 1994.

Organizations listed in the database were distributed largely in accordance with population levels across the country (see Table 6.3). Over-representation occurs in the case of South Australia (13 per cent of organizations in the database compared to 8 per cent of the Australian (1991) population) and Tasmania (5 per cent database to 3 per cent population). Queensland is under-represented with only 10 per cent of the organizations in the database compared with 18 per cent of the national population. These rates of differential representation are consistent with those found by Milligan et al. (1984: 23) and we conclude that the particular histories and conditions of each state and territory account for these differences, rather than sample error.

Conclusion

Our database analysis is generally consistent with findings of other national studies in that the Australian voluntary welfare sector is large and diverse (even though we focus on the welfare aspect while others focus on the whole sector). This classificatory approach is a useful first step, but given that our research aim was to develop an analysis of effects of marketization on forms of active citizenship, we needed to go forward by utilizing the database again, this time as a sampling frame for further research.

Notes

1 Milligan, Hardwick and Graycar's pioneering study was able to estimate the number of 'non-government welfare organizations' in Australia at between 26,000 and 49,000 in 1981, but their use of local government areas (LGA's) as the basis for the initial sampling frame meant that not only were these units large and diverse in terms of population characteristics but also non-comparable without the researcher's reconstruction of 'LGA-type' areas for Brisbane, the Northern Territory and the Australian Capital Territory (Milligan et al., 1984: 17–20). The present study used statistical local areas, which provides national coverage and achieves smaller and less diverse units. The database was constructed between October 1993 and September 1994 using secondary sources for 100 Australian Bureau of Statistics (ABS) statistical areas.

2 At the first stage, the ABS statistical local areas (comprising 1,298 populated areas) were stratified on the basis of population distribution (strata 1 by state and territory and strata 2 by capital city and remaining populations). Second, a cluster of 100 statistical local areas (Castles, 1991: 40) was drawn randomly to achieve a proportionate sample.

3 A neighbourhood house in Australia is a multi-focused, non-profit organization centred on a physical house location. Programmes typically include one or more of the following: emergency aid; refuge; childcare; adult education; disability programmes; drop-in centres; advocacy and referral; youth projects. Essentially, this is the same form of organization as its namesakes in North America and Canada, but should not be confused with neighbourhood housing offices in the UK, which are specialist accommodation centres.

7
Welfare and the Voluntary Sector in Australia

Introduction

While the database gives some idea of the shape of the sector across Australia, it provides no information on how the organizations are constituted or operate. To address these issues, 14 focus groups were conducted with workers and participants from the community sector across Australia between February 1995 and August 1996. Groups were arranged using a random sample of towns and metropolitan suburbs and their listed organizations from the database, stratified in order to ensure national coverage within all states and territories and reflect population levels.[1]

Group discussions centred on the subjects' experiences of the sector and upon current areas of concern and possibility. The aim was to provide qualitative data within an inductive framework, the insights of which would later be tested by means of a sample survey. As such, the management of the focus groups by the researchers tended towards a non-directive moderation that Morgan calls 'self-managed groups' (Morgan, 1988: 49). That is, a fairly low level of moderator direction intended to maximize the exploratory potential of this research stage.

In accordance with what we already knew of the Australian voluntary welfare sector from the database, the range of focus group participants was broad – from full-time paid workers and administrators of state government community services departments to retired voluntary workers from thrift shops.

Through the course of the discussions, particular themes re-emerged with little or no prompting from the moderator of the group. These themes are introduced below through the broad issues of work, funding, volunteers, competition and active and passive voices.

Working in the sector

Key to transcripts:	[additional information]
	... pause
	(...) material edited out
Key to participants:	PW paid worker
	UW unpaid worker
	GE government-funded organization
	NGF non-government-funded organization

There was a strong sense across participants of feelings about the worth of working in the sector. This was usually expressed through ideas often associated with a community development model and present to some degree in all focus groups:

Well its all about bringing the community together to work out ways forward. We can do it but you have to struggle to get the chance, and you don't always win [laughs].

(PW/GF, Marrickville, NSW)

At the end of the day you are about what you do with other people and so that's why I'm here.

(UW/NGF, Sunshine, VIC)

So many people just couldn't care less but all people need sometimes is a little help to be able to help themselves. There's enormous talent and creativity all around us but so often it's overlooked or kept down. I couldn't imagine doing something else outside this area.

(PW/NGF, Dubbo, NSW)

Clearly present though slightly less commonly articulated was a charitable approach:

It's sad to see the position of some of our families and we feel we can help.

(PW/NGF, Alexandra, VIC)

We have an obligation to help them I feel ... we are in a position to do so and they cannot help themselves.

(UW/NGF, Belconnen, ACT)

Perhaps the best summary of the underlying ethos, whether community-development or charity based, is from the coordinator of a centre for gender issues. Simply, 'we are important'.

This strong sense of worth was tied to a closeness to and a feeling of belonging within the community which often translated into the structures of operation:

> We are guided by the people in the community and they set the priorities, it's been very successful.
>
> (PW/NGF, Springvale, VIC)

> Some of the health workers are frightened by community input ... but ... they [the community] come up with very creative solutions, once they're given the information and understand the problems and work with you.
>
> (PW/GF, Leichart, NSW)

> I first came here [neighbourhood house] to ask about some legal thing I couldn't understand and they helped me out good, then later I started coming more sometimes just for a chat sometimes and now I'm on the committee to run the place [smiles] and I've told my family and neighbours and now they come here too.
>
> (UW, Fremantle, WA)

> Because I'm from the [Anglican] church we are nearly always invited onto committees set up to look at social problems or funding or priorities or whatever else the government sees fit to talk about. The thing is that I can see the government people usually nodding away when I speak but in the end they rarely listen. I regard myself as nothing other than part of the community and so I try to make my voice theirs and that's not always what they want to hear.
>
> (PW/NGF, Prospect, SA)

This general level of a feeling of worth in this work is in line with other research (Onyx, 1993) and is connected to the commonly expressed sentiment that their work is desperately required because of the weight of unmet need in the community:

> Mental disorder needs here are just the tip of the iceberg, we wouldn't have the resources to deal with the real number here.
>
> (PW/GF, Belconnen, ACT)

When I feel upset with things here I just think what would it be like without even the little that we are doing, it's frightening but you've just got to get on with it.

(UW/NGF, Sunshine, VIC)

What would we do with a doubled budget? [laughs] We'd knock over about a twentieth of the need in just this one area.

(PW/GF, Fremantle, WA)

Funding

Often funding determines the direction of your service and not what the community would like.

(PW/GF, Hobart, TAS)

The issues of funding are central to those working in the sector and were a common theme in group discussions. Participants were almost always a mix of workers from both government and non-government funded organizations. For those with government funding, the pressure to adopt practices and directions tied to that funding were often voiced as a problem and one that contradicted their views of their own work:

I think it was better in a way when the organization was not government funded ... at least we made our own decisions then about the ways to go without having to think about how we could justify that in a strategic plan or whatever.

(UW/GF, Alice Springs, NT)

We wrestled with accepting government funding for years, a lot of people now say we should never have accepted the first dollar from them.

(PW/GF, Alexandra, VIC)

We're becoming more like a government department every day.

(PW/GF, Prospect, SA)

Clearly, the time taken up in the added bureaucratic tasks associated with funding intended to increase accountability and evenness of provision are regularly seen as imposts:

Over the last two years I've become more and more stuck away down the back in my office or in meetings ... if I wasn't then we wouldn't have funds but sometimes I just think, what ever happened to that person who wouldn't take a step without knowing it was part of what the people around here were about? I feel I'm losing touch sometimes with the reason I'm here.

(PW/GF, Leichart, NSW)

Last week we had two of three workers away for an all-day meeting in town about strategic planning (...) when we can't even keep up with the demand here.

(PW/GF, Springvale, VIC)

They [funding bodies] have very little contact with the community.

(UW/GF, Sunshine, VIC)

Such complaints are often accentuated in remote and regional areas:

It's unbelievable, we just got a fax saying that so and so was arriving from community services in Brisbane the next day and then he turned up with three others and expected that we would just sit around all day and talk about meeting objectives as if we didn't have anything else to do.

(PW/GF, Mt Isa, QLD)

Canberra haven't got a clue about what its like out there [the community].

(PW/GF, South Brisbane, QLD)

Behind this though, there is a level of support for the regulating features inherent in centralized state funding provision:

Well we complain about it [collecting and reporting data on numbers of people seen by the organization] but obviously if we didn't do it who would really know what we're doing overall?

(PW/GF, Marrickville, NSW)

I'm trying to help my staff realize how important it is to collect data, analyse it and how accurate data has a role to play in planning services.

(PW/GF, Springvale, VIC)

It's certainly the case that before they brought in the twelve-month justifications there were some organizations that just funded themselves from project money and without any comebacks.

(PW/GF, South Brisbane, QLD)

The problem, though, is generally seen on balance to be one of the extent of the payoff – long hours spent on reporting and submission tasks seen as the very opposite to community-oriented 'people' work:

We're becoming more bureaucratic, we have to if we're going to develop three-year strategic plans.

(PW/GF, Fremantle, WA)

The demand for government accountability is getting worse and worse, state and federal and all the funding bodies want a different format. It's all about money and numbers.

(PW/GF, Springvale, VIC)

The pity of it all is that lots of great and committed people end up burnt-out behind a desk somewhere.

(PW/GF, Prospect, SA)

Ultimately the dilemma remains as an unresolved tension between accountability and commitment to the ideals of the sector:

The positive side of this accountability is we do get to understand what our service is, we become more focused, clearly specified, objective. I think it is sad you lose the grass-roots response.

(PW/GF, Belconnen, ACT)

As well, many organizations are always in the process of putting in the next submission. This leads to a situation where funding (and often survival) is a year-to-year matter while the perceived needs demand longer-term solutions:

We are constantly chasing money checking what the flavour of the month is.

(PW/NGF, Fremantle, WA)

Communities are hard to access it can take you twelve months just to get started then your funding runs out.

(PW/GF, Hobart, TAS)

To be an effective worker to an extent you have to be emotionally involved ... form-filling and evaluation just adds to your work load and actually takes away from your involvement.

(PW/GF, Dubbo, NSW)

In some organizations, a formal division of labour has taken place to address these problems:

Before we shared out the tasks we all pretty much tried to do everything because obviously you want to be involved at the desk in the community and everything. Now we each stick with our own area of things like I do all the submissions and evaluations and Val does mainly the project work.

(PW/GF, Springvale, VIC)

For government funded organizations, there exists a daily tension around balancing the justifications and administration of the funds, their work in the community and putting in the submission for next year. Organizations not in receipt of government grants are funded through member fees, fees for service, charitable trusts, fundraising activities or are unfunded. These alternatives bring their own sets of characteristics:

We rely on fundraising and some fees. It's alright most of the time but you know ... it's also a constant thing about wondering if it'll all add up at the end of the year.

(UW/NGF, Mt Isa, QLD)

Our playgroup is funded ourselves, 60 children plus families ... we fund raise, but we need to be more expert ... stories from Melbourne with private agencies taking over, it sounds terrible.

(UW/NGF, Alexandra, VIC)

We're not funded and we don't want to be really. It'd be nice to have a proper office and even a telephone for the group and a mailbox you know, but look I've seen other [self-help] groups go the funding path and six months down the track they're not recognizable and I don't mean they're better, they're worse (...) because the money brings different ways of having to do the things you've done for years ... it's just not worth it.

(UW/NGF, South Brisbane, QLD)

Volunteers

While unfunded and non-government funded organizations rely more heavily on unpaid workers (volunteers), government-dependent organizations are also characterized by volunteer work in conjunction with paid work. The question of volunteers was a topic which was constantly raised.

In what might be called the traditional notion of volunteers, participants viewed them as valuable members who help the collective good of the community through activities which at the same time act back to increase the volunteer's own sense of self-worth:

> Lots of people want to give back to the community.
>
> (PW/GF, Sunshine, VIC)

> Working with volunteers in community education is wonderful, they bring a lot of energy and enthusiasm. A lot of people who don't have the qualifications to teach say at TAFE teach here as volunteers. They are not seen as experts and it helps to build a sense of community.
>
> (PW/GF, South Brisbane, QLD)

> It's my way of putting something back into the community.
>
> (UW/NGF, Fremantle, WA)

However, many participants claimed that while their organizations could not work without volunteers, it was not always an ideal situation when there were also paid workers alongside them:

> More volunteers can put pressure on workers who have to oversee them, can add difficulties in some circumstances... often you are unsure of where the line is drawn between what volunteers should and shouldn't be doing both from their point of view and the community member's.
>
> (PW/GF, Dubbo, NSW)

Both the professionalization of organizations and the tightening of legislation around their activities can create tensions between legal and managerialist structures on one hand and volunteers on the other:

> With paid workers you can say 'do it' but you have to look after volunteers, you have to respect what they're doing.
>
> (PW/GF, Mt Isa, QLD)

We provide mediation for any dispute so we're getting pressure from above [changes to the Family Law Act requiring qualified mediators for family disputes] to say no longer recruit from the community. Whereas before mediation came from the community and we'd say we want to be able to resolve disputes in a different way.

(PW/GF, Prospect, SA)

A solution to this last problem may be found in increasing the skills and 'professionalism' of the volunteers:

We couldn't operate without volunteers, we're looking at how to maintain them by running workshops, skills training and updates.

(PW/GF, South Brisbane, QLD)

In fact, the volunteers of today are already a different breed from the point of view of many in the sector:

When I met the old bunch [of volunteers] who look at volunteering as giving their time freely and the new bunch who say 'will you pay for my parking, my lunch, my training' ... some of the old ones can't believe it.

(PW/GF, Sunshine, VIC)

I'm hoping to eventually get a job in this area [of work] so for the time being doing this voluntary work gives me some experience and of course contacts. I'm hoping to get a place on the management committee.

(UW/GF, South Brisbane, QLD)

Let's face it, most of the volunteers we see here are getting their foot in the door, and good luck to them. Volunteering is not like it used to be, though; today you almost have to think about if you're dressed well enough to go off to work today 'cause such and such a volunteer will be in and they're *so* serious [laughs].

(PW/GF, Springvale, VIC)

Competition and tendering

With few exceptions, the participants were aware of the moves towards compulsory competitive tendering (CCT), even if they had not experienced it personally. During the period of the focus group research, CCT

measures were introduced in Victoria and scheduled for South
Australia. Much discussion took place over the relative merits of introducing competition into the voluntary welfare sector in relation to
tendering for funds. Many opposed the notion on the grounds of the
perceived erosion in standards:

> My concern is looking at the quality of services being tendered for,
> who's doing it?
>
> (PW/GF, Alexandra, VIC)

> 'Meals on wheels' went to the cheapest tender; now the person
> knocks on the door three times and runs, no quality of service. Is
> the person in there breathing or not?
>
> (PW/GF, Sunshine, VIC)

The CCT 'threat' was seen partly as being linked to moves towards
deprofessionalization and therefore a shift away from the model which
many (particularly government funded) organizations had felt com-
pelled to follow in the 1980s and 1990s:

> We've filled in all the forms, dotted all the I's and crossed all the T's
> and now they'll give funding to some cheapo charity outfit or
> maybe something even worse.
>
> (PW/GF, Prospect, SA)

> This year the council has had to expose 30 per cent of its operating
> budget to CCT, next year it's 50 per cent. Meals on wheels could be
> picked up by the Uniting Church.
>
> (PW/GF, South Brisbane, QLD)

The other major worry over the process, and a deep-seated one, was
the likely effects of introducing competition into a sector traditionally
based on cooperation:

> It [CCT] hasn't been good, I don't know what I can say in this room
> because any of you could be competing for the same tender.
>
> (PW/GF, Footscary, VIC)

> Before we would just ring each other up and say 'what do you put in
> this section of the submission?' Now you've got to think that who-
> ever you ring is probably a competition for the same money. It's
> rotten.
>
> (PW/GF, Springvale, VIC)

The smaller community resource bases of regional Australia perceived particular problems from such a change:

> Tender issues could be quite damaging in a small town. We're used to pulling together here but that would force us apart.
>
> (PW/GF, Mt Isa, QLD)

However, not all participants saw it as a negative development:

> It makes you ask strategic questions.
>
> (PW/GF, Springvale, VIC)

> [CCT] asks you to sharpen up, it does challenge you, I think it does make you go into a period of reflection and moving forward.
>
> (PW/GF, Sunshine, VIC)

> Well I know this sounds hard but we've done a damn good job here for years and I've seen other places 'round here just sit there doing not very much sometimes and always seem to get funding, often better resourcing than us ... so I don't know ... I know I shouldn't like it but maybe it won't be a totally bad thing.
>
> (PW/GF, Springvale, VIC)

Active and passive voices

The focus group discussions often highlighted differences between passive and active voices on behalf of the participants. Passivity was not usually confined to one area such as funding, but would often characterize a more generalized view of themselves, their organization and wider forces, in particular the government:

> It's the government's responsibility to provide money, if they're not going to match the need how does it get done?
>
> (UW/NGF, Fremantle, WA)

> Do you know that no one *ever* writes to us and says they have money available?
>
> (UW/NGF, Dubbo, NSW)

> Why do we have to justify our spending every twelve months?
>
> (PW/GF, Marrickville, NSW)

We've waited and waited for someone from government to come and hear us … its unfair.

(UW/NGF, Prospect, SA)

The passivity is similar to that of the welfare recipient waiting for the centralized handout and complaining to no one in particular in the meantime. On more than one occasion, focus group participants left the group immediately upon learning that the researchers' University had not convened the meeting in order to confer grants to community groups (despite the fact that our invitation made it very clear that nothing like this was on offer).

Interestingly, passivity did not appear confined to one type or funding or location. Participants seemed equally likely to voice a passive outlook whether they were from a federally funded, large organization in Sydney or an unfunded self-help group in Mt Isa. This was also true for more active voices which similarly ranged across organizational types and locations:

The government is always using failed ideas from overseas … we're trying to develop ways of using the ideas that we have here.

(PW/GF, Dubbo, NSW)

It's no good waiting for things to fix themselves … we' ve just got to think of different ways to solve problems as they come up.

(UW/GF, Isa, QLD)

I've worked in places [voluntary associations] where if it had been a person we'd be still standing at the tram stop even after being told that there were no more trams 'till next week … talk about hitting your head against a brick wall.

(PW/GF, Springvale, VIC)

Of course, the passive and active extremes reflect a contested space both within the voluntary sector itself and very often within the individuals who work in it. Movement between the two must be regarded as the usual situation, as one or other voice seems to make more sense or better resolve the particular matter at hand.

We end this section by considering some of the characteristics of organizations which seemed to us to highlight the more dynamic elements of the voluntary sector and those that might contribute to the development forms of active citizenship:

- Perhaps the most pervasive feature of the dynamic and active association lies in the centrality of the idea of accountability to members. Members are the most important thing about the organization and the reason it exists. This is connected to a strong sense of integrity which comes from being true to the member base: 'authenticity is it'.
- For associations with a defined workforce (probably a mix of paid and unpaid), a relatively flat structure of organization best promotes the subsidiarity features inherent in the member-driven focus.
- Multiple sources of funding also help the creation of spaces within which new ideas, strategies and plans can be tried out. With a single or a restricted funding source, the association is vulnerable to pressures from that source. Being unfunded, the association is freed from those strings but it is debatable how effective associations with no funding base can be. In general the goal of associations would be: 'funding on our own terms'.
- Working strategically (pragmatically) is an important factor. This especially relates to ensuring that plans are likely to lead to outcomes which will be best for members.
- Networking to create both an information base and opportunities is crucial. We would expect the use of electronic communications to grow rapidly within active-oriented associations.

As such, this list of features and characteristics may be a useful general description of voluntary associations which are working to extend active citizenship. Nevertheless, the importance of contextualization needs to be stressed, as the list could also describe sectors of organized crime. As we note in Chapter 3, the main distinguishing difference between the Mafia and a legal voluntary association is the freedom of entry and exit. This underlines the importance of the notion of voluntary we employ in this book.

Summary

The data which emerge from the focus group research indicate that underlying the voluntary welfare sector in Australia is a strong current of belief in 'a fair go' and in the value of working in and through communities at a local level.

While the sector is in some way united through such community-based ideas, other factors work to divide organizations and workers.

Many of these are linked to funding and regulation and are heightened by the consequences flowing from economic slowdown.

While the sector operating in remote and regional areas of Australia has enhanced concerns over issues to do with control from afar and the impacts of government policies on smaller communities, the pattern of concerns in fact appears highly regular across the country.

Both active and passive voices are evidenced by workers in explaining and dealing with their concerns and everyday situations. We would not characterize part of the sector as passive and part as active, however. The actual situation seems altogether more mixed.

In terms of the frameworks discussed in Chapters 4 and 5, there is clear evidence for the existence and continuing relevance of ideas linked to what we have identified as the activist, charity, market and welfare state industry frameworks.

If one thing characterizes the picture that emerges from the focus groups it is that of a sector that has long existed and coped with uncertainty, constant change and, for many organizations, life on the margins. Perhaps this history equips the sector better than most with the abilities needed to chart paths through the projections of future welfare possibilities.

Demographic data

What emerges from the database and the focus groups is a picture of a large and vibrant voluntary welfare sector characterized by a broad range of function and focus, and one which has experienced recent rapid growth. Within the associations that comprise the sector, there are indications that conditions are present for the voluntary welfare sector to play a part in the sort of moves away from traditional welfare state provision and towards structures of 'associative democracy' discussed in Part I. The extent to which this apparent potential may be realized cannot of course be answered wholly from within the sector itself, for legislative, economic and political frameworks must first be developed in order to provide enabling environments for change. Nevertheless, we were concerned to look in finer detail at the characteristics of the sector, including a range of attitudinal dimensions suggested by the focus group research.

To achieve these ends, a sample survey of organizations was planned utilizing the data from the focus groups as a starting point. From these data a questionnaire was devised and a random sample survey conducted.[2] The survey utilized telephone interviews with the coordinators

- There are an estimated 542,000 paid workers and 1,134,000 unpaid or voluntary workers in the Australian voluntary welfare sector
- The use of unpaid work is constant across the sector at an average (median) of 2 to 1 (unpaid to paid hours)
- 66% of organizations have at least 1 paid worker
- 18% of organizations have no unpaid workers
- There are an average (median) of 6 paid workers across organizations
- There are an average (median) of 12 unpaid workers across organizations
- Women workers outnumber men by factor of 5 to 1 in paid positions
- Women workers outnumber men by factor of 3 to 1 in unpaid positions
- Unpaid workers did all the work in 41% of organizations
- Unpaid workers did more than 50% of work in 56% of organizations
- 76% of organizations had less than half their paid workers as full-time positions
- 28% of organizations gained paid workers compared to 14% of organizations that lost paid workers
- 43% of organizations gained unpaid workers compared to 11% of organizations that lost unpaid workers
- The median age of organizations is 14 years
- 67% of all organizations provide free or mostly free services
- High levels of dependency on government funding characterize service provision organizations (refuges, crisis counselling, neighbourhood houses)
- Low levels of dependency on government funding characterize mutual-aid organizations (support, self-help, action/rights)
- Over 64% of organizations were principally funded by government in NSW, TAS and WA
- 50% to 54% of organizations were principally funded by government in SA, QLD and VIC

Figure 7.1   Summary of demographic findings: Australian voluntary welfare sector, 1996–7

of 495 organizations drawn from the database as a random stratified sample. Demographic, organizational and attitudinal data were elicited. The survey has enabled us to test the generalizability of the qualitative data from the focus groups and to probe for demographic and attitudinal data for the sector. (See Figure 7.1 for a summary of demographic findings.)

Age

Organizations were on average well established. The median age of the organizations was 14 years,[3] with a range of one year to 103 years. Nine and a half per cent of organizations were 5 years old or less, 30 per cent were 10 years old or less, and 32 per cent were older than 20 years (the last group includes larger and long-established charitable organizations such as the Salvation Army). Median organizational age varied little between capital cities (16 years), main population centres (14 years) and towns or smaller (14 years). Victoria and New South Wales recorded the highest median ages (16 years and 15.5 years respectively), other states being grouped around the 14 years median (South Australia, 14 years; West Australia, 14 years; Queensland, 13.5 years). Tasmania had the lowest median age of any state at 9.5 years.

Resources

A measure of organizational 'connectivity' is the use of fax and email by the organizations. While nearly two-thirds (63 per cent) of organizations had a fax number, only 16 per cent had ever used email (9 per cent were regular users ('in the last week'), 3 per cent 'in the last month', and 3 per cent 'more than one month ago'). There was little or no difference in 'connectivity' on the basis of location either by state or by population centre. Given that the survey was administered in 1996–7, we might expect that by now a larger proportion of the better resourced organizations would have become equipped with email. Indeed the major split is between organizations funded largely by government and those not. Eighty-three per cent of organisations whose principal funding was from federal, state or local government had a fax number, compared to 35 per cent of organizations not funded principally by government. Government funding recipients also had higher email usage rates (20 per cent compared to 11 per cent).

Funding

When we look at the mix of funding (Figure 7.2), state governments are the single largest source for 39 per cent of all 'organizations, followed by Federal government (13 per cent), fundraising (12 per cent), membership and/or service fees (8 per cent), local government and charity (contributions made by charitable institutions or benefactors) (7 per cent) and private funding (4 per cent). Eleven per cent of organizations were unfunded. The low percentage for local government is probably the result of the question which asked for the single largest source of funding. Local government may therefore be under-represented in the data in so far as it may contribute more than data suggest there as a secondary or tertiary source.

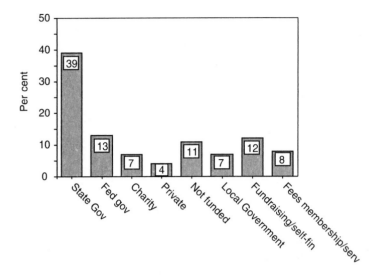

Figure 7.2 Principal source of funding (survey data $n = 493$)

When funding source is broken down by state (Table 7.1), there is a split between high (over 60 per cent) levels of government funding for organizations in Tasmania (80 per cent), West Australia (65 per cent) and New South Wales (64 per cent), and lower levels of government funding in the cases of South Australia (54 per cent), Queensland (52 per cent) and Victoria (50 per cent). There is a small to moderate association overall (Phi = .153).

Funding differences tend to group organizational types (by function) into two categories depending upon the level of government funding as demonstrated in Table 7.2.

High levels of dependency on (State) government funding are characterized by the service types of organizations: refuges; crisis counselling; childcare and neighbourhood houses which ranged from a high of 70 per cent principal funding from government (across organizations within that function) for refuges to 48 per cent for neighbourhood houses. Low levels of dependency on government funding are associated with the mutual support and aid organizations: support (29 per cent); self-help (modal category = unfunded); and action/rights (modal category = unfunded).

Table 7.1   Principal funding source by state

State		Principal source of funding		
		Fed., state and local gov.	Non-gov.	Total
VIC	Count	66	65	131
	% within State	50.4%	49.6%	100.0%
NSW	Count	115	65	180
	% within State	63.9%	36.1%	100.0%
SA	Count	37	31	68
	% within State	54.4%	45.6%	100.0%
QLD	Count	24	22	46
	% within State	52.2%	47.8%	100.0%
TAS	Count	16	4	20
	% within State	80.0%	20.0%	100.0%
WA	Count	31	17	48
	% within State	64.6%	35.4%	100.0%
Total	Count	289	204	493
	% within State	58.6%	41.4%	100.0%

Significance = 0.04.
Phi = 0.153.[5]

Email usage rates between the two categories are similar and reflect the overall low rate across the sector, but facsimile access is noticeably higher in the first group. This differential in basic office communication equipment probably indicates a more general resourcing disparity between the two groups and clearly suggests that high levels of dependency on government funding probably equate with higher levels of funding overall. Services are free or mostly free for both groups, suggesting that user-pays principles had not achieved any substantial foothold at the time of the survey. The median services category for childcare is still low at 50/50 for an area more usually thought of as an 'obvious' user-pays situation, but this serves to underline the strength of mutuality in the sector. Generally no restrictions are placed on access to these organizations, the understandable exceptions being self-help groups and refuges. Numbers of paid and unpaid workers show some differences, with slightly more paid workers in the high government funding level group and (with the exception of crisis counselling) higher ratios of unpaid to paid workers in the low government funding level group. The age profile of both groups is similar.

Table 7.2 Organizational function, principal funding and selected characteristics

Function	Funding (mode) (modal %)	Use email (%)	Have fax (%)	Services (median)	Access (mode)	Workers (median) Paid	Workers (median) Unpaid	Organization age (median yrs)
High-level dependency on government funding								
Refuge	State G.(70)	10	90	Mostly free	Restriction	7.5	10.5	17
Crisis/Coun.	State G.(63)	25	75	Wholly free	No restriction	5	43	15.5
Childcare	State G.(53)	15	73	50/50	No restriction	8	10	10
N. House	State G.(48)	21	76	Mostly free	No restriction	5	12.5	14
Low-level dependency on government funding								
Support	State G.(29)	15	51	Mostly free	No restriction	6	12	17
Self-help	Unfunded (31)	13	44	Wholly free	Restriction	4	12	14
Action/rgts	Unfunded (24)	12	60	Wholly free	No restriction	4.5	12	14.5

Work

Coordinators

Data on the coordinators (the respondents of the survey) show a consistent pattern across organizations. In all organization types, women coordinators were in the majority – 77 per cent for the entire sample This corresponds to the gender breakdown pattern for paid workers in the sample as a whole (80 per cent women) and unpaid workers (64 per cent women). Childcare (92 per cent women), crisis counselling/refuges (89 per cent women) and neighbourhood houses (88 per cent women) recorded the highest rates, while-self help (59 per cent women) and action/rights (60 per cent women) contained proportionately more male coordinators even though women coordinators were still found in the majority of those organizations. The median time worked by coordinators in their current position was 6 years (range = 4 to 8 years), and in the community sector overall the median time was 12 years (range = 10–13 years). Median age and highest level of completed education for the sample were 47 years (range = 42–50 years) and diploma/certificate (range = year 11–diploma/certificate). Action/rights (median highest education completed = year 11) and self-help (year 12) were the only types of organizations that deviated from the diploma/certificate average.

Workforce

By combining the data on the numbers of paid and unpaid workers in the surveyed organizations together with the database, we were able to estimate the total national workforce both in total and broken down by organizational function and focus. This is presented in Table 7.3.

The sector has an estimated total workforce of 1,670,000, of which the ratio of unpaid to paid is approximately two to one. Workforce by function is dominated in absolute terms by support, neighbourhood houses and childcare organizations, which between them have an estimated 491,000 paid and 983,000 unpaid workers. Within the areas of focus, health organizations have the largest estimated number of paid workers (98,500). While poverty-focused organizations have the lowest median survey score of any focus area for paid workers (median = 3) giving an estimate of 37,000 paid workers nationally, they have the highest score for unpaid workers (median = 17), which makes them the single highest users of unpaid workers (national estimate = 207,000 unpaid workers).

Table 7.3 National estimates for paid and unpaid workers by organization function and focus

| Organizational function | Projected national estimate (range 000's)[a] | |
	Number paid workers[b]	Number unpaid workers[b]
Support/Social Org.	27 0000 (200–346)[c]	541 000 (401–692)
Neighbourhood house	13 1000 (125–137)	329 000 (314–343)
Childcare centre	90 000 (86–94)	113 000 (108–118)
Action/Rights group	21 000 (20–22)	56 000 (54–59)
Self-help	19 000 (18–20)	56 000 (54–59)
Crisis/counselling[d]	11 000 (11–12)	39 000 (38–41)
Est. Population Total	542 000 (460–631)	1 134 000 (969–1312)
Organization focus		
Health	98 500 (73–124)	162 000 (121–204)
Disability	85 000 (82–89)	134 000 (128–140)
Poverty	37 000 (35–38)	207 000 (198–217)
Youth	90 000 (86–94)	84 000 (81–88)
Women	72 000 (69–76)	93 000 (89–97)
Elderly	56 000 (54–59)	122 000 (117–128)

[a] Estimates rounded to 500 (ranges rounded to 1,000).
[b] Survey median score × (total N. SLA/sample n. SLA × [total n. organizations in sample] = 1278/100 × (7233) given in figure above).
[c] Range estimates for function and focus areas based on median score + −4.5% sample error applied to proportion of sample applied to estimations of total population range. NB: restricted to non-ranged high/low estimates for clarity of presentation.
[d] Includes category of 'refuge' (sample comprised: women's refuge 70%, youth refuge 30% for these calculations).

In a preliminary report to their forthcoming study of the Australian non-profit sector (within the Johns Hopkins comparative project), Lyons and Hocking (1998: 3) provide a breakdown for organizations by field of activity with operating expenditures and numbers of employees. Because they use a more inclusive classification than our project, their organization fields are not directly comparable to ours and include many fields such as leisure, political parties, trade unions and employment services that fall outside our definitions. However, their field of 'health' can be compared to our data. Their study uses a number of aggregated data sources together with targeted survey data. The preliminary result for the health field gives the number of (paid) employees as 105,000 for Australia in 1995–6 (Lyons and Hocking, 1998: 3). Table 7.3 shows our estimate for the same field using inference from the survey (question on the number of paid workers in each organization)

Table 7.4 Comparison of estimates for paid and unpaid workers in selected fields, Australia

| | | Estimates | | |
| | | 'Health' field | | 'Community welfare' field |
Study	Year	Paid workers	Unpaid workers	Unpaid workers
ABS	1995	–	181 000	1 064 600
Lyons and Hocking	1995–6	105 000	–	–
Present study	1996–7	98 500	162 000	1 134 000

and database. We estimate the number of paid workers in the community welfare health field to be 98,581 (with a range between 73,480 and 124,440) for the period 1996–7. This congruence (a difference of only 6 per cent between the two estimates) is helpful in suggesting a degree of validation for our health-focus employment data (arrived at by different methods and procedures), and by extension for our other estimates for paid and unpaid workers across the sector. In addition, the national survey of voluntary work in 1995 (ABS, 1996) estimated 181,000 volunteers in the field of 'health' and 1,064,600 in the combined fields of health, welfare/community and environmental (ABS, 1996: 10, Table 8).

Funding and location profiles

By combining (principal) funding and location we can further group organizations into capital cities and government funding ('metropolitan state'), capital cities and non-government funding ('metropolitan non-state'), outside capitals and government funding ('regional state') and outside capitals and non-government funding ('regional non-state').[5] The data which follow have been organized in this way in order to examine remainder of the demographic variables.

The median age for all organizations is 14 years. Metropolitan non-state (median = 17 years) and regional non-state (median = 16.5 years) organizational profiles have median ages higher than their state funded counterparts (3 years older for metropolitan and 2.5 years older for regional). The median number of paid workers for the sector is 6 and for unpaid workers 12. Perhaps surprisingly given the discussion following Table 7.2 on the resource differences between state and non-state funded organizations, regional non-state organizations have the highest median number of paid workers (median = 8), followed by

Table 7.5 Organization profiles by age of organization and workforce data

Profiles		Age of organization (yrs)	Total number paid workers	Paid men	Paid women	Total number unpaid workers	Unpaid men	Unpaid women
Metropolitan state	Median	14.00	6.00	1.00	5.00	13.00	4.00	10.00
	N	136	125	125	125	94	94	94
Metropolitan non-state	Median	17.00	3.00	1.00	2.00	13.50	4.00	8.50
	N	73	29	29	29	68	68	68
Regional state	Median	14.00	5.00	1.00	5.00	12.00	2.00	8.00
	N	145	141	141	141	107	109	107
Regional non-state	Median	16.50	8.00	1.50	6.00	10.00	3.00	5.00
	N	126	28	28	28	128	128	128
Total	Median	14.00	6.00	1.00	5.00	12.00	3.00	8.00
	N	480	323	323	323	397	399	397

metropolitan state (median = 6), regional state (median = 5) and metropolitan non-state (median = 3). This high median for regional state may be accounted for by the relatively small number of organizations involved ($n = 28$). Ratios of women to men in both paid and unpaid work remain close to the overall pattern across the profiles.

For the sector, 66 per cent of organizations have at least one paid worker of some kind. When the profiles are broken down by the presence or absence of paid workers, the effects of state funding are marked. In Table 7.6, both metropolitan state and regional state have ratios of over nine to one in terms of the presence:absence of paid workers, while for non-state the ratios are reversed – four to six for metropolitan and two to eight for regional. The dominant pattern then for organizations not receiving government funding as their principal income, is a heavy and often total reliance upon unpaid workers. For those that do have principal government funding, less than 10 per cent have no paid workers.

Eighty-two percent of all organizations have at least one unpaid worker, and across all profiles the pattern holds with the majority of organizations using unpaid workers. There is a difference between state

Table 7.6 Organization profiles by presence of paid workers

| Profiles | | Any paid workers | | |
		Yes	No	Total
Metropolitan state	Count	124	13	137
	% within 4 org profiles on loc and funds	90.5%	9.5%	100.0%
Metropolitan non-state	Count	29	45	74
	% within 4 org profiles on loc and funds	39.2%	60.8%	100.0%
Regional state	Count	141	10	151
	% within 4 org profiles on loc and funds	93.4%	6.6%	100.0%
Regional non-state	Count	29	101	130
	% within 4 org profiles on loc and funds	22.3%	77.7%	100.0%
Total	Count	323	169	492
	% within 4 org profiles on loc and funds	65.7%	34.3%	100.0%

Significance = 0.000.[4]
Phi = 0.669.

Table 7.7 Organization profiles by presence of unpaid workers

Profiles		Any unpaid workers		
		Yes	No	Total
Metropolitan	Count	94	44	138
state	% within 4 org profiles of loc and funds	68.1%	31.9%	100.0%
Metropolitan	Count	69	4	73
non-state	% within 4 org profiles on loc and funds	94.5%	5.5%	100.0%
Regional state	Count	112	39	151
	% within 4 org profiles on loc and funds	74.2%	25.8%	100.0%
Regional non-state	Count	128	2	130
	% within 4 org profiles on loc and funds	98.5%	1.5%	100.0%
Total	Count	403	89	492
	% within 4 org profiles on loc and funds	81.9%	18.1%	100.0%

Significance = 0.000.
Phi = 0.336.

and non-state in the case of unpaid workers, but not as strong a difference as was noted with paid workers. While both non-state profiles have over 90 per cent of their organizations engaging unpaid workers, the state profiles have lower proportions, between 68 per cent and 74 per cent. A summary indication of the different strength of these relationships is given by the values of Phi: 0.669 in the case of the presence of paid workers and 0.336 in the case of the presence of unpaid workers.

In those organizations that employ paid workers, it is unusual to find those personnel working either as full-time (36 hours or more per week) workers or amongst high proportions of other full-time paid workers. Per the sector, only 11 per cent of organizations comprised full-time paid workers in proportions of 75 per cent or above of the organization's workforce. This rises only to 26 per cent of organizations that had full-time paid workers constituting a quarter or more of the organization's workforce. There are slight differences between the profile groups, but the overall pattern holds for each. Undoubtedly, the effects of the importance of unpaid workers to the sector as a whole explain much of these data. The picture is one of a sector in which

Table 7.8 Organization profiles by proportion of full-time paid workers in workforce

		Paid workers working more than 36 hrs per week				
		0–25%	25–50%	50–75%	75–100%	Total
Metropolitan state	Count	75	10	13	15	113
	% within 4 org profiles on loc and funds	66.4%	8.8%	11.5%	13.3%	100.0%
Metropolitan non state	Count	27	2	2	3	34
	% within 4 org profiles on loc and funds	79.4%	5.9%	5.9%	8.8%	100.0%
Regional state	Count	97	7	9	16	129
	% within 4 org profiles on loc and funds	75.2%	5.4%	7.0%	12.4%	100.0%
Regional non-state	Count	42	2	3	1	48
	% within 4 org profiles on loc and funds	87.5%	4.2%	6.3%	2.1%	100.0%
Total	Count	241	21	27	35	324
	% within 4 org profiles on loc and funds	74.4%	6.5%	8.3%	10.8%	100.0%

Significance = 0.217.
Phi = 0.179.

Table 7.9 Organization profiles by proportion of work done by unpaid workers in the last week

Profiles		Proportion of work done by unpaid in the last week					
		0–25%	25–50%	50–75%	75–100%	All of the work	Total
Metropolitan state	Count	38	18	11	7	14	88
	% within 4 org profiles on loc and funds	43.2%	20.5%	12.5%	8.0%	15.9%	100.0%
Metropolitan non-state	Count	8	3	5	10	41	67
	% within 4 org profiles on loc and funds	11.9%	4.5%	7.5%	14.9%	61.2%	100.0%
Regional state	Count	55	20	9	9	11	104
	% within 4 org profiles on loc and funds	52.9%	19.2%	8.7%	8.7%	10.6%	100.0%
Regional non-state	Count	13	5	5	3	90	116
	% within 4 org profiles on loc and funds	11.2%	4.3%	4.3%	2.6%	77.6%	100.0%
Total	Count	114	46	30	29	156	375
	% within 4 org profiles on loc and funds	30.4%	12.3%	8.0%	7.7%	41.6%	100.0%

Significance = 0.000.
Phi = 0.371.

Table 7.10 Organization profiles by turnover of paid workers in the last six months

Profiles		Same number	Net loss of workers	Net gain of workers	Total
Metropolitan state	Count	71	16	36	123
	% within 4 org profiles on loc and funds	57.7%	13.0%	29.3%	100.0%
Metropolitan non-state	Count	20	4	5	29
	% within 4 org profile on loc and funds	69.0%	13.8%	17.2%	100.0%
Regional state	Count	75	21	41	137
	% within 4 org profiles on loc and funds	54.7%	15.3%	29.9%	100.0%
Regional non-state	Count	20	2	7	29
	% within 4 org profiles on loc and funds	69.0%	6.9%	24.1%	100.0%
Total	Count	186	43	89	318
	% within 4 org profiles on loc and funds	58.5%	13.5%	28.0%	100.0%

Significance = 0.587.
Phi = 0.117.

unpaid work is the norm; and even where full-time paid workers exist, they share their workplace with greater numbers of unpaid colleagues. For organizations with unpaid workers, 42 per cent reported that all of the work in the organization had been done by unpaid workers in the last week. There is a marked difference between the state and non-state profiles in this case, with the state organizations having the highest proportion in the range of zero to 25 per cent (state metropolitan = 43 per cent, state regional = 53 per cent) and the non-state having the highest proportion in the category of all the work (metropolitan = 61 per cent and regional = 78 per cent).

Tables 7.10 and 7.11 show rates of turnover for paid and unpaid workers in the six-month period before the survey.

Most organizations (59 per cent) had kept the same number of paid workers over the six-month period, while net gains (28 per cent of organizations) outweighed net losses (14 per cent of organizations). The pattern generally holds across the profiles, but the state organizations show higher rates of net gains than the non-state organizations.

The reported turnover of unpaid workers is greater than that for paid workers, with 46 per cent of organizations registering the same number against 43 per cent with net gains and 11 per cent with net losses. State organizations had higher rates of net gains, with both state profiles

Table 7.11 Organization profiles by turnover of unpaid workers in the last six months

Profiles		Same	Net loss	Net gain	Total
Metropolitan state	Count	38	6	42	86
	% within 4 org profiles on loc and funds	44.2%	7.0%	48.8%	100.0%
Metropolitan non-state	Count	32	9	22	63
	% within 4 org profiles on loc and funds	50.8%	14.3%	34.9%	100.0%
Regional state	Count	41	7	55	103
	% within 4 org profiles on loc and funds	39.8%	6.8%	53.4%	100.0%
Regional non-state	Count	60	18	42	120
	% within 4 org profiles on loc and funds	50.0%	15.0%	35.0%	100.0%
Total	Count	171	40	161	372
	% within 4 org profiles on loc and funds	46.0%	10.8%	43.3%	100.0%

Significance = 0.041.
Phi = 0.187.

Table 7.12 Organization profiles by levels of service charges

Profiles		Service free of charge?					
		Wholly free	Mostly free	About 50/50	Mostly paid for	Wholly paid for	Total
Metropolitan state	Count	54	43	8	23	9	137
	% within 4 org profiles on loc and funds	39.4%	31.4%	5.8%	16.8%	6.6%	100.0%
Metropolitan non-state	Count	38	15	2	11	8	74
	% within 4 org profile on loc and funds	51.4%	20.3%	2.7%	14.9%	10.8%	100.0%
Regional state	Count	47	42	27	31	4	151
	% within 4 org profiles on loc and funds	31.1%	27.8%	17.9%	20.5%	2.6%	100.0%
Regional non-state	Count	68	34	3	21	4	130
	% within 4 org profiles on loc and funds	52.3%	26.2%	2.3%	16.2%	3.1%	100.0%
Total	Count	207	134	40	86	25	492
	% within 4 org profiles on loc and funds	42.1%	27.2%	8.1%	17.5%	5.1%	100.0%

Significance = 0.000.
Phi = 0.311.

having the more organizations reporting net gains than either the same or net losses (metropolitan state net gains = 49 per cent, regional state net gains = 53 per cent). Non-state organizations were more stable than their state counterparts, having most of their organizations reporting the same number of unpaid workers (metropolitan non-state, same number = 51 per cent, regional non-state, same number = 50 per cent). The situation appears dynamic in terms of the large numbers of organizations reporting net gains of unpaid workers.

Sixty-nine percent of organizations operate wholly free or mostly free services, with 24 per cent of organizations providing services mostly or wholly paid for. Non-state organisations are more likely to be wholly or mostly free than state organisations; however, the general pattern holds across the profiles.

Inside the sector

A base of activism

The demographic data above indicate that the sector is large and growing, diverse in terms of function and focus and divided by funding arrangements and locations which throw up large differences in areas such as the presence of paid and unpaid workers and levels of resources. However, there is also much evidence here which suggests similarities across the different types and situations of organizations, such as average numbers of workers, the strong reliance on unpaid work across the board, the dominance of free or mostly free provision and the established nature (in terms of average age) of organizations. On the basis of these data there are perhaps as many reasons to retain the notion of a sector as to abandon it, as Evers (1995) proposes.

In order to further help answer questions about the validity of sectoral assumptions and the potential for mutuality and subsidiarity amongst community welfare organizations, the analysis now turns to attitudinal data in order to probe for further areas of homogeneity and heterogeneity.

As well as the demographic and organizational data, the survey sought to elicit an attitudinal dimension from the sector. The attitudinal questions were designed to gauge organizations in relation to a series of issues including: privatization; competition; volunteer work; participation; standards; charges; planning and funding. The design of these questions was heavily influenced by the focus-group data, and in this way the survey provided the opportunity to test those findings on a larger scale.[6]

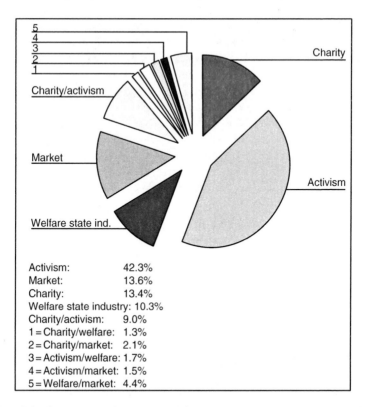

Figure 7.3   Organizational stance (modal category). Based on responses to 17 attitudinal questions[6]

The first stage of the analysis involved the creation of scales using answers to 17 attitude questions designed to measure an organization's stance in terms of the frameworks outlined in the last section (charity, activism, welfare state industry, and market). This provided an initial indication of organizational stance or ideology. When split on organizations' operating rationales (modal ideology), the results are seen in Figure 7.3. From Figure 7.3, it can be seen that the activism framework is dominant in 42.3 per cent of organizations, followed by market (13.6 per cent), charity (13.4 per cent) and welfare state industry (10.3 per cent). This survey result therefore shows, in a generalizable way, the strength of the activism undercurrents noted in the analysis of the data from the focus groups. A strong base of activism exists within the sector which comprises a segment larger than the other three frameworks

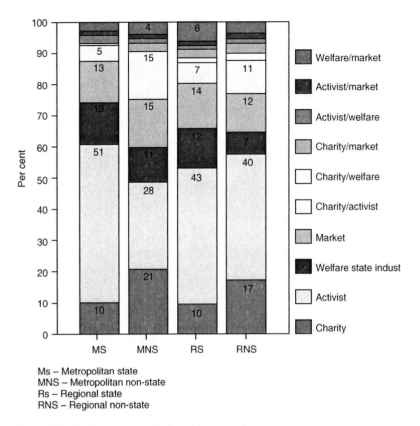

Ms – Metropolitan state
MNS – Metropolitan non-state
Rs – Regional state
RNS – Regional non-state

Figure 7.4   Profiles by organizational frameworks

put together. In terms of the possibilities of a move towards forms of welfare based around conceptions of subsidiarity, mutuality, equality and active citizenship, this indeed suggests a conducive terrain.

In the last section, four profiles were employed to assess some of the demographic features of the sector. Here, in the first application of the frameworks to the empirical data, it is useful to examine its constituent organizational frameworks.

The results show an across-profile consistency in that activism is in each case the largest constituent framework ranging from a high of 51 per cent in the metropolitan state profile to a low of 28 per cent in the metropolitan non-state profile.

Operating factors

While this initial analysis is useful in developing an overall view of the sample in terms of the shape of the frameworks, a further stage of analysis was undertaken. In the context of this book, it is the next stage of factor analysis which we wish to concentrate on. Factor analysis was pursued in order to: (a) minimize the possible effects of question focus weighting; and (b) allow a fuller consideration of the possible complexity of the data set and its interrelations. All 22 attitude questions were loaded in the initial factor analysis. Four factors were identified which accounted for 36 per cent of the total variance.[7]

Factor 1 identifies issues of *marketization*, factor 2, *professionalization* and factors 3 and 4 indicate different aspects of an activist outlook. To achieve a workable typology (Table 7.20) based on the factor analysis, factors 1, 2 and 4 were used. Factor 4 can be taken to stand for 3 and includes more facets of the activist position. We have called this factor *grass-roots*.

Factor 1: competition in the sector will produce better services; competition will lead to greater efficiency; cuts to welfare are reasonable as a result of budget deficits; planning should be left to professionals; the organization has more control over its work than 2 years ago; client participation makes for less efficiency.

Factor 2: there is a need for more highly trained staff; volunteers should have formal training; government-set minimum standards are important; marketing skills are now important; volunteers are not used as the only way of operating; the best organizations are not run by clients; the best organizations have strong leadership.

Factor 3: community-run services should be free; government should guarantee grants; the best organizations are run by clients; the organization cannot run without volunteers.

Factor 4: client participation should be encouraged; client-run organizations are not less efficient; planning should not be left to professionals; the best organizations are run by clients; political activity by the organization is preferred; it is not reasonable to have cuts to funding because of budget deficits; competition does not increase effectiveness.

Factor scores were calculated for each organization on each factor. Table 7.13 shows these scores as rankings by grouped organizational function. The lower (numerically) the ranking, the more important the factor is to that organizational function relative to the other functions.

Table 7.13 Organizational function (percentage in sample) and ranking on three factors

Function		Rank		
		Marketization	Grass-roots	Professionalization
Support/social organization	1 (48)	3	4	6
Neighbourhood house	2 (22)	6	3	3
Childcare centre	3 (14)	5	2	4
Self-help	4 (7)	2	1	7
Action/rights group	5 (5)	4	6	5
Refuge	6 (2)	7	5	2
Crisis counselling	7 (2)	1	7	1

The organizations grouped by function exhibit different patterns of rankings across the three factors. Crisis counselling is ranked first in both marketization and professionalization, and ranked last on grass-roots. Self-help is similar to crisis counselling in respect of marketization (being ranked second), but highly dissimilar with regard to grass-roots, where self-help is ranked first (to crisis counselling's last). Grass-roots is also important for childcare (rank = 2) and neighbourhood house (rank = 3); and indeed, these groups also exhibit similar rankings for marketization (ranks 5 and 6 and professionalization (ranks 4 and 3). The largest single function group, support and social organizations, is a mirror image to neighbourhood house on marketization and professionalization, but similar on grass-roots. Organizations identified above as low-level government funded (support/social; action/rights and self-help) show similarities in occupying the last rankings for professionalization and rankings 2, 3 and 4 for marketization, but are dissimilar for grass-roots.

Table 7.14 shows the organizations ranked on the three factors by grouped focus. Of the more numerically important focus areas, 'women' is strongly ranked on grass-roots (rank = 4) and very weakly ranked on marketization (rank = 10) and professionalization (rank = 11). 'Elderly' is ranked first for marketization and in the bottom half of the rankings for both grass-roots (rank = 7) and professionalization (rank = 7). 'Disability' achieves top-half rankings for all factors. 'Health' and 'youth' have comparable patterns across the factors, with professionalization ranked more strongly than grass-roots, which in turn is ranked more strongly than marketization. 'Poverty' is ranked in the lower half for all three factors, being almost a mirror image of 'disability'.

Table 7.14 Organizational focus (and percentage in sample) and ranking on three factors

Focus	Rank		
	Marketization	Grass-roots	Professionalism
Health	1 (15)	7	6	4
Youth	2 (14)	9	8	5
Poverty	3 (13)	8	10	8
Disability	4 (13)	4	3	6
Women	5 (11)	10	4	11
Elderly	6 (10)	1	7	7
Special accommodation	7 (7)	6	5	2
Ethnicity	8 (7)	2	9	3
Environment	9 (4)	5	1	9
Housing	10 (3)	11	2	1
Men	11 (2)	3	11	12
Legal	12 (1)	12	12	10

Table 7.15 Median ranking scores for three factors by principal funding (rank expressed on scale 1 [highest ranked] to 100 [lowest ranked])

Principal source of funding	Median rank		
	Marketization	Grass-roots	Professionalization
Government funded	55	47	38
Non-government funded	45	57	69
Unfunded	45	44	64

The following tables (7.15 to 7.18) consider the organizations grouped in variables with six or fewer categories in relation to the factors. For each category, the median ranking score is expressed on a percentile scale allowing a relatively immediate comparison of similarities and differences.

The difference between government and non-government funded organizations comes out clearly in relation to marketization and professionalization, where the two groups stand far apart. While government funded organizations achieve their highest rank of 38 on professionalization, non-government funded organizations achieve their lowest in this factor (rank = 69). The pattern is repeated inversely for marketization, with government funded organizations' lowest rank (55) and non-government funded organizations' highest rank (45). The profile for unfunded organizations is similar to the non-government funded group in respect of both marketization and professionalization, but for grass-roots, unfunded (rank = 44) is closer to government funded (rank = 47) than to non-government funded (rank = 57). Indeed, when broken down by funding, the factor which shows the least variation between the categories is grass-roots. The factor analysis appears to correspond with the earlier application of the frameworks to the data in suggesting a certain consistency of activism across, in this case, funding groups.

This is further emphasized when looking at the high and low levels of government funding (Table 7.16).

Table 7.16 Median ranking scores for three factors by level of government funding (rank expressed on scale 1 [highest ranked] to 100 [lowest ranked])

Level of government funding	Median rank		
	Marketization	Grass-roots	Professionalization
High	55	45	41
Low	46	50	62

Table 7.17 Median ranking scores for three factors by organizational profiles (rank expressed on scale 1 [highest ranked] to 100 [lowest ranked])

Funding and location profile	Median rank		
	Marketization	Grass-roots	Professionalization
Metropolitan state	60	48	36
Metropolitan non-state	53	58	64
Regional state	51	46	39
Regional non-state	40	50	69

The pattern noted for table 7.15 is repeated for levels of funding. There are clear divisions between the two groups for marketization and professionalization, and a much smaller difference for grass-roots. Returning to the four-profile grouping, we can see that location has little effect on professionalization, with the pattern of high rankings for government funded organizations and low rankings for low and non-government organizations (seen in tables 7.15 and 7.16) holding across metropolitan and regional groups. Location has some effect on marketization, with higher rankings for regional groups. Within this location pattern the funding pattern holds, so that metropolitan non-state is more highly ranked than metropolitan state and regional non-state more highly ranked than regional state. Grass-roots is again the least affected factor on this grouping of funding and location.

Tables 7.15, 7.16 and 7.17 together suggest that while marketization and professionalization are connected with differences in funding, grass-roots is much less affected by funding type. Similarly, location has little effect on grass-roots, some effect on marketization, and a strong effect on professionalization where metropolitan locations are associated with higher rankings.

When split by state of origin, we see a distinct difference within grass-roots for the first time, with Queensland (rank=61) and West Australian organizations (rank=62) attributing much less importance to the factor than the other states (range=40-49). This grouping is repeated for marketization, with Queensland (rank=29) and West Australia (rank=41) ranked first and second.

Relationships between significant organizational groupings and factors are reported in summary form in Table 7.19.

The strongest correlation is between funding and professionalization (0.355) and this is at least double the strength of any other correlation.

Table 7.18 Median ranking scores for three factors by state location (rank expressed on scale 1 [highest ranked] to 100 [lowest ranked])

State	Median rank		
	Marketization	Grass-roots	Professionalization
NSW	52	49	43
VIC	60	48	57
QLD	29	61	58
SA	49	40	48
WA	41	62	50
TAS	70	42	47

Table 7.19 Selected correlations with factors

Pearson correlations	Factor ranking		
	Marketization	Grass-roots	Professionalization
Principal funding			
(1: Government 2: Non-	−.118**	0.52	.355**
government)	.008	.251	.000
Significance (2-tailed test)			
Location			
(1: Metropolitan 2: Regional)	−.071	−.024	.126**
Significance (2-tailed test)	.114	.590	.005
Organization Age (1–108)	−.156**	.160**	.040
Significance (2-tailed test)	.001	.000	.379
State			
(1: NSW, VIC, SA, TAS	−.168**	.127**	−.005
2: QLD, WA)	.000	.005	.904
Significance (2-tailed test)			

**Significant at the 0.01 level.

A significant result also occurs for marketization and funding (-0.118), but not for grass-roots. Government funding is therefore a predictor (0.355) of higher levels of professionalization (as measured by the professionalization factor) and lower levels of commitment to marketization (-0.118) (as measured by the marketization factor). Funding type is not a good predictor of activism (as measured by the grass-roots factor).

Metropolitan locations are a predictor (0.126) of higher levels of professionalization but are not predictors of marketization or grass-roots.

Increasing age of organizations is a predictor (-0.156) of higher levels of marketization and lower levels of activism (0.16). Age is not a predictor of professionalization.

State of origin is a predictor (-0.168) of higher levels of marketization and lower levels of activism (0.127) in Queensland and West Australia. State of origin is not a predictor of professionalization.

The growth of hybridity: a typology of voluntary welfare sector organizations

The ranking tables are able to identify organizations grouped by various categories on each separate factor. This has been useful in determining which variables appear to effect changes in averaged ranking scores.

A further stage of analysis is to create a typology by considering variations of the three factors in combination for each organization (rather than relying on averaged scores on one factor at a time).

Using the original factor scores every organization was ranked below or above the mean score for each factor. The various combinations can then form a typology as in Table 7.20.

The typology allows the construction of four 'pure' types relating to the general model developed from the earlier analysis ('marketer', 'activist', 'professional' and 'charity oriented'). As well, four hybrid types are created ('combinational', 'market activist', 'market professional' and 'professional activist'). In applying the typology to the sample, factor scores below the mean were taken to represent rejection of the factor, and scores above the mean, acceptance. This results in the distribution in Figure 7.5.

The results of the factorial analysis and the construction of the typology present a more complex picture of the voluntary welfare sector. Activist as a 'pure' type makes up 11.5 per cent of the total and 41 per cent in combination forms (excluding the type, combinational). The latter figure is almost the same as that for the original category of the activist framework (Figure 7.3). By providing a way of bringing out shared and hybridized types and constituents, the factor analysis enables a way of understanding different forms of the activist position and shows that the largest of these is professional activist (17 per cent). Market activist (12 per cent) and the 'pure' type activist (12 per cent) follow this. Whereas the market category in the original application of

Table 7.20 A typology of third-sector community welfare organizations (3 factor analysis)

Type	Factor 1 Marketization	Factor 4 Grass-roots	Factor 2 Professionalization
1. Combinational	+	+	+
2. Market activist	+	+	−
3. Market professional	+	−	+
4. Marketer	+	−	−
5. Professional activist	−	+	+
6 Activist	−	+	−
7. Professional	−	−	+
8. Charity oriented	−	−	−

+ = acceptance.
− = rejection.

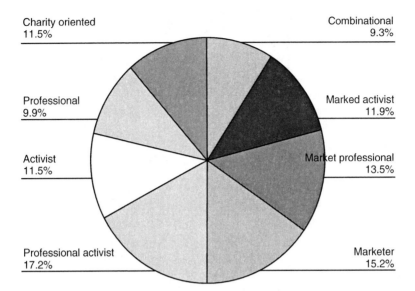

Charity oriented
11.5%

Combinational
9.3%

Professional
9.9%

Marked activist
11.9%

Activist
11.5%

Market professional
13.5%

Professional activist
17.2%

Marketer
15.2%

Figure 7.5 Distribution of organizational type: Australian national data (based on ranked factor research)

the frameworks comprised at maximum 17 per cent in combination forms, here, market types are much more important, holding 15 per cent in the type marketer and equalling the total activist share with a total in combination of 41 per cent of organizations typed in ways that include a marketization component. Similarly, professional types comprise 41 per cent, which is up from the 13 per cent that the welfare state industry framework achieved in the earlier modelling.

In the remainder of this section, the types are considered within the categories of organizational function and focus, age and workforce, funding arrangements and locational differences.

Organizational function and focus

Table 7.21 lists the two most frequently occurring organizational types for organizations broken down by function. Marketization types are important in the organizational functions identified above as being characterized by low levels of government funding – support/social, self-help and action/rights. For the remaining functions, there is a mix of professionalization and activist types. Indeed, underscoring the trend noted above for activism to form wide representation across the

Table 7.21   Organizational function (and percentage in sample) and two most frequently occurring organizational types

Function		Type 1 (%)	Type 2 (%)	'Hybridity scale' (% outside top 2 types)
Support/social organization	1 (48)	MP (31)	M (17)	52
Neighbourhood house	2 (22)	PA (23)	C (14)	63
Childcare centre	3 (14)	C (18)	PA (17)	65
Self-help	4 (7)	A (31)	M (19)	50
Action/rights group	5 (5)	MA (28)	M (16)	56
Crisis counselling/Refuge	6 (4)	PA (22)	P (22)	56

Key: C = Combinational
MA = Market activist
MP = Market professional
M = Marketer
PA = Professional activist
A = Activist
P = Professional

Table 7.22   Organizational focus (and percentage in sample) and two most frequently occurring organizational types

Focus (top 6)		Type 1 (%)	Type 2 (%)	'Hybridity scale' (% outside top 2 types)
Health	1 (15)	MP (20)	PA (13)	67
Youth	2 (14)	PA (22)	MP (18)	60
Poverty	3 (13)	M (24)	Ch (23)	53
Disability	4 (13)	PA (22)	MA (18)	60
Women	5 (11)	A (20)	M (18)	62
Elderly	6 (10)	M (25)	PA (19)	56

Key: MA = Market activist
MP = Market professional
M = Marketer
PA = Professional activist
A = Activist
P = Professional
Ch = Charity oriented

sector, only the support/social function has no activist component. The trend to hybridity is also indicated here, with all functions having at least half of their organizations in types other than the top two. In the case of childcare, 65 per cent of organizations lie outside combinational and professional activist types.

Table 7.22 lists the two most frequently occurring organizational types for organizations broken down by focus. All organizational focus areas contain marketization types within the top two, with poverty and elderly having marketer as their most frequent type. Activist types are present in all but poverty. Professionalization types are found in all but poverty and women focus areas. The hybridity measures here are in the same order as for organizational function, with all focus areas over 50 on the hybridity scale and health having 67 per cent of organizations outside the top two types.

Age and workforce

All types have median ages of between 13 and 17 years and median total workforces of between 13 (activist) and 25 (professional) workers. Two groups are apparent here in terms of numbers of workers. Market activist, activist, marketer, charity, and market professional share similar characteristics in terms of median paid (range = 4 to 5) and unpaid (range = 7.5 to 16) workers. Professional activist, combinational and professional exhibit higher median paid (range = 7 to 7.5 and unpaid workers (range = 13 to 18). The higher number of paid workers in the latter group may simply reflect a higher funding base, but this cannot be substantiated at this time.

Funding

From Table 7.24 we can see that three clusters emerge. Firstly, types with over twice the representation in government funded organizations: professional activist, combinational and professional. Secondly, types with over twice the representation in non-government organizations: marketer, market activist and activist. Thirdly, types with roughly equal representation between funding types: market professional and charity.

Location

The clusters noted in Table 7.24 are present again in Table 7.25 in terms of organizational location. Professional, professional activist and combinational increase their representation as we move from towns to capital cities. Market activists and marketers increase their representation moving from capital cities to towns; and market professionals, activists and charity oriented display no general pattern across the categories of location.

Table 7.23 Organizational type, age and workforce

Typology based on rank factors		Age of organization (yrs)	Total number paid workers	Paid workers: men	Paid workers: women	Total number unpaid workers	Unpaid workers: men	Unpaid workers: women
Combinational	Median	14.00	7.50	1.00	6.50	16.50	6.00	11.50
	N	46	38	38	38	34	34	34
Market activist	Median	17.00	4.00	.00	4.00	12.00	2.50	7.00
	N	57	21	21	21	54	54	54
Market professional	Median	14.00	5.00	1.00	4.00	11.00	4.00	7.00
	N	63	51	51	51	45	45	45
Marketer	Median	14.00	5.00	1.00	4.50	12.00	2.00	7.00
	N	72	34	34	34	65	65	65
Professional activist	Median	13.00	7.00	1.00	6.00	13.00	4.00	9.00
	N	83	79	79	79	63	63	63
Activist	Median	14.00	5.50	1.00	4.50	7.50	2.50	5.00
	N	55	24	24	24	52	52	52
Professional	Median	16.00	7.00	1.00	4.00	18.00	3.00	12.00
	N	49	42	42	42	33	35	33
Charity oriented	Median	16.00	4.00	.00	3.00	12.00	3.00	8.00
	N	57	35	35	35	53	53	53
Total	Median	14.00	6.00	1.00	5.00	12.00	3.00	8.00
	N	482	324	324	324	399	401	399

Table 7.24   Organizational type by funding (2 categories)

Type		Fed., state and local gov.	Non-gov.	Total
Combinational	Count	37	8	45
	% within recoded funding source into 2 cats	12.8%	3.9%	9.1%
Market activist	Count	20	38	58
	% within recoded funding source into 2 cats	6.9%	18.6%	11.8%
Market professional	Count	43	24	67
	% within recoded funding source into 2 cats	14.9%	11.8%	13.6%
Marketer	Count	30	45	75
	% within recoded funding source into 2 cats	10.4%	22.1%	15.2%
Professional activist	Count	73	12	85
	% within recoded funding source into 2 cats	25.3%	5.9%	17.2%
Activist	Count	21	36	57
	%within recoded funding source into 2 cats	7.3%	17.6%	11.6%
Professional	Count	35	14	49
	% within recoded funding source into 2 cats	12.1%	6.9%	9.9%
Charity oriented	Count	30	27	57
	% within recoded funding source into 2 cats	10.4%	13.2%	11.6%
Total	Count	289	204	493
	% within recoded funding source into 2 cats	100.0%	100.0%	100.0%

Significance = 0.000.
Phi = 0.396.

There is a marked decrease in the importance of 'professional' when moving from capital cities (13 per cent), through main population centres (8 per cent) to towns (7 per cent). The reverse trend is indicated in the case of 'market activist', which accounts for 7 per cent in capital cities, 14 per cent in main population centres and 17 per cent in towns. This implied negative association between the professional type and provincial third-sector Australia appears to result in a market/ activist hybrid in the ascendancy there. Comparative work over time and within the day-to-day operations of the third sector may allow us to chart further moves towards, for example, either associational democracy or market hegemony.

Table 7.25 Organizational types by location (3 categories)

Type		Capital city	Main population centre	Town or smaller	Total
Combinational	Count	25	8	13	46
	% within typology based on ranked factors	54.3%	17.4%	28.3%	100.0%
	% within LOCATION	11.7%	9.3%	6.7%	9.3%
Market activist	Count	14	12	33	59
	% within typology based on ranked factors	23.7%	20.3%	55.9%	100.0%
	% within LOCATION	6.5%	14.0%	16.9%	11.9%
Market professional	Count	29	15	23	67
	% within typology based on ranked factors	43.3%	22.4%	34.3%	100.0%
	% within LOCATION	13.6%	17.4%	11.8%	13.5%
Marketer	Count	27	13	35	75
	% within typology based on ranked factors	36.0%	17.3%	46.7%	100.0%
	% within LOCATION	12.6%	15.1%	17.9%	15.2%
Professional activist	Count	41	18	26	85
	% within typology based on ranked factors	48.2%	21.2%	30.6%	100.0%
	% within LOCATION	19.2%	20.9%	13.3%	17.2%
Activist	Count	23	4	30	57
	% within typology based on ranked factors	40.4%	7.0%	52.6%	100.0%
	% within LOCATION	10.7%	4.7%	15.4%	11.5%
Professional	Count	28	7	14	49
	% within typology based on ranked factors	57.1%	14.3%	28.6%	100.0%
	% within LOCATION	13.1%	8.1%	7.2%	9.9%
Charity oriented	Count	27	9	21	57
	% within typology based on ranked factors	47.4%	15.8%	36.8%	100.0%
	%within LOCATION	12.6%	10.5%	10.8%	11.5%
Total	Count	214	86	195	495
	% with typology based on ranked factors	43.2%	17.4%	39.4%	100.0%
	% within LOCATION	100.0%	100.0%	100.0%	100.0%

Significance = 0.007;   Phi = 0.242

Using the profiles to look at the effects of funding and location together stresses that non-government funded organizations are strongholds of marketer and activist organizations, while over one-quarter of government funded organizations are professional activists.

Table 7.26 Organizational type by profiles

Type		Metropolitan state	Metropolitan non-state	Regional state	Regional non-state	Total
Combinational	Count	19	5	18	3	45
	% within 4 org profiles on loc and funds	13.8%	6.8%	11.9%	2.3%	9.1%
Market activist	Count	6	7	14	31	58
	% within 4 org profiles on loc and funds	4.3%	9.5%	9.3%	23.8%	11.8%
Market professional	Count	21	8	22	16	67
	% within 4 org profiles on loc and funds	15.2%	10.8%	14.6%	12.3%	13.6%
Marketer	Count	12	15	18	30	75
	% within 4 org profiles on loc and funds	8.7%	20.3%	11.9%	23.1%	15.2%
Professional activist	Count	38	3	35	9	85
	% within 4 org profiles on loc and funds	27.5%	4.1%	23.2%	6.9%	17.2%
Activist	Count	8	15	13	21	57
	% within 4 org profiles on loc and funds	5.8%	20.3%	8.6%	16.2%	11.6%
Professional	Count	18	10	17	4	49
	% within 4 org profiles on loc and funds	13.0%	13.5%	11.3%	3.1%	9.9%
Charity oriented	Count	16	11	14	16	57
	% within 4 org profiles on loc and funds	11.6%	14.9%	9.3%	12.3%	11.6%
Total	Count	138	74	151	130	493
	% within 4 org profiles on loc and funds	100.0%	100.0%	100.0%	100.0%	100.0%

Significance = 0.000; Phi = 0.444.

Table 7.27 Organizational type by state

Type		VIC	NSW	SA	QLD	TAS	WA	Total
					State			
Combinational	Count	8	16	9	3	1	9	46
	% within state	6.1%	8.8%	13.2%	6.5%	5.0%	18.8%	9.3%
Market activist	Count	12	25	7	11		4	59
	% within state	9.1%	13.8%	10.3%	23.9%		8.3%	11.9%
Market professional	Count	11	27	6	10	2	11	67
	% within state	8.3%	14.9%	8.8%	21.7%	10.0%	22.9%	13.5%
Marketer	Count	22	20	13	9	3	8	75
	% within state	16.7%	11.0%	19.1%	19.6%	15.0%	16.7%	15.2%
Professional activist	Count	25	37	13	3	6	1	85
	% within state	18.9%	20.4%	19.1%	6.5%	30.0%	2.1%	17.2%
Activist	Count	24	15	8	2	4	4	57
	% within state	18.2%	8.3%	11.8%	4.3%	20.0%	8.3%	11.5%
Professional	Count	16	18	7	3	2	3	49
	% within state	12.1%	9.9%	10.3%	6.5%	10.0%	6.3%	9.9%
Charity oriented	Count	14	23	5	5	2	8	57
	% with state	10.6%	12.7%	7.4%	10.9%	10.0%	16.7%	11.5%
Total	Count	132	181	68	46	20	48	495
	% with state	100.0%	100.0%	100.0%	100.0%	100.0%	100.0%	100.0%

Significance = 0.002.

Phi = 0.345.

Activist is highly under-represented in metropolitan state organizations (6 per cent), suggesting that the foothold for an activist standpoint in this profile lies in combination with professionalized outlooks. Regional non-state organizations are highly under-represented in professional types (3 per cent) and strongly represented in market activists (24 per cent).

The wide variation between the states, which we can see here, is an extension of the patterns noted above in Tables 7.19 and 7.20. While professional activist is important in New South Wales (21 per cent), South Australia (19 per cent) and Victoria (19 per cent), combinations of marketization tend to dominate elsewhere, with Queensland having 65 per cent of its organizations as either marketer, market professional or market activist.

Conclusion

While it is important to keep in mind the apparent unevenness and irregularity of these processes and to recognize that shifts within the voluntary welfare sector will not be uniformly distributed, the underlying base of an activist framework seems clear.

Earles makes the point that spatial difference may be at least as important as organizational 'shape' in explaining the nature of change in the third sector (Earles, 1997). Our data support this to some extent, especially in regard to the different states which have an effect on levels of marketization and grass-roots (see also Table 7.19). While the static nature of the data elicited by the survey alone leaves analysis unclear as to the shape or direction of movement within or between these types, the context of change in the sector and the results of our qualitative research suggest strongly that key areas of change and contestation are those in which market ideologies and practices interact with and potentially penetrate other systems of organization more traditional to the area. Organizations typed as 'market professional', 'market activist' or 'combinational' stand on this shifting ground, where voluntary associations deal with and routinize aspects of market orientation within activized and professionalized positions.

We have found, generally, a high level of activism, which corresponds to Hirst's ideas of what associationalism would require or even produce. Hirst utilizes rational choice theory, he says, because he is providing a minimal argument – people would embrace associationalism *even if* we accept rational choice theory: that is, we are all calculating and individualistic. Our data may suggest that Hirst is perhaps being too cautious in this way – that there is evidence here that associationalism could be taken up more easily then he might think *if* the political and economic facilitation was made (see also Chapter 9).

Notes

1   Focus groups were held in the following locations: NSW (Dubbo, Leichhart, Marrickville); VIC (Alexandra, Springvale [twice], Sunshine); SA (Prospect); WA (Fremantle); QLD (Mt Isa, South Brisbane); NT (Alice Springs); ACT (Belconnen); TAS (Hobart).

2   The survey was conducted between November 1996 and March 1997 and used a stratified random sample of organizations from the database of 7,233 (n = 495; response rate = 89%). Inferences from the survey data are subject to a sample error of $+/-$ 4.5% based on the n of 495.

   The sample was representative of the database in terms of organization focus and function having been stratified, 1: state and location (capital city or regional); 2: organizational function and focus (see Table 7.1 above for a comparison between the percentages of organizations by state in the database and the survey). Because of low rates of representation in the database, which reflects population size, organizations from the Australian Capital Territory and the Northern Territory were not included in the sample, as numbers would be too small for meaningful comparison to be made. The survey therefore represents a national basis of all Australian states.

3   Median scores have been used rather than means, to minimize the problems of interpretation associated with large standard deviation scores.

4   Significance for all cross-tabulations is chi-square likelihood ratio significance. Measures of significance relate to inference from the sample to the database which was the sampling frame. Phi is used throughout as a measure of association based on assumptions that all cross-tabulation tables presented contain at least one variable that should be treated as nominal.

5   The classification was made using Australian Bureau of Statistics divisions of Capital City; and 'Main population centres' (Australian Bureau of Statistics, 1997b: 17–18). Locations of respondents outside these areas were classified as 'town or smaller'.

6   A full version of the questionnaire is available at:

   http://www.deakin.edu.au/~kevinb/arcq.htm

A random sample of 100 ABS statistical areas was drawn from the national frame of 1,112. The sample was stratified on the basis of inter- and intra-state population levels. Part of the questionnaire comprised a series of 22 statements with which respondents were asked to strongly disagree, disagree,

agree or strongly agree. These are as follows:

1. More competition in the community sector will lead to better services [comp]
2. In an ideal world our organization would never use volunteers [ideal]
3. Marketing skills are now centrally important for workers in community organizations [market]
4. Participation by clients in the running of community organizations makes the organization run less efficiently [lesseff]
5. Minimum standards set by government are important providing quality programmes [min]
6. Volunteers should receive formal training [vtrain]
7. Community-run services should be free of charge to the user [free]
8. Workers in community organizations must try to encourage clients to participate in planning for the organization [plan]
9. In our organization we have more control over planning and doing our work today than we had 2 years ago [control]
10. Our organiztion is less accountable to clients now than it was 2 years ago [account]
11. Our organization's major responsibility is to the funding body, not the clients [resp]
12. When there is a federal or state budget deficit it is reasonable to have cuts to programmes [deficit]
13. Competition for funding increases the effectiveness of programmes [compet]
14. Governments should guarantee grants to community organizations [guar]
15. It is better to leave community planning to professionals rather than clients [profs]
16. It is reasonable to go to many sources for funding [many]
17. Our organization prefers not to be involved in political activity [politic]
18. It is more important for our organization to be trusted by the clients than to achieve government-defined targets [trust]
19. We use volunteers because this is the only way we can operate [only]
20. The best community provision has strong leadership [strong]
21. Community organizations like ours need staff who are more highly trained [more]
22. The best community organizations are run by clients [clients]

Attitudinal scale construction:

Question	01	02	03	04	05	06	07	08	09	10	11	12	13	14	15	16	17	18	19	20	21	22
Charity	0	0	0	1	0	0	1	0				1	0	0	0		1			0	0	0
Activism	0	0	0	0	0	0	1	1				0	0	1	0		0			0	0	1
Welfare state ind.	0	1	0	1	1	1	1	0				1	0	1	1		1			1	1	0
Market	1	0	1	1	0	0	0	0				1	1	0	0		1			1	0	0

1 = agreement; 0 = disagreement.

7 Factor Pattern Matrix of Attitudinal Data – 4 factors (based on principal components analysis)

Structure matrix:

Variable	Factor 1	Factor 2	Factor 3	Factor 4
COMP	**.75768**	.05420	.01818	−.02604
IDEAL	.07232	.05848	.09212	−.05802
MARKET	−.06783	**.42453**	−.13620	.06372
LESSEFF	.20826	−.01300	−.01688	**.69241**
MIN	.17104	**.55679**	−.03495	−.04899
VTRAIN	−.08969	**.63539**	−.03235	.09234
FREE	−.06154	.06963	**.67559**	.04945
PLAN	.02639	.16734	.05968	**.74706**
CONTROL	**.27183**	.11545	.12114	.00418
ACCOUNT	−.02658	−.08336	−.09792	−.04399
RESP	.16169	.02606	.00071	−.10722
DEFICIT	**.51621**	−.14042	−.18057	−.26797
COMPET	**.79199**	−.03082	−.11703	−.26209
GUAR	.00653	.21820	**.66455**	.18371
PROFS	**.41214**	.01057	.09820	−**.64832**
MANY	.07431	.08001	−.07891	−.04256
POLITIC	**.40345**	−.19366	.09841	−.28352
TRUST	−.12317	−.20982	**.6014**	−.06790
ONLY	.0787	−**.38840**	**.30685**	.00730
STRONG	.20273	**.32730**	.05934	−.09863
MORE	−.06383	**.64688**	.18082	.03484
CLIENTS	.01282	−**.33489**	**.35567**	**.55756**

(Kaiser–Meyer–Olkin measure of sampling accuracy = .69634; Bartlett test of sphericity = 1200.0902; significance = 0.00000).

The factors weighted as important, answers indicating that (in order of importance):

Factor 1: competition in the sector will produce better services; competition will lead to greater efficiency; cuts to welfare are reasonable as a result of budget deficits; planning should be left to professionals; the organization has more control over its work than 2 years ago; client participation makes for less efficiency.

Factor 2: there is a need for more highly trained staff; volunteers should have formal training; government-set minimum standards are important; marketing skills are now important; volunteers are not used as the only way of operating; the best organizations are not run by clients; the best organizations have strong leadership.

Factor 3: community-run services should be free; government should guarantee grants; the best organizations are run by clients; the organization cannot run without volunteers.

Factor 4: client participation should be encouraged; client-run organizations are not less efficient; planning should not be left to professionals; the best organizations are run by clients; political activity by the organization is preferred; it is not reasonable to have cuts to funding because of budget deficits; competition does not increase effectiveness.

Part III
The Search for Active Citizenship

8
Activating the Public Sphere and Social Capital

The settings for active citizenship are also those which facilitate a robust public sphere and engender social capital. In this chapter we will consider how the operating frameworks of voluntary associations might contribute to the development of the public sphere and social capital. We have already identified in Chapter 3 the current narrowness of liberal representative democracy and those theorists who argue that the public sphere is in decline. Indeed, Dahlgren (1991: 1–2) argues that the democratic character of a society can be judged according to how well the public sphere functions, and therefore the imperfections of liberal representative democracy are marked by parallel imperfections of the public sphere. In regard to social capital, we have suggested the much research is still required to inform the debates regarding the production, maintenance and value of social capital. However, because trust, norms and networks are identified as critical elements of the activity of voluntary associations, the voluntary sector can be identified as an important site for generating social capital.

The decline of the public sphere

Most of the recent discussions and debates concerned with the public sphere have tended to focus on the imperfections and withdrawal of the citizenry from the arena known as the public arena. These discussions almost without exception draw on the work of Jürgen Habermas, and particularly *Strukturwandel der Offentlichkeit* (1962). Although not translated into English until 1989 as *The Structural Transformation of the Public Sphere,* Habermas's concept of the public sphere has been debated for a number of years (Bryant, 1995: 258). While there is no universal definition of the public sphere, Habermas claims it is the sphere between the private realm of the family and civil society and the public authority of the state, in which 'critical public discussion of matters of general interest could be institutionally guaranteed' (Habermas, 1989: xi). The public sphere was intrinsically connected to the implementation and maintenance of democratic principles. The question Habermas asks is: 'under what social conditions does rational-critical debate about public issues, conducted by private persons willing to let arguments and not statuses determine decisions', take place? (Calhoun, 1992: 1).

The public sphere was extremely important to Habermas since he believed it was as much a possible mode of coordination of human life as either state power or market economics, and in fact was essential to counterbalance the pressures of both the state and the market. Indeed, since money and power are non-discursive modes of coordination, tending towards domination and reification, and with no opportunity for the expression of reason and will, the state and the economy are antagonistic to a democratic public sphere (Calhoun, 1992: 6; London, 1995: 38).

The Enlightenment notion of the public sphere developed in conjunction with the construction of the modern state; and on the basis, therefore, of the capitalist economy. Given that this period was dominated by laissez-faire politics, private persons were left to themselves and civil society was established as a private sphere emancipated from public authority. As the modern state developed it did so in such a way that the public was constructed as a separate realm where private individuals came together to discuss and debate matters pertaining to state authority. This had not been the case of course during the Middle Ages, when there was little or no opportunity for the citizenry to engage in discussion regarding the exercise of the state's authority and power. Critically, as citizens came together to discuss the issues raised by the state administration they did so in a way that was without historical precedent, in their use of reason and rational critical debate. Initially formed in the world of letters, the literary public sphere which at the time produced literary critique, extended into the political sphere and institutionalized rational critical discourse in political discussion (Calhoun, 1992; Dahlgren, 1991; Habermas, 1989).

This was a fleeting moment, however. Rational–critical debate soon gave way to negotiation and the consumption of culture. As the size and composition of civil society changed and inequalities increased, the basis of discussion and action became negotiated compromise among interests as opposed to rational–critical debate. Further, with the development of mass culture, Habermas argues that rather than a sharing in culture there was a move to a joint consumption of culture; and rather than active participation in mutual critique (and production), rational–critical debate was replaced by consumption. For Habermas, the world fashioned by the mass media is a public sphere in name only, with the form of participation fatally altered from that of the early bourgeois public sphere. As individuals experience radio, television and film with an immediacy in a way not possible in the printed word, rational–critical discourse becomes more difficult if not impossible. Clearly this opens the door for personalized politics and special interest groups, and a public relations industry which focuses on engineering consent among the consumers of mass culture. Attempts are made to increase the prestige of the political party or special interest group through publicity work, without making the topics of their positions subject to genuine public debate. Publicity becomes only an occasion for the manipulation of popular opinion (group psychology rather than democratic practice), and as such, not only is the public sphere weakened but democracy too is undermined with little opportunity for discursive will formation (Calhoun, 1992: 21–9).

London (1995: 38) suggests the concept of the public sphere discussed by Habermas includes several requirements for authenticity. He summarizes them as follows:

> open access, voluntary participation outside institutional roles, the generation of public judgement through assemblies of citizens who engage in political deliberation, the freedom to express opinions, and the freedom to discuss matters of the state and to criticise the way state power is organised.

Since its publication, *The Structural Transformation of the Public Sphere* has generated much debate and a wide range of responses. Criticisms point to an apparent unsystematic treatment of the 'classical' bourgeois public sphere versus its post-transformation counterpart. For example, Habermas pays considerable attention to the role of intellectuals in his account of the bourgeois public sphere, yet gives them scant regard in accounting for the twentieth-century public sphere, placing more emphasis on 'the typical television viewer'. Alternatively, his account of the bourgeois public sphere does not include less rational–critical branches of the press, and therefore appears optimistic and even idealizes the role of the media in early capitalism. Further, too little attention is given to culture and identity, religion, and social movements. Feminist critiques have addressed the essentially gendered nature of the bourgeois public sphere. Also, while idealizing the early public sphere, in the view of many critics Habermas is unduly pessimistic about the present, where new social movements and new communication technology might be two examples of a more vibrant and progressive communication environment than that described by Habermas (Calhoun, 1992: 33–8; Golding, 1995: 26–30; Bryant, 1995: 257–61; Holub, 1991: 1–3; Dahlgren, 1991: 1–26). Before moving on to the debates regarding voluntary associations, we first pay some attention to the issues concerning digital technologies.

London (1995: 33–55) draws attention to the potential contribution of electronically mediated communication to the development of the public sphere. London claims that from Aristotle (legislation through reasoned dialogue and deliberation) to Rousseau (the formation of a general will through deliberation) and to John Stuart Mill (government by discussion), political thinkers have stressed the importance of public discourse and debate. However, the advent of new technologies such as telephone, radio, television, and now the World Wide Web, have radically changed the nature of public discourse in the twentieth century. Indeed, London claims it may well be that voluntary associations, public spaces, local newspapers and neighbourhood assemblies are giving way to computer bulletin boards, satellite television, and radio call-in programmes, as those who advocate 'teledemocracy' (literally 'democracy at a distance') suggest.

The advocates of teledemocracy would certainly regard Habermas as unduly pessimistic. The public sphere can be greatly enhanced through electronically mediated political discourse, they argue, where civic participation can be enhanced and where citizens can be connected across boundaries of time and space. Links between citizens and government can increase transparency and allow unmediated communication between citizens and their leaders. Teledemocracy provides a way for improved political agenda-setting and planning, and can involve large numbers of people more directly who can be informed and educated on public issues more quickly (London, 1995).

London (1995) also identifies the potential risks of electronically mediated communication. Firstly, there is the argument that plebiscitary democracy (e.g. tele-voting) is 'din not democracy'. It leaves no room for reasoned dialogue and debate and amounts to no more than a collection of opinions. This is especially the case when discussion is highly specific, technical or regionalized. Secondly, consulting the citizenry through such mechanisms atomizes individuals and is time-consuming and inefficient. Thirdly, experiments thus far have achieved low rates of participation. Finally, there are also a number of criticisms that London identifies which are related to politics and policy formation based on public opinion rather than teledemocracy *per se*, for example the influence of news media, and advertising which sees the Australian federal government 'selling' tax reform to the electorate at a cost of $15 million.

It is certainly not clear yet whether teledemocracy can reinvigorate the public sphere and allow reasoned dialogue and debate to take place. However, to dismiss the concept under the pressure of the many criticisms is premature. Our research certainly found some evidence of the take-up of email among voluntary organizations, but this was small nevertheless. It will be interesting to see how increases in this usage might facilitate broader information and power sharing. There is clearly an opportunity for the exchange of views, knowledge and opinions, and while competitive tendering might reduce the level of communication and collaboration between associations competing in the same local 'market', voluntary associations might be inclined to 'network' into other regions and internationally. As such, new information technologies could be an area leading to the strengthening of the contribution of voluntary associations to the public sphere. Indeed, 'acting locally and thinking globally' might become all the more real for those citizens and voluntary associations that embrace such technologies. That is not to deny, and in fact it might point to the growing significance, of debates regarding access to such information technology, since equality of access is not guaranteed. Organizations that have polyvalent characteristics (Evers, 1995), in that they have economic functions (e.g. through service delivery) and undertake lobbying and advocacy roles, might find that they are able to function more effectively by utilizing communication technology. Thus the two functions may be less conflict laden. It was certainly the case in our research that the organizations with higher rates of connectivity were generally the better resourced. Whether this remains the case or not will be an interesting and important question.

More recently, debates regarding the public sphere have begun to focus on 'deliberative democracy', which appears to be more consistent with the questions raised by Habermas (1989) regarding the nature of social conditions where 'rational-critical debate' about public issues can be developed through a focus on argument rather than status. While there are a number of definitions, it is clear that deliberative democracy privileges the strength of the argument over the status of the arguer. Further, Giddens (1994: 113–15) asserts that one of the important points regarding deliberative democracy is that it does not assume the existence of a general will. There are clearly many questions to which there is no single answer, and all solutions can be contested. In deliberative democracy a settlement can be reached where those involved might agree on norms and/or procedures that can guide the assessment of policy decisions. Alternatively, Benhabib (1996: 69) claims that where 'decisions are in principle open to appropriate public processes of deliberation by free and equal citizens', democratic institutions can gain and/or increase their legitimacy.

Criticisms of deliberative democracy tend to focus on the conformity component of group decisions (as opposed to genuine unanimity) and the fact that decisions are closed in direction, shutting out alternative views and/or minority issues. Further, because consensus is near impossible, the mechanisms for aggregating group ideas undermine the very notion of and purpose of deliberation. Finally, as with other forms of democracy, deliberative democracy requires public participation and there may not be the inclination to participate. Deliberative democracy might be quite unrealistic (indeed, only an ideal) in contemporary mass society (London, 1995: 44). However, we argue that with the increasing size of the voluntary sector and the fact that mass society is also a plural society, voluntary associations are a potential site for deliberative democracy and a reinvigoration of the public sphere through such means. However, according to the frameworks developed in Chapters 4 and 5, there will clearly be differences regarding the degree to which the operating rationales facilitate or curb the restoration of the public sphere. The existence of a strong base of activism could lead to positive outcomes in light of this discussion, but as we point out in Chapter 9, not all paths lead to such ends.

The form of market operation constructed around the concept of what we have previously called the quasi-capitalist market of buyers and sellers has a distributional logic based on entrepreneurial skills, money, power and individual self-determination. This logic does not encourage deliberative democracy. Further, privatization and contracturalism have not facilitated deliberative democracy. Similarly, the 'enterprise culture' is not compatible with deliberation, dialogue, cooperation, collaboration and communication, given its focus on competition, performance, efficiencies, user-pays, and a propensity for managerialism with its focus on output and outcomes. The communication in the 'can-do' managerial style is more directed towards getting people to do something rather than genuine exchange of knowledge. Further, in the 'contract culture' there is one-way accountability and clear lines of authority are being drawn, with voluntary associations accountable to governments. This power relation unquestionably reduces the opportunity for any kind of deliberative democracy and is more likely to cultivate the continuing decline of the public sphere. However, we would want to argue that the second form of market operation we identified – social markets – might indeed be compatible with notions of deliberative democracy and a robust public sphere. Accordingly, we claim social markets emphasize the construction of the market as a place where there is a maximum number choices and a variety of market agents, such as publicly owned or municipal companies, worker communes, consumer cooperatives and non-profit organizations of different kinds. These agents, while functioning in the market, have their origins outside the market (Walzer, 1992). In this type of market, devolution is based on the principle of subsidiarity and occurs when activities, processes and responsibility are passed from high levels of power to lower ones, where there is more flexibility and a greater degree of responsiveness. If the principles of devolution of responsibility, subsidiarity and autonomy are adhered to there is reason to believe there would be space for activism, deliberation and communication.

The activist framework attempts to balance local determinism with an interest in the question of universal rights. Activism is oriented to a degree of social change, and activist rationales are directed towards the importance of community participation with an emphasis on trust, mutuality, civic virtue and moral obligation. As we argued in Chapter 4, associations utilizing an activist framework are unique in opening up sites for the celebration of difference, and the activist framework privileges the rhetoric of community participation, democratization and empowerment. The organizational structure of associations utilizing an activist framework attempts to maximize input and control with a non-hierarchical structure and open decision-making processes. Adhering to democratic principles is a priority in many such associations, and social relations are characterized by a high degree of symmetry, with accountability that is both horizontal and reciprocal. The activist framework resonates with the signifiers of deliberative democracy and an open and vigorous public sphere. However, we have also identified the debates and issues that might suggest that there are factors that undermine the ideals of the activist framework and its potential to democratize democracy. For example the informality of the decision-making processes does not necessarily ensure democratic practice, as the most articulate and active people can have a tendency to dominate (Keane, 1988). Further, we re-emphasize Everingham's (1998) argument that despite the democratic rhetoric of participatory politics, participation has been replaced with processes of consultation, advocacy and self-help.

We do not believe the charity framework offers very much in the way of enhancing democratic processes and/or the public sphere. This framework is historically organized around the distinction between the deserving and undeserving poor. It also draws on the discourses of virtue, service and compassion, moral discipline, ideas of dependency and patronage. We have suggested there is reciprocity, but that it is vertical reciprocity, where the giver is bestowed with moral redemption and the receiver is provided with material or moral sustenance. While deliberative democracy privileges the argument over the status of the arguer, not all citizens are free and equal, indeed recipients are clearly not fellow-citizens. There is little motivation to engage in democracy, deliberative or otherwise, since the 'crusade' does not include structural or collectivist solutions to the issues of poverty, disadvantage, social justice or inequality.

Within the welfare state industry framework there are opportunities for democracy and the public sphere to be strengthened. As we have noted, empowerment processes are invoked, but they are flawed since empowerment is constructed in an individualist rather than collectivist way. However, there is consultation and communication, but these are constrained by the existence of asymmetrical power relations. There is a focus on formal equality and social rights, but it is left up to the state to ensure these, through standardized rules, procedures and programmes. There is no room for the politics of difference.

In summary, then, we conclude that of the four frameworks the quasi-capitalist market and the charity framework have least to offer and are most unlikely to contribute to the strengthening of democracy and the public sphere. The welfare state industry model perhaps in a limited way shares some common ground with the ideas outlined at the beginning of this chapter, though social markets and the activist base of the voluntary sector generally provide the most fertile ground for optimism.

Social capital and voluntary associations

The term social capital has gained increasing prominence in recent years. While Coleman and Bourdieu were the first to apply the term, it is Robert Putnam's (1993) work that has generated much of the recent debate. For the most part Putnam's definition has been widely accepted, though more recent literature (as we outlined in Chapter 3) has began to question of the validity of the definition (Newton, 1998; Levi, 1996; Sabetti, 1996; Kenworthy, 1997) and whether it is consistent with the Coleman thesis of social capital (Edwards and Foley, 1998).

However, while we acknowledge the fact that Putnam's definition of social capital is becoming increasingly contested, we will utilize it in this section in order to facilitate the examination of the critical aspects of the social relations in the four operating frameworks of voluntary associations (charity, activist, welfare state industry, and market). In this chapter social capital is defined as the 'features of social organization, such as trust, norms, and networks, that can improve the efficiency of society by facilitating coordinated action' (Putnam, 1993).

Whenever social capital is analysed, theorists point to the importance of trust and reciprocity. Concepts such as empathy, cooperation, mutuality, the 'common good', active, civic, and risk taking in a social context are invariably included, and the hypothesis proposed is principally that increasing social capital will remedy the decline towards the Hobbesian version of society as brutish and nasty. If Margaret Thatcher was right and society really no longer exists, then social capital as an answer to the Hobbesian version is futile, since individuals acting on their own clearly cannot produce and/or reproduce social capital. Social capital is a concept that privileges the social rather than individual virtues.

Since the publication of Putnam's (1993) *Making Democracy Work* there has been considerable interest in the notion of social networks. Indeed, in the spirit of Putnam (and clearly de Tocqueville) voluntary associations have taken centre stage as the site for the production and/or reproduction of social capital. The literature, in terms of its focus, tends to lead to the view that such associations have a monopoly on social capital, both in terms of generating it and because they require social capital to survive. This view is open to question. For example, Fukuyama (1995) argues that markets are linked to and depend on norms of reciprocity and trust. Indeed, surely the family is also a site where social trust can be generated. Further, not all voluntary associations will/can be sites for the production and reproduction of social capital.

There are also negative aspects of social capital (Levi, 1996; Onyx and Bullen, 1997), as evidenced in the debates around the concept of trust. The type of trust proposed under the rubric of social capital is generalized and reciprocal trust (Putnam, 1993; Cox, 1995), and is the product of weaker ties such as those associated with organic solidarity and *gesellschaft* communities. Alternatively, the trust associated with mechanical solidarity or *gemeinschaft* communities, that is, socially homogeneous and exclusive communities with unitary social forms and authoritarian social structures, is not seen to be congruent with social capital. It is assumed that of the two forms the former carries with it far more positive connotations. The 'dangers' of the latter have been tragically played out late in the century in the Balkans, the Middle East and parts of Africa. Further, some voluntary associations, such as certain self-help and consciousness raising groups, might be 'skewed' more towards the latter type of trust, with high levels of trust internally and low levels of trust with non-members and institutions outside the organization. Thus it is important to examine the nature of trust according to the frameworks we propose.

Voluntary associations operating within the charity framework have their genesis in pre-welfare state systems where responsibility for welfare provision lay largely outside state institutions, such as in the family and the church. Further, this model operates under the principle of social amelioration, directed at filling the gaps in provision and at those identified as most in need, who are generally passive recipients with little power for self-determination. The provider/welfare recipient relationship is based on patronage. The questions arising out of this framework and relating to social capital concern the fact that the recipients lack power and opportunity to determine the services they receive. The notion of duty is clearly at odds with notions of reciprocity and trust. Indeed, trust in the charity framework might tend towards 'thick' trust as described above: that is, high levels of trust between those sharing the sense of 'calling to work with the poor', and low levels of trust with recipients (who are plainly not fellow-citizens) and institutions outside the organization. Relationships and structures that are vertical, as they clearly are in this framework, generate dependent relations that encourage passivity, lead to absence of choices, and engender trust that is dependent on the good will of the powerful (Onyx and Bullen, 1997). Participatory democracy is clearly not part of the language of the charity framework. It might be argued that there is a strong sense of reciprocity between providers and recipients of welfare, understood as 'short-term altruism for long-term self interest' (Taylor, 1982), and there might also be notions of empathy, articulated formally or informally within the organization, which might also be considered an important aspect of the social capital argument. However, given the fact that relationships are unquestionably paternalistic, the strength of such reciprocity and empathy is without doubt diminished. We would argue that the charity form of operation is unlikely to achieve favourable outcomes in terms of production and/or reproduction of social capital.

The welfare state industry framework attempts to standardize programmes and welfare delivery drawing on the tenets of the modernist welfare state. It would appear to be unlikely to generate much, if any social capital. The framework relies on professional expertise to identify recipients and priorities, and while the concept of enablement and active engagement may be invoked it is constructed in an individualist rather than collectivist way. The fact that organizations are funded and largely controlled by centralized welfare bureaucracies means they are subject to the same characteristics of these bureaucracies – vertical coercive sanctions, relations of dependence, passivity where reciprocity and mutuality are discouraged, an absence of choice and trust that is dependent on the goodwill of the powerful (Onyx and Bullen, 1997). Further, contractual relations, where voluntary associations are set in competition against each other, does not enhance notions of cooperation, and relations of trust between agencies are clearly weakened. Indeed, it is difficult to imagine where there would be an opportunity for the production and/or reproduction of social capital under this framework.

To summarize: the activist framework welfare is seen as a site for effective struggle and embracing a whole range of activities that can enhance well-being. Further, there is a professed commitment to non-hierarchical structures and a commitment to principles of subsidiarity, democracy and mutuality, with lines of accountability to co-members. Participants in our focus-group discussions conducted as part of this study often used expressions such as 'acting from the ground up' and 'involvement of everyone'. The activist framework is compatible with the development of social capital. It is most likely to maximize the opportunities for the enhancement of social capital where the organizational structure is flat and open and includes widespread decision-making by the members. Important to the generation of social capital for these activist organizations is their ability to maintain active face-to-face participation where trust and reciprocity can thrive. There are clearly high levels of generalized trust and opportunities to test such trust with 'fellow-citizens' who might be both co-workers and recipients of programmes. The commitment to active citizenship and participatory democracy obviously make this framework a potential site for the generation of social capital. However, the activist framework also points to the assumption that organizations might already have high levels of social capital if, at the point of formation, the founding members bring it with them and therefore commit to such a structure. Putnam (1993) and Fukuyama (1995) appear to differ regarding the direction of causation where trust and voluntary associations are concerned. Putnam claims the strengthening of trust occurs as a result of joining voluntary associations. Fukuyama seems to suggest it is the prior existence of trust that facilitates the formation of voluntary associations in society.

As noted at the beginning of this section, Fukuyama (1995) argues that where there are ample stores of social capital markets perform better. Certainly there is nothing in Putnam's definition that at first glance could not apply equally to market relations as to those of the family, social groups and the community, and economists have become increasingly interested in the concept since Putnam (1993; 1995) indicated there are economic benefits associated with large stores of social capital. Fukuyama (1995) argues that the economic benefits for the commercial world flow because people cooperate in a relationship of trust and shared norms. To do business in an environment of little or no trust requires a system of formal rules and regulations. The associated 'transaction costs' of a legal system that has to be in place to replace trust imposes a tax on all forms of economic activity and therefore reduces efficiency. Further, trust increases, or at least can contribute to, cooperation which can complement the competition of the market. However, Lyons (1997) points out that where markets are pervasive other parts of society where social capital is produced are damaged, and the capitalist marketization of voluntary associations may well result in the weakening of social capital. Terms such as flexibility, output, efficiencies and competition are not necessarily incompatible with effective welfare provision; however, we argue that a commitment to profit-driven competition and efficiencies undercuts ideas of equality, mutuality, active engagement and generative practice.

According to Lyons (1997: 5) those voluntary associations that have the greatest potential for generating social capital are member-serving organizations such as bowling clubs, choral groups, professional and trade organizations. For Lyons this is because they provide opportunities for people to collaborate voluntarily with strangers. They encourage enthusiasm among members to remain involved and to take responsibility. Lyons further argues that associations that are established to serve others can be an important sign of social capital but are more focused on the services they provide than on the activities that specifically contribute to social capital. Public-serving organizations can generate social capital at two sites: the way they are governed and the services they offer (1997: 4–6). Interestingly, such associations usually also have the features of social markets. Members of the public can come and go in such organizations. They can decide the level of their involvement in the association. There are choices for prospective members when there is a plurality of organizations offering services, and democratic procedures for existing members to decide whether they wish to accept membership applications. There is strong horizontal trust and mutuality amongst the members. Thus it would be fair to say that the strong incompatibilities between social capital and capitalist markets is not transferred to social markets.

In terms of governance, organizations that are formed by strangers to address a common problem clearly draw on social capital in their formation: however, they can continue to generate social capital in the way of operating. This is impossible if members remain active, seek to involve others in decision-making, and continue to attract/recruit more people into active membership (Lyons, 1997: 6). This form of operation is most clearly associated with the activist framework. The services offered can generate social capital if they are developed according to community development principles. Accordingly they are developed to 'engender norms of trust and generalised reciprocity, by building networks, encouraging people in these networks to form new associations, and by persuading people to provide services for themselves or to advocate for other bodies to do so' (Lyons, 1997: 6). It appears that only the activist framework shares any of these values, aims and ambitions.

Lyons (1997: 7–8) makes two final points. Firstly, generating social capital in the way an organization is governed is only possible for organizations that are member-owned. Secondly, according to much research-based literature, the characteristics of a well-run organization and the management practices and approaches to governance mitigate against the principles of social capital. Efficiency, quality, responsiveness to 'customers', regular evaluation of services, and commitment to best practice are activities opposed to those that might generate social capital. This is particularly important given the findings of our own study and the push towards marketization and professionalization.

While we need further research into the role of voluntary associations in the production and reproduction of social capital, our analysis indicates that where the welfare state industry and capitalist market rationales are applied to the operation of voluntary associations, it is unlikely that there will be much social capital generated. Where the charity framework is applied there is some potential for the social capital to be produced, but clearly if any of the operating rationales has the ability to generate social capital, the activist model is the one.

9
Facing Uncertainty

Introduction

In this final chapter we return to the question posed at the beginning of this book: can active citizenship survive the marketization of welfare provision through the medium of voluntary associations?

Our view is that the analyses and empirical evidence we have presented warrant an answer which is affirmative, although we do acknowledge that the market framework remains unsettled and is still developing. To argue our case fully we need to return to the discussion of Chapter 5 on the forms of market discourse and operation in the voluntary sector and the features of voluntary associations.

What has been evident in our analyses of market discourses and operations is that the market framework is far from a unitary construct. Market mechanisms have been applied to the voluntary sector very selectively. Governments have developed what we have described as quasi-market processes in their attempts to introduce an enterprise culture and 'business-like' approach to the management of voluntary associations. Voluntary associations themselves have selected different aspects of market processes which are compatible with their own operations. Where they are subjected to the quasi-market processes implemented by governments, they respond in pragmatic ways, for example, embracing government contracting regimes strategically, rather than complicitly.

Let us consider each of these points in more detail. First, as discussed in Chapter 5, the application of market logic to voluntary associations is circumscribed in several ways. Like the operation of market principles in for-profit companies, the way this actually works means that the pure market form just does not exist. Fiscal and information monopolies mean that not all players in the market-place are equal and choices are circumscribed by features external to market logic. For all the argument about 'rolling back the state', it is necessary for the state to intervene to regulate market operations. In voluntary associations market processes only operate on the principles of capitalist quasi-markets. For example, the relation between consumers of services and providers (or sellers) of services is generally mediated by a third party, the purchaser of a service, which is generally the government. A welfare client has a very tenuous role as consumer, because she is generally not the purchaser of services. Consumer sovereignty and the other requirements for an open market (a plurality of providers and purchasers, and free choice of entering the market-place or not) only exist in pseudo form. If we take it that market processes existing in voluntary associations are of a capitalist quasi-market form, it might be more appropriate to interpret the capitalist quasi-market system as no more than just another form of the welfare state, constructed upon new disciplinary mechanisms. If this is the case, then the voluntary sector has no more to fear from the incursions of capitalist quasi-market than it does from the disciplinary mechanisms of the welfare state industry.

Again, if the market mechanism in voluntary associations is a capitalist-driven market, then there is an argument that voluntary associations should embark upon a strategic response. This might involve taking market discourse at face value and demanding that the government implement policies that ensure consumer sovereignty, and provide welfare consumers with real consumer choices in services.

However the sector responds to capitalist quasi-markets, it has always had the capacity to draw out its own space and resolutions. There is no evidence that the strategic and creative thinking that form part of the activist model, in particular, will disappear under the weight of capitalist quasi-market discourses. Our data indicate that despite extensive reliance on government funds amongst some sections of the voluntary welfare sector, it has so far managed to maintain a reasonable degree of autonomy from the state, at least in terms of the framework of activist principles that underlie the whole sector.

Secondly, and as we argue in Chapter 5, although there are many problems in the application of capitalist quasi-markets, some elements of marketization can be applied to the voluntary sector in useful ways. We have identified these elements as comprising a social market. The emphasis in the social market is the provision of a maximum number of choices for all who enter into market arrangements. People must be free to enter and exit from market arrangements. In the present (social) market voluntary associations may or may not enter into funding arrangements with governments. Stronger forms of social markets exist in cooperatives such as childcare cooperatives and LETS. In fact, the social market has already been in operation in the sector but has not been recognized as such.

In Australia we have numerous examples of voluntary associations that combine elements from both capitalist and social quasi-markets and several examples of organizations committed to the development of social quasi-markets. For example, Australia has a long history of cooperatives, which people join freely, and in which they are able to choose their type of membership and participation (Mathews, 1989). Of relevance to voluntary associations are examples of local community groups establishing small non-profit businesses such as food cooperatives and printing activities. Aboriginal organizations have established businesses which are not for private profit, but which do generate surpluses used to run welfare programmes. Sometimes such cooperatives seek funding from a range of different funding sources. At other times they prefer maximum autonomy from governments. When interviewed in focus-group discussions, representatives from cooperatives emphasized their commitment to a plurality of sources of funds, and maximum choice for members in their form of participation in the organization and the type of services provided.

There appears to be a trend in larger voluntary associations towards the idea of separating an organization's activities into several administrative areas, such as a fundraising area, an activist area and a service-provision area. While there have been some criticisms of this organizational arrangement, because it could open the way for governments to withdraw from their obligation to fund welfare voluntary associations, the effects have yet to be analysed thoroughly. Those we have interviewed who have been involved in this type of organization are positive in their stance towards these trends of diversification.

The activist engagement

Our empirical research has revealed several features of the voluntary welfare sector in Australia. The dominant framework is an activist one. While, as we have discussed in Chapter 4, there are some shortcomings in the activist contribution to civil society, this outlook is our best bet for the survival and development of active citizenship. The activist framework is resilient. It has had to survive in hostile environments, where voluntary associations have been starved of resources, stigmatized and marginalized.

The uncertainty of day-to-day existence, which characterizes many voluntary associations, has led to the development of strategies to deal with risk. These strategies are embedded in the commitment to mutuality and self-determination. For example, the principles of mutuality enable risk sharing within and between organizations. The practice of survival has also opened the way for dealing with market logics. Interestingly, the possibility of some compatibility between market and activist logics has always existed, especially for those voluntary associations concerned with political mobilization. Both market and mobilizing activist discourses are concerned with social change, initiative and strategic action. The rhetoric of both the activist and market frameworks is to provide programmes that are responsive to people's needs, rather than being imposed upon them from above.

However, the processes of survival in voluntary associations have not always rested upon their capacity to accommodate different operational frameworks. For many organizations utilizing an activist framework, the survival path has been very different. It has involved carving out territory in which marginal groups can construct identity politics and develop oppositional interpretations of needs. As indicated in Chapter 4, activism in voluntary associations has historically provided sites for the development of alternative politics and the circulation of counter-discourses. This survival trek has often been based on the sheer strength of commitment, mutuality and solidarity which appear to be enduring features of so many voluntary associations that operate within the activist framework.

Voluntary associations have been able to sustain the commitment, mutuality and solidarity required for survival in quite hostile operating contexts in at least two ways. First, commitment can be achieved through authoritarian leadership, as has occurred within conditions of unreflective political modernism. Secondly and more recently, as faith in strong political leadership and grand political narratives has faded, there has been another source of dedication and commitment. This source is the very interpretation of society that takes as its starting point the reflexive nature of social existence. It places self-determining active citizens at the centre of political analysis. Within this second position, then, the way to develop commitment, solidarity and mutuality is to provide sites and processes that will enable the self-development of individuals and society. Commitment here comes through general knowledge and self-knowledge, and the belief that it is worth participating in any particular social or political venture, for the purpose of sociability and mutuality as ends in themselves, or because individuals can contribute usefully to some form of social or political change. But in the contemporary context where there is also a commitment to pluralism, diversity and listening to the voices of others, it is necessary to establish sites for articulating concerns and negotiating conflicting views. What is needed, then, is a place for extending and radicalizing democracy. The desire to develop these spaces in the voluntary sector is what lies behind the claim that voluntary associations provide a training ground for participatory democracy. While there is a long way to go before we can pronounce activist-centred voluntary associations to be successful in providing model settings for extending and radicalizing democracy, the activist framework does offer a set of logics that at least make the extension of democracy and the strengthening of active citizenship possible.

The threats to active engagement

Yet the potential for the advancement of forms of active citizenship through the development of social market mechanisms set within such a voluntary sector framework of activist ideas remains largely unrealized at this time.

The exigencies of post-Fordist economies around the world and their changing social and demographic patterns contain tendencies that not only press against the twin commitments of social democratic welfare – full employment and high levels of social entitlements through redistributive direct taxation – but also oversee a series of trends which contain distinctly double-edged possibilities for the building of associationalist structures. This rolling social crisis, which we discussed in Part I, is characterized by, among others things, the decline of traditional work forms, chronic unemployment and under-employment and the growth of a working poor. These factors, combined with declining trust in all public institutions, reduce the power of the labour movement, important historically in the promotion of universalistic welfare regimes. At the same time, welfare demand is increasing, especially in relation to the 'greying' of populations.

On the one hand, associationalism can be seen to provide answers to the problems of remote, centralized, bureaucratic and inappropriate welfare solutions. On the other, there are question-marks against the ability of voluntary associations to play a core or a major role in welfare.

Firstly there are the issues of the sector's reliance on and autonomy from the state. We have shown this reliance to be strong in Australia, where 60 per cent of our surveyed organizations were principally funded by government. While this result is not surprising given the historical development of the voluntary welfare sector in Australia, only 8 per cent of organizations had their main funding from local government, meaning that dependence on government is to a large degree dependence on a relatively remote source. This is exacerbated in the case of federal and state-funded organizations in regional and remote Australia, where an us/them theme in relation to the national or state capital city has strong reverberations in voluntary associations (see the focus-group analysis in Chapter 7). Against this, however, is the finding that the strength of an activist framework (as measured by the 'grass-roots' factor in our survey) does not change significantly between regions or funding regimes.

State influence, direction and control loom large either directly through bureaucratic fiat (endless justifications of last year's budget and endless submissions for next year's), or more indirectly through the sector possibly becoming a 'shunting yard' (Seibel, 1990) or a casualty ward (Roelofs, 1995) buffering the remainder from the marginalized. This situation calls into question the ability of the voluntary welfare sector to operate more independently from the state – a necessary condition in any move towards the strengthening of associationalist tendencies and structures. We would argue that in any such move, a proportion of existing organizations (perhaps characterized by the dominance of the passive voice discussed in relation to the focus-group data) would be unlikely to survive the necessary 'de-corporatization' and would likely be replaced.

Secondly, the continuing ability of the voluntary sector to cope with the most marginalized must be questioned. These groups are likely to be the most socially isolated and consequently least able to respond to new forms of social market driven structures. It is quite likely that some form of bifurcation of the sector would occur in response to associationalism with, in this instance, a section of organizations developing different relations with the state and 'clients' and acting in relative isolation from the social market structures. Because of the potentially incremental nature of an associationalist path this would no doubt be regarded as being in the realm of the possible and sectoral bifurcation in such a manner would merely continue a trend already noted within the activist framework, for example in the difference between activisms based on politics and mutuality. Yet the prospect of a specially serviced 'undermarket' of the least privileged raises disturbing questions which associationalism would need to resolve.

In Chapter 2 we also considered the idea that the development of a constant interplay between audit (regulation) and risk (unregulatable) society results in increasingly hybridized social environments. In thinking of the possibilities for radicalizing democracy we must expect this hybridity to be expressed in moves towards bifurcation and plurality – for example, the possible widening of the split in the voluntary welfare sector between service and advocacy functions.

Constituting citizens

To assess the possibilities inherent in this discussion we return to our focus on the voluntary welfare sector and project five possible welfare paths. While some involve the sustenance and growth of forms of active citizenship, others quite clearly do not. We utilize for this schema the possibilities inherent in combinations of the contrasts between consumer–communitarian citizenship on the one hand and active–passive citizenship on the other.

Both Habermas (1992) and van Gunsteren (1992) point to the opposing traditions of individualistic or liberal citizenship and communitarian citizenship. The individualistic tradition from Locke stresses an instrumentalist relationship between citizen and state, a calculatedly distancing one which regards citizenship rights and obligations as something negotiated between the already formed individual and the state (Habermas, 1992: 25–6). The idea of communitarian citizenship can be traced to Aristotle and holds that the individual is derivative of the integrated community which is the realm of shared tradition (van Gunsteren, 1992: 41–2). Here, citizenship-as-membership must be achieved through engagement in the processes of belonging. Within our focus on welfare here, we utilize these distinctions but give particular emphasis to marketization processes through the notion of consumer citizenship, by which we mean a particular type or form of individualistic citizenship which can develop in societies undergoing extreme marketization. It shares with individualistic citizenship ideas of instrumentalism and a stress on individual rights and obligations, but significantly raises the possibilities of a profound non-integration of the populous as a result of the effects of a sustained and atomizing market hegemony (cf. Walzer's notion of 'radical disengagement', Walzer, 1992: 106).

The passive–active contrast is set out in Part I and elsewhere (Turner, 1992). Briefly, active citizenship is the result of citizenship development

| | Audit Society | Risk Society |
	Passive Citizenship	**Active Citizenship**
Consumer Citizenship	McWelfare	Welfare.com
Consumer/ Communitarian Citizenship	Contractual Welfare	Market-bounded Associationalism
Communitarian Citizenship	Social Democratic Welfare	State-bounded Associationalism

Figure 9.1   Classification of welfare regimes.

from below (such as citizen/local initiatives of many kinds), whereas passive citizenship is 'bestowed' from above.

Five paths for welfare

Here we shall argue that we stand at a point in time where a choice must be made between associationalist structures of welfare or mass welfare production and consumption within a thoroughly marketized environment. The present arrangements characterized as contractual welfare will not in our view persist in the longer term.

The pressures of post-Fordism and increasing globalization are likely to have profound effects upon citizenship. We wish to argue that questions of passive and active citizenship together with those of consumer and communitarian citizenship lie at the heart of the possible changes and effects which will push welfare towards one of five ideal-typical destinations portrayed in Figure 9.1 (the two associationalist types are grouped together for the purposes of this summary argument). The role of the voluntary welfare sector changes according to the direction taken but every path leads to bifurcation.

Social democratic welfare – communitarian and passive citizenship

This is the combination of communitarian and passive forms of citizenship. While collective rights and obligations are stressed at all levels, a strong collective state actor ensures that the ultimate control over the definition and operation of these principles resides ultimately at the level of the state. The social democratic welfare model is a path only likely for the Nordic countries who have developed this further and remain closer to it than have others, despite the rigours of the 1980s and 1990s.

Welfare is a central player in the social democratic state model, with centralized provision and administration designed to ensure redistributive equity. At such points we see the combination of passive and communitarian citizenship resolved in favour of the structures of the former. The consequence of holding to unitary concepts and mechanisms is the silencing of alternative voices. There will certainly be the need for a chronic crisis management style. Such a style would be aimed at the containment and partial resolution of the pulls and pushes of post-Fordist pressures from without, and probable declining levels of trust, together with the claims of marginalized groups from within.

It is likely that the voluntary sector would remain largely concentrated on non-welfare concerns as is characteristic of contemporary Sweden, but new organizations would almost certainly appear to answer the unmet needs of the marginalized. These smaller welfare-centred groups would be likely to grow in times of the relaxation of centralizing legislations, but the periodic legislative U-turns characteristic of crisis management would mean that any upsurge would be part of a cyclical existence.

This path leans firmly towards the apparent stability of audit society, but the threat of rupture lies just below the surface.

Contractual welfare – consumer/communitarian and passive citizenship

Contractualism is the current path that welfare is taking in Australia and a number of other Western democracies. It produces a middle point between communitarian and consumer citizenship, and with the pole of audit society again ascendant, combines these with passive forms of citizenship. In many ways contractual welfare is a halfway house in that it contains within its makeup distinct pulls in (at least) two directions. The first is to the market and the sovereignty of choice ideas associated with consumer citizenship in that the systems of contracting-out are claimed to give people more 'choice' over welfare provision. This is counterpointed by the pull back towards the more obvious top-down control characteristic of social democratic welfare through the state intermediary control of the contracting and tender processes. As we discuss in Chapter 5, contractual welfare regimes can be seen as simply different arrangements of state control.

This halfway house may prove to be tenable – after all, both likely paths away lead to places we are constantly warned about through dominant media thinking (ideas of the unfettered market or the Nanny State). The model has the rhetoric of the market seemingly without many of the attendant risks. Weighing against this, however, are the same factors which pulled welfare in this direction in the first place. The rhetoric of a smaller state cannot for long disguise the realities of state control through welfare quasi-markets. Popular resentment towards state 'hand-outs' of welfare, together with continuing suburban disquiet over questions of redistribution, are not likely to be removed by contractual welfare, no matter how many glossy leaflets are produced (indeed the state's public relations messages in the letterbox have become the most ubiquitous and visible 'hand-outs' of the 1990s, and ones more-over which merely serve to remind us of who is in charge of the choice).

The pulls of a full engagement with consumer citizenship through a widening of the idea of choice may be too much for this model to handle. Having introduced 'choice', the full consequences may not be far away if the perception of state 'failure' cannot be contained.

The voluntary welfare sector can certainly exist and even expand under contractual welfare. The bifurcation here will likely be between those who are state contractors and the remainder. Active citizenship forms will be played out in both, but always under the shadow of the structures of passive citizenship within an audit society trajectory.

McWelfare – consumer and passive citizenship

In Chapter 1 we discussed in passing the idea of 'McDonaldization' (Ritzer, 1996; 1998). Ritzer claims that the drive for profitability through the application of the principles of efficiency, calculability, predictability and control has set in train a process that threatens to remake the world in the image of a fast-food restaurant. The audit society road for welfare in a more thoroughly marketized environment results in what we could call McWelfare. Here, passivity combined with consumer citizenship leads to the mass consumption of standardized welfare from large and monopolistic providers driven by efficiencies of scale and market domination. A kind of mirror image of the standardized state provision is constructed by private and probably also transnational monopolistic enterprises such as the Lockheed corporation.

This can be seen as a 'fuller' version of the ideas of choice encapsulated in the contractual welfare model. The dilemma of the modern state's relationship to welfare which mitigates against a total withdrawal (Offe, 1984) is resolved here by sharing the burden of that responsibility with transnationals whose commitment to the prevention of a 'war of all against all' is a purely economic one, but rational in its own terms of keeping a customer base.

Crisis counselling, for example, could be no more than a phone call away, connecting the user to a call centre in Atlanta or Dublin where counsellors work in quasi-factory conditions with one eye on the time taken by each call. The unemployed might sign up with the job agency of their choice where they would be directed towards the ever opening (and revolving) door of 'McJobs' (Ritzer, 1998: 6–7) – a realm of work where forms of production and consumption merge.

The old idea of membership of civil society institutions and voluntary associations, which gave access to the provision of forms of welfare in a broad sense, becomes here the world of welfare club memberships.[1] One's preferred job agency is linked to a counselling service, a health centre, a supermarket chain, a bank and credit system and so on, all giving discounts for their valued members. What better than accumulating 'welfare' points in the process of buying a burger? These cartels of welfare services therefore compete to gain market share and would provide, at least initially, a seemingly dazzling array of choices.

Yet all of this is cast within the passivity of the audit sphere, and the mass production inherent in this model demands mass consumption. This in turn provides merely the illusion of choice, as in the end all choices blend into one. Ironically, the problems of homogenous state provision of welfare are recreated here. Having said this, the market seems more capable than the state of convincing us that more of the same is better and this is done precisely through the mechanism of choice – should we buy the same old tried and tested burger yet again or try the new 'Mexican' version in the limited time it will be available? These abilities to contain possible ruptures through constant appeals to 'choice' give McWelfare a certain stability and chance to persist.

The voluntary welfare sector would likely split in at least two directions within McWelfare. Some would ally themselves to the large corporations always on the lookout for some 'community' ties, and others would be actively created by the corporations ('astro-turf' organizations which on the surface look like grass-roots organizations but are imposed from the corporation above). For this sector, the corporation would become a surrogate state provider. Other associations would retreat to the margins where forms of more active citizenship could be developed amongst the refugees from McWelfare.

Welfare.com – consumer and active citizenship

The pulls of risk society, especially on McWelfare, creates a combination of active and consumer citizenship which we call welfare.com. The drive to homogeneity, a potential problem for McWelfare as it tends to undercut the notion of choice, is here answered from within a (quasi-capitalist) market model through the mass creation of 'niche' markets which promise the individual the means by which to put together their own tailored welfare package.

We would see this being tied closely to the development of digital technology which would allow both tailored packages and open up possibilities for decentred virtual voluntary associations such as worldwide advocacy, advice and self-help groups.

Citizenship is still highly individualized but the activation of choice provides a means to escape some of the standardization traps of McWelfare. We would expect the relationship between state and corporations to be similar to that of McWelfare but more thoroughly contingent and decentered.

In Chapter 8 we considered some of the ideas inherent in the teledemocracy debate. It is clear that welfare.com is a path which will open up the notion of choice in welfare, but probably only for those sections of the population who are able to achieve high levels of connectivity initially through personal computer ownership. The choice would therefore have a price and one too high for many to pay. For the connected, welfare becomes a series of choices within niche markets. For the rest, the choice is likely to be McWelfare.

Such a combination of McWelfare and welfare.com would oversee the dispersion of voluntary associations in a number of ways. First, a large body of associations would exist under the auspices of the corporations as discussed above. They are likely to be major service-providing organizations such as health care, care of the aged, childcare and possibly education offering a mass product. Second, one would see marginalized groups of associations working with those for whom McWelfare fails to deliver. Third would be virtual associations dealing primarily in niche middle-class welfare markets, including customizable versions of McWelfare together with new forms of looser connections made possible by communications technologies.

It would seem that the second and third types of associations offer possibilities for active citizenship, but this would still be encountered through the individuating medium of consumer citizenship. In such a scenario, the activation of choice is only available for the elites who have the resources to escape the blandness of McWelfare.

Associationalism: consumer/communitarian and active citizenship

We have discussed ideas of associationalism in Chapters 1 and 3. Such a path requires moves towards active citizenship together with a retreat from consumerism in the direction of communitarian citizenship.

Political power is required to create the conditions under which systematic forms of social markets are created in welfare which in the process replace those of the state, mass or niche markets characteristic of the contractual, McWelfare and welfare.com paths. As Hirst (1996) points out, associationalism can be incremental in its growth; so the hope would be that the building-up of social capital following early implementations of associationalist structures would be sufficient to then provide conducive political conditions for the introduction of redistributive mechanisms by the state.

As we argued in Chapter 1, associationalism might be one of two types depending upon the extent of communitarian citizenship forms. Social market associationalism combines the active form with a middle point between consumer and communitarian citizenship, whereas state-bounded associationalism is more fully structured by the latter. In both versions we would expect high levels of social capital and a strong civil society due to the effects of this citizenship mix.

In our view, the social market variant is the more likely (possibly with the exception of the Nordic countries) as it does not require so profound a retreat from the mesmeric world of consumerism. Choice as such is actually enhanced in the move to the social market where subsidiarity is a defining feature. The problem may simply be that while this path holds all the cards in the longer term, its immediate and short-term appeal could well be limited. As Walzer (1992: 106) puts it, the activities of associationalism seem so ordinary. We would argue that there is a problem if we expect people to immediately see the benefits of leaving the queue at McDonalds to join a neighbourhood food co-op. Yet when we look at the results of our research we see that there are large numbers of people and associations who are already engaged with everyday activities of the kind that would characterize associationalism – and this in a climate not conducive in many ways to voluntary association.

The associationalist path for welfare offers the brightest hope for active citizenship, but the alternatives to the appeals of out and out consumer society need to be effectively set out.

Conclusions

In conclusion, what is the prognosis for active citizenship as we move into the next century? On balance we would argue that we have reached a crossroads. With the post-war consensus gone and consumerism in the ascendancy, welfare has finally and painfully begun to be detached from the state. There is a very good chance that contractual welfare is only a stop on the path to McWelfare, a short period of taking breath before starting on again. This would not be good news for those who advocate active citizenship. However, we would expect a viable voluntary welfare sector to persist in that scenario but to do so in a more marginalized capacity. Our research shows the breadth of the activist framework that currently exists, and we have suggested that this has proved in the past to offer adaptable and innovative solutions to difficult circumstances.

The other path, which we could still take at this point, is towards social market associationalism. If the political power could be mobilized, the strengths of the voluntary welfare sector would be a firm base on which to build. Hirst (1994) argues that associational structures could still be built even if we accept a rational choice model to explain motivation. He may well be correct but we would point out that moving to associationalism now, with an already existing base of active citizenship forms, offers our best hope before we are drawn instead into the world of McWelfare.

The tasks of promoting food co-ops over McDonalds or neighbourhood health centres over 'one-stop doctor shops' are challenging to say the least, but through their successes and failures mark the routes to the welfare of the next century.

Note

1 On this point see Lundström and Wijkström (1997: 266), who discuss the 'marketization of membership'.

References

Abercrombie, N., Hill, S. and Turner, B. S. (1980), *The Dominant Ideology Thesis*. London: Allen & Unwin.

Abercrombie, N., Hill, S. and Turner, B. S. (1986), *Sovereign Individuals of Capitalism*. London: Allen & Unwin.

Alford, J. and Consodine, M. (1994), 'Public sector employment contracts', in Alford and O'Neil (1994).

Alford, J. and O'Neil, D. (1994), *The Contract State: Public Management and the Kennett Government*. Centre for Applied Social Research, Deakin University Geelong.

Alford, J., O'Neil, D., McGuire, Consodine, M., Muetzelfeldt, M. and Ernst, J. (1994), 'The contract state', in Alford and O'Neil (1994).

Alinsky, S. (1972), *Rules for Radicals*. New York: Vintage.

Althusser, L. (1984), *Essays on Ideology*. London: Verso.

Altman, D. (1979), *Coming Out in the Seventies*. Sydney: Wild and Woolley.

Amin, A. (ed.) (1994), *Post-Fordism. A Reader*. Oxford: Blackwell Publishers.

Anheier, H. K. and Seibel, W. (1997) 'Germany', in L. M. Salamon and H. K. Anheier (eds), *Defining the Nonprofit Sector: a Cross-national Analysis*. New York: Manchester University Press, 128–68.

Archambault, E. (1997), *The Nonprofit Sector in France*. Manchester: Manchester University Press.

Arnold, M. (1960), *Culture & Anarchy*. Cambridge: Cambridge University Press.

Australian Bureau of Statistics (1996), *Voluntary Work, Australia [4441.0]*. Canberra: Australian Bureau of Statistics.

Australian Bureau of Statistics (1997a), *Australia's Welfare [8905.0]*. Canberra: Australian Bureau of Statistics.

Australian Bureau of Statistics (1997b) *Australian Demographic Trends (3102.0)*. Canberra: Australian Bureau of Statistics.

Bailey, P. (1977), Task force on co-ordination in welfare and health, first report: *Proposals for Changes in the Administration and Delivery of Programs and Services*. Canberra: AGPS.

Baistow, K. (1994/5), 'Liberation and Regulation? Some paradoxes of empowerment', *Critical Social Policy*, 42, winter, pp. 34–46.

Baldry, E. and Vinson, T. (eds) (1991), *Actions Speak*. Melbourne: Longman Cheshire.

Barbetta, G. P. (ed.) (1997), *The Nonprofit Sector in Italy*. Manchester: Manchester University Press.

Bauman, Z. (1998) *Work, Consumerism and the New Poor*. Buckingham: Open University Press.

Beck, U. (1992), *Risk Society*. London: Sage.

Beilharz, P., Considine, M. and Watts, R. (1992), *Arguing about the Welfare State, The Australian Experience*. North Sydney: Allen & Unwin Pty. Ltd.

Bell, D. (1976), *The Cultural Contradictions of Capitalism*. New York: Basic Books.

Bellah, R., et al. (1985), *Habits of the Heart: Individualism and Commitment in American Life*. Berkeley: University of California Press.

Benhabib, S. (ed.) (1996), *Democracy and Difference – Contesting the Boundaries of the Political*. Princeton: Princeton University Press.

Benhabib, S. (1996), 'Towards a deliberative model of democratic legitimacy', in S. Benhabib (ed.) *Democracy and Difference: Contesting the Boundaries of the Political*. Princeton: Princeton University Press.

Billis, D. and Harris, M. (1996), *Voluntary Agencies: Challenges of Organisation and Management*. London: Macmillan.

Boddy, M. and Fudge, C. (1984), *Local Socialism*. London: Macmillan.

Boli, J. (1991), 'Sweden: Is there a viable third sector?', in R. Wuthnow (ed.), *Between States and Markets*. Princeton: Princeton University Press.

Boli, J. (1992), 'The ties that bind: The non profit sector and the state of Sweden', in K. McCarthy, et al. (eds), *The Nonprofit Sector in the Global Community*. San Franscisco: Jossey-Bass.

Bourdieu, P. (1984), *Distinction: a Social Critique of the Judgment of Taste*. London: Routledge.

Brown, K., Elder, J., Kenny, S., Paddle, S. and Spratt, P. (1992), *Managing the Community: the Identification of Needs and the Politics of Resource Distribution*. Melbourne: Deakin University Press.

Brown, K., Kenny, S. and Spratt, P. (1990), *Community Development in the 1990s: Industrial, Educational and Training Issues*. Melbourne: Victoria College.

Brown, K., Kenny, S. and Turner, B. S. (1994), 'The transformation of the welfare state: Developments in the non-profit community based welfare sector', paper delivered at The Australian Sociological Annual Conference, Deakin University, Geelong.

Bryant, C. G. A. (1995), 'Of matters public and civil', in S. Edgell, S. Walklate and G. Williams (eds), *Debating the Future of the Public Sphere*. Hants., UK: Avebury.

Bryson, L. (1992), *Welfare and the State*. Basingstoke: Macmillan.

Buchanan, J. (1995), 'Managing Labour in the 1990s' in S. Rees and G. Rodley (eds), *The Human Costs of Managerialism*. Leichhardt: Pluto Press, pp. 49–54.

Burger, A., Dekker, P., van den Ploeg, T. and van Veen, W. (1997), 'Defining the nonprofit sector: The Netherlands', *Working Papers of the Johns Hopkins Comparative Nonprofit Sector Project*, 23. Baltimore: Johns Hopkins Institute for Policy Studies.

Burgmann, V. (1993), *Power and Protest*. St Leonards: Allen and Unwin.

Burgmann, V. and Lee, J. (eds) (1988) *Staining the Wattle*. Fitzroy, Aus.: McPhee Gribble/Penguin.

Butcher, T. (1995), *Delivering Welfare: The Governance of the Social Services in the 1990s*. Buckingham: Open University Press.

Calhoun, C. (1992), 'Introduction: Habermas and the public sphere', in C. Calhoun (ed.), *Habermas and the Public Sphere*. Cambridge, Mass.: MIT Press.

Castells, M. (1983), *The City and the Grassroots: a Cross-cutural Theory of Urban Social Movements*. London: Arnold.

Castles, I. (1991), *Australian Standard Geopraphical Classification (ASGC) Manual (1991 update)*. Canberra: Australian Bureau of Statistics.

Castles, F. (1985), *The Working Class and Welfare: Reflections on the Political Development of the Welfare State in Australia and New Zealand, 1890–1980.* Wellington: Allen and Unwin.

Clarke, J., Cochrane, A. and Smart, C. (1987), *Ideologies of Welfare: from Dreams to Disillusion.* London: Hutchinson.

Cochrane, A. (1986), 'Community politics and democracy', in D. Held and C. Pollitt (eds), *New Forms of Democracy.* London: Open University, Sage.

Cockburn, C. (1977), *The Local State.* London: Pluto Press.

Cohen, J. and Arato, A. (1992), *Civil Society and Political Theory.* Cambridge, Mass.: MIT Press.

Cohen, J. and Rogers, J. (1995), *Associations and Democracy.* London: Verso.

Collins, H. (1985), 'Political ideology in Australia: the distinctiveness of a benthamite society', *Daedalus*, 114(1), pp. 147–70.

Considine, M. (1996), 'Market bureaucracy? Exploring the contending rationalities of contemporary administrative regimes', in *Labour and Industry*, 7(1), June, pp. 1–27.

Considine, M. and Painter, M. (eds) (1997), *Managerialism – the Great Debate.* Carlton South: Melbourne University Press.

Cox, E. (1995), *A Truly Civil Society: 1995 Boyer Lectures.* Sydney: ABC Books.

Craig, G., Mayo, M. and Sharman, N. (eds) (1979), *Jobs and Community Action.* London: Routledge & Kegan Paul.

Croft, S. and Beresford, P. (1989), 'User-involvement, citizenship and social policy', *Critical Social Policy*, 26 (Autumn), pp. 5–18.

Culpitt, I. (1992), *Welfare and Citizenship: Beyond the Crisis of the Welfare State?* London: Sage.

Dahl, R. A. (1989), *Democracy and its Critics.* New Haven: Yale University Press.

Dahlgren, P. (1991), 'Introduction', in P. Dahlgren and C. Sparks (eds), *Communication and Citizenship: Journalism and the Public Sphere.* London: Routledge.

Dahrendorf, R. (1959), *Class and class Conflict in Industrial Society.* London: Routledge & Kegan Paul.

Dalton, T., Draper, M., Weeks, W., and Wiseman, J. (1996), *Making Social Policy in Australia: an introduction.* St Leonards: Allen and Unwin.

Davidson, A. (1997), *From Subject to Citizen: Australian Citizenship in the Twentieth Century.* Cambridge: Cambridge University Press.

Davis, G. (1997), 'Implications, consequences and futures', in G. Davis, B. Sullivan and A. Yeatman (eds), *The New Contractualism?* South Melbourne: Macmillan, pp. 224–38.

Davis, G., Sullivan, B. and Yeatman, A. (eds) (1997), *The New Contractualism?* South Melbourne: Macmillan Education Australia.

Davis Smith, J., Rochester, C. and Hedley, R. (eds) (1995), *An Introduction to the Voluntary Sector.* London: Routledge.

Dekker, P. and van den Broek, A. (1998), 'Civil society in comparative perspective: involvement in voluntary associations in North America and Western Europe', *Voluntas: International Journal of Voluntary and Nonprofit Organisations*, 9(1), pp. 11–38.

Dennis, N., Henriques, F. and Slaughter, C. (1957), *Coal is Our Life.* London: Eyre and Spottiswoode.

Denzin, N. (1970), *The Research Act*. Chicago: Aldine Press.

Dickey, B. (1980), *No Charity There: a Short History of Social Welfare in Australia*. Melbourne: Nelson.

Dixon, J. (1987), 'The dilemma of community management', in P. Dunn (ed.), *Community Welfare Services – Rural Focus Proceedings from Conference,* Riverina Murray Institute of Higher Education, Wagga Wagga.

Duncan, T. and Fogarty, J. (1984), *Australia and Argentina: on Parallel Paths*. Melbourne: Melbourne University Press.

Durkheim, E. (1947), *The Division of Labour in Society*. New York: Free Press.

Durkheim, E. (1957), *Professional Ethics and Civic Morals*. London: Routledge & Kegan Paul.

Drucker, P. (1973), *Management: Tasks, Responsibilities, Practices*. New York: Harper and Row.

Drury, S. B. (1988), *The Political Ideas of Leo Strauss*. Basingstoke: Macmillan.

Earles, W. (1997), 'Contracting and devolution: Centralisation of decentralisation for third sector organisations?', *Third Sector Review*, 3, pp. 87–100.

Edwards, B. and Foley, M. W. (1998), 'Civil society and social capital beyond Putnam', *American Behavioural Scientist*, 40(5), pp. 575–87.

Engels, F. (1956), *The Peasant War in Germany*. Moscow: Progress Publishers.

Ernst, J. (1994), 'Privatisation, competition and contracts', in J. Alford and D. O'Neill (eds), *The Contract State: Public Management and the Kennett Government*. Centre for Applied Social Research, Deakin University. Geelong: Deakin University Press, 101–35.

Esping-Andersen, G. (1990). *The Three Worlds of Welfare Capitalism*. Cambridge: Polity Press.

Etzioni, A. (1993), *The Spirit of Community: Rights, Responsibilities and the Communitarian Agenda*. London: Fontana.

Evers, A. (1995), 'Part of the welfare mix: the third sector as an intermediate area', *Voluntas*, 6(2), pp. 159–82.

Everingham, C. (1998), 'Making and breaking the corporist welfare state: "New Left" politics for participation to consultation', *Third Sector Review*, 4(1).

Fairclough, N. (1992), *Discourse and Social Change*. Cambridge: Polity Press.

Feher, F. and Heller, A. (1983), 'Class, democracy, modernity', *Theory and Society*, 12(2), pp. 211–44.

Flynn, R. (1997), 'Quasi-welfare, associationalism and the social division of citizenship', *Citizenship Studies*, 1(3), pp. 147–51.

Foley, G. (1988), 'For Aboriginal sovereignty', *Arena*, 83, pp. 20–4.

Foucault, M. (1975), *Discipline and Punish: the Birth of the Prison*. London: Tavistock.

Franklin, J. (ed.) (1998), *The Politics of Risk Society*. Malden: Blackwell Publishers.

Franzway, S., Court, D. and Connell, R. W. (1989), *Staking a Claim: Feminism, Bureaucracy and the State*. Sydney: Allen and Unwin.

Fraser, N. (1985), *Unruly Practices – Power, Discourse and Gender in Contemporary Social Theory*. Minneapolis: University of Minnesota Press.

Fraser, N. (1995), 'From redistribution to recognition? Dilemmas of justice in a "post-socialist" age', *New Left Review*, 212, July–August, pp. 68–93.

Fraser, N. and Gordon, L. (1994) ' "Dependency" demystified: Inscriptions of power in a keyword of the welfare state', *Social Politics*, spring, pp. 4–31.

Friedman, M. (1989), 'Feminism and modern friendship: Dislocating the community', *Ethics*, 6(2), spring.

Fukuyama, F. (1992), *The End of History and the Last Man*. London: Hamish Hamilton.

Fukuyama, F. (1995), *Trust: The Social Virtues and the Creation of Wealth*. London: Penguin Books.

Galaskiewicz, J. and Bielefeld, W. (1998), *Nonprofit Organizations in an Age of Uncertainty: a Study of Organizational Change*. New York: Aldine De Gruyter.

Gee, C. D. and Lankshear, C. (1995) 'The new work order: Critical language awareness and "fast" capitalism texts', *Discourse: Studies in the Cultural Politics of Education*, 16(1), pp. 5–14.

Gerard, D. (1983), *Charities in Britain: Conservatism or Change?* London: Bedford Square Press.

Gerth, H. H. and Mills, C. Wright (eds) (1991), *From Max Weber: Essays in Sociology*. London: Routledge.

Giddens, A. (1990), *The Consequences of Modernity*. Cambridge: Polity Press.

Giddens, A. (1994), *Beyond Left and Right: The Future of Radical Politics*. Stanford: Stanford University Press.

Giner, S. and Sarasa, S. (1996), 'Civic altruism and social policy', *International Sociology*, 11(2), pp. 139–59.

Goldberg, E. (1996), 'Thinking about how democracy works', *Politics and Society*, 24(1), pp. 7–18.

Golding, P. (1995), 'The mass media and the public sphere: The crisis of information in the "information society"', in S. Edgell, S. Walklate and G. Williams (eds), *Debating the Future of the Public Sphere*. Hants., UK: Avebury.

Goldmann, L. (1973), *The Philosophy of the Enlightenment*. London: Routledge and Kegan Paul.

Goodall, H. (1988) 'Cryin out for land rights', in V. Burgmann and J. Lee (eds), *Staining the Wattle*. Fitzroy, Aus.: McPhee Gribble/Penguin, pp. 181–97.

Gorz, P. (1992), 'On the difference between society and community, and why basic income cannot by itself confer full membership of either', in P. van Parijs (ed.), *Arguing for Basic Income*. London: Verso, pp. 178–84.

Gumprecht, N. (1986), 'Strategies for change: Women employees in social service agencies', in H. Marchant and B. Wearing (eds), *Gender Reclaimed: Women in Social Work*. Sydney: Hale and Iremonger, pp. 212–22.

Gyford, J. (1985), *The Politics of Local Socialism*. London: Allen and Unwin.

Habermas, J. (1976), *Legitimation Crisis*. London: Heinemann.

Habermas, J. (1989), *The Structural Transformation of the Public Sphere*. Cambridge: Polity Press.

Habermas, J. (1992), 'Citizenship and national identity', in B. van Steenbergen (ed.), *The Condition of Citizenship*. London: Sage, pp. 20–35.

Hadley, R. and Hatch, S. (1981), *Social Welfare and the Failure of the State*. London: George Allen and Unwin.

Harris, M. (1994), 'The power of boards in service providing agencies: Three models', *Administration in Social Work*, 18(2), pp. 1–15.

Healy, J. (1982), 'The status of women in the Australian welfare industry', *Australian Social Work*, 35(3), pp. 19–26.

Held, D. and Pollitt, C. (eds) (1986), *New Forms of Democracy*. London: Sage Publications.

Hewitt, J. N. (1997), 'Re-conceptualising the voluntary sector: Associative democracy in the pluralist public sphere and the legacy of Tocqueville, Gierke and Durkheim', *Third Sector Review,* 3, pp. 67–86.

Hilmer, F. (1993), *Independent Committee of Inquiry Into Competition Policy in Australia: National Competition Policy.* Canberra: Australian Government Publishing Service.

Hirst, P. Q. (1990), *Representative Democracy and its Limits.*Cambridge : Polity Press.

Hirst, P. Q. (ed.) (1993), *The Pluralist Theory of the State.* London: Routledge.

Hirst, P. Q. (1994), *Associative Democracy: New Forms of Economic and Social Governance.* Cambridge: Polity Press.

Hirst, P. Q. (1995), 'Can secondary associations enhance democratic governance?', in J. Cohen and J. Rogers (eds), *Associations and Democracy.* London: Verso.

Hirst, P. Q. (1996), 'Associative democracy – a comment on David Morgan', *Australian and New Zealand Journal of Sociology,* 32(1), pp. 20–6.

Hirst, P. Q. (1997), *From Statism to Pluralism: Democracy, Civil Society and Global Politics.* London: UCL Press.

Hirst, P. Q. and Thomson, G. (1996), *Globalisation in Question.* Cambridge: Polity Press.

Hoatson, L., Dixon, J. and Sloman, D. (1996),'Community development, citizenship and the contract state', *Community Development Journal,* 31(2), April, pp. 126–36.

Hoggart, R. (1957), *The Uses of Literacy.* London: Chatto & Windus.

Hollinsworth, D. (1996), 'Community development in indigenous Australia: Self-determination or indirect rule', *Community Development Journal,* 31(2), April, pp. 114–25.

Holton, R. J. and Turner, B. S. (1986) *Talcott Parsons on Economy and Society.* London: Routledge & Kegan Paul.

Holton, R. J. and Turner, B. S. (1989), *Max Weber on Economy and Society.* London: Routledge & Kegan Paul.

Holub, R. C. (1991), *Jürgen Habermas: Critic in the Public Sphere.* London: Routledge.

Hooper, A. (1998), *Community Development and Enterprise Culture,* MA thesis, Deakin University.

Hutton, D. (1982), 'Anarchism and the anti-militarist movement in Australia', *Social Alternatives,* 2(3), February, pp. 17–21.

Ife, J. (1995), *Community Development: Creating Community Alternatives–Vision, Analysis and Practice.* Longman: Melbourne.

Jacubowicz, A. (1983), 'Ethnic welfare: Problems in policy formation and implementation', *Social Alternatives,* 3(3), July, pp. 51–5.

James, E. (1989), 'The provision of public services: A comparison of Sweden and Holland', in E. James (ed.), *The Nonprofit Sector in International Perspective.* New York: Oxford University Press.

Janoski, T., Musick, M. and Wilson, J. (1998), 'Being volunteered? The impact of social participation and pro-social attitudes on volunteering', *Sociological Forum,* 13(3), pp. 495–519.

Janoski, T. and Wilson, J. (1995), 'Pathways to voluntarism: Family, socialization and status transmission', *Social Forces,* 74(1), pp. 271–92.

Jones, D. and Mayo, M. (ed.) (1974), *Community Work One*. London: Routledge & Kegan Paul.

Kamali, M. (1997), *Distorted Intergration: Clientalization of Immigrants in Sweden*. Uppsala University: Uppsala Multiethnic Papers.

Keane, J. (1988), *Democracy and Civil Society*. London: Verso.

Keat, R. (1991), 'Introduction: Starship Britain or international enterprise?', in R. Keat and N. Abercrombie (eds), *Enterprise Culture*. London: Routledge.

Kendall, J. and Knapp, M. (1996) *The Voluntary Sector in the United Kingdom*. Manchester: Manchester University Press.

Kennedy, R. (1982), *Australian Welfare History*, South Melbourne: Macmillan.

Kenny, S. (1994a), 'The art of compromise – Community development in the 1990s', Paper presented at The Australian Sociological Association Annual Conference, Deakin University, Geelong, December.

Kenny, S. (1994), *Developing Communities for the Future: Community Development in Australia*. South Melbourne: Thomas Nelson Australia.

Kenny, S. (1995), 'Privatisation and the community sector', *Public First Conference Proceedings*, Royal Melbourne Institute of Technology, Melbourne, pp. 91–107.

Kenny, S. (1996), 'From charity to industry to charity industry? Community welfare organisations in Australia', paper presented at The Australian Sociological Association Annual Conference, University of Tasmania, Hobart, December.

Kenny, S. (1996), 'Contestations of community development in Australia', *Community Development Journal*, 31(2), pp. 104–13.

Kenny, S. (1997), 'Configurations of community welfare organisations and associative democracy', *Third Sector Review*, 3, pp. 41–65.

Kenny, S. and Muetzeldfeldt, M. (1996), 'Welfare citizenship and the turn to market discourse', Culture and Citizenship Conference, Australian Key Centre for Cultural and Media Policy, Griffith University, Brisbane.

Kenny, S. and Turner, B. (1996), 'The search for active citizenship? The community welfare sector and associative democracy', paper presented at The Australian Sociological Association Annual Conference, University of Tasmania, Hobart, December.

Kenworthy, L. (1997), 'Civic engagement, social capital, and economic cooperation', *American Behavioural Scientist*, 40(5), pp. 645–57.

Kitchen, R. (1982), 'Sexual differences', *Social Alternatives,* 2(4), June, pp. 7–11.

Knapp, M. (1996), 'Are voluntary agencies really more effective?', In D. Billis and M. Harris (eds), *Voluntary Agencies: Challenges of Organisation and Management*. Basingstoke: Macmillan, pp. 166–86.

Krieger, L. (1957), *The German Idea of Freedom*. Chicago: University of Chicago Press.

Kuti, E. (1996), *The Nonprofit Sector in Hungary*. Manchester: Manchester University Press.

Latham, M. (1998), *Civilising Global Capital: New thinking for Australian Labor*. St Leonards: Allen and Unwin.

Lee, P. and Raban, C. (1988), *Welfare Theory and Social Policy – Reform or Revolution?* London: Sage Publications Ltd.

Le Grand, J. (1990), 'The state of welfare', in J. Hills (ed.), *The State of Welfare: the Welfare State in Britain since 1974*. London: Oxford University Press, pp. 338–62.

Le Grand, J. and Robinson, R. (ed.) (1984), *Privatisation and the Welfare State*. London: George Allen & Unwin (Publishers) Ltd.

Leonard, P. (1997), *Postmodern Welfare – Reconstructing an Emancipatory Project*. London: Sage Publications Ltd.

Levi, M. (1996), 'Social and unsocial capital: A review essay on Robert Putnam's *Making Democracy Work*', *Politics and Society*, 42(1) pp. 45–55.

Liffman, M. (1983), 'Multiculturalism: Where to, with whom – and why?', in *Social Alternatives*, 3(3), July, pp. 13–17.

London, S. (1995), 'Teledemocracy versus deliberative democracy: A comparative look at two models of public talk', *Journal of Interpersonal Computing and Technology*, 3(2), pp. 33–55.

London Edinburgh Weekend Return Group (1980), *In and Against the State*. London: Pluto Press.

Lundström, T. and Wijkström, F. (1998), *The Nonprofit Sector in Sweden*. Manchester: Manchester University Press.

Lyons, M. (1994), *Defining and Counting Australia's Charitable Organisations*. CACOM Working Paper no 19, Centre for Austaralian Community Organisations and Management, University of Technology, Sydney.

Lyons, M. (1997), 'Capacity of nonprofit organisations to contribute to social capital formation under market style government regimes', *CACOM Working Paper* no. 40, December, Sydney: University of Technology.

Lyons, M. and Hocking, S. (1998), *Australia's Nonprofit Sector: Some Preliminary Data*. Australian Nonprofit Data Project: University of Technology, Sydney.

Lyons, M. and Pocklington, J. (1992), *Data Sources for Research on Private Not-for-Profit Organisations in Australia*. Working Paper no. 9, Centre for Australian Community Organisations and Management, University of Technology, Sydney.

Lyotard, J.-F. (1984), *The Postmodern Condition. A Report on Knowledge*. Manchester: Manchester University Press.

MacIntyre, A. (1981), *After Virtue: a Study in Moral Theory*. London: Duckworth.

MacIntyre, S. (1985), *Winners and Losers*. Sydney: Allen and Unwin.

Mackintosh, M. and Wainwright, H. (1987), *A Taste of Power: the Politics of Local Economics*. London: Verso.

Macpherson, C. B. (1962), *The Political Theory of Possessive Individualism*. Oxford: Clarendon Press.

Macpherson, C. B. (1981), *Thomas Hobbes*. Harmondsworth: Penguin Books.

Mansbridge, J. (1996), 'Using power/fighting power: The polity', in S. Benhabib (ed.), *Democracy and Difference: Contesting the Boundaries of the Political*. Princeton: Princeton University Press.

Marshall, T. F. (1996), 'Can we define the voluntary sector?', in D. Billis and M. Harris (eds), *Voluntary Agencies: Challenges of Organisation and Management*. Basingstoke: Macmillan, pp. 46–60.

Marshall, T. H. (1950), *Citizenship and Social Class*. Cambridge: Cambridge University Press.

Marshall, T. H. (1965), *Class, Citizenship and Social Development*. New York: Anchor.

Marshall, T. H. (1981), *The Right to Welfare and Other Essays*. London: Heinemann Educational Books.

Marshall, T. H. and Bottomore, T. (1992), *Citizenship and Social Class*. London: Pluto.

Martin, B. (1982), 'Disruption vs. organisation', *Social Alternatives*, 2(4), June, pp. 42–3.

Mathews, J. (1989), *Age of Democracy: the Politics of Post-Fordism*. Oxford: Oxford University Press.

McMichael, P. (1984), *Settlers and the Agrarian Question: Foundations of Capitalism in Colonial Australia*. Melbourne: Widescope.

Melville, R. and Nyland, J. (1997), 'On the starting blocks of contracting: Will NSW take the dive?', *Third Sector Review* (special issue), pp. 45–66.

Milligan, V., Hardvick, J. and Graycar, A. (1984), *Non-Government Welfare Organisations in Australia: a National Clarification*. Report. no. 51, Social Welfare Research Centre, Sydney.

Mishra, R. (1984), *The Welfare State in Crisis*. London: Harvester Press.

Morgan, D. E. (1996), 'Associative democracy: Decentralisation of societal and industrial governance? A critical discussion', *The Australian and New Zealand Journal of Sociology*, 32(1), March, pp. 1–19.

Morgan, D. L. (1988), *Focus Groups as Qualitative Research*. Newbury Park: Sage.

Mouffe, C. (ed.) (1992), *Dimensions of Radical Democracy: Pluralism, Citizenship, Community*. London: Verso.

Mowbray, M. (1985), 'The medicinal properties of localism: A historical perspective', in R. Thorpe and J. Petruchenia (eds), *Community Work or Social Change?* London: Routledge & Kegan Paul.

Muetzelfeldt, M. (1994), 'Contracts, politics and society', in J. Alford and D. O'Neill (eds), *The Contract State: Public Management and the Kennett Government*. Centre for Applied Social Research, Deakin University, Geelong, pp. 136–57.

Mundey, J. (1981), *Green Bans and Beyond*. Sydney: Angus and Robertson.

Mune, M. (1989), 'Implausible dreams: Community work and the human services', Paper delivered to AASW 21st National Conference, Townsville, Qld.

Najam, A. (1999), 'Citizen organizations as policy entrepreneurs', in D. Lewis (ed.), *International Perspectives on Voluntary Action: Reshaping the Third Sector*. London: Earthscan, pp. 142–81.

Neville, A. (1999), 'Competing interests: Competition policy in the welfare sector', the Australia Institute and Anglicare Australia: Lyneham, ACT. Discussion paper no. 21 (June).

Newton, K. (1998) 'Social capital and democracy', *American Behavioural Scientist*, 42(1), pp. 124–40.

Nozick, R. (1974), *Anarchy, State and Utopia*. Oxford: Basil Blackwell.

O'Brien, M. and Penna, S. (1998), *Theorising Welfare – Enlightenment and Modern Society*. London: Sage Publications.

O'Connell, B. (1996), 'A major transfer of government responsibility to voluntary organisations? Proceed with caution', *Public Administration Review*, 56(3), pp. 222–5.

O'Connor, J. (1973), *The Fiscal Crisis of the State*. New York: St. Martin's Press.

Offe, C. (1976), *Disorganized Capitalism: Contemporary Transformations of Work and Politics*. Cambridge: Polity.

Offe, C. (1984), *Contradictions of the Welfare State.* London: Verso.

Onyx, J. (1993), 'Career paths in the third sector: Implications for human resource management', Queensland University of Technology Working paper no. 30. Sydney: Queensland University of Technology.

Onyx, J. and Bullen, P. (1997), Measuring social capital in five communities in NSW', CACOM Working Paper 41 (December), Sydney, University of Technology of Sydney.

Orr, S. (1995), *Jerusalem or Athens: Reason and Revelation in the Work of Leo Strauss.* Lanham: Rowman and Littlefield.

Osborne, D. and Gaebler, T. (1993), *Reinventing Government – How the Entrepreneurial Spirit is Transforming the Public Sector.* Reading: Addison-Wesley.

Paddon, M. (1993), 'Taking contracting seriously: The current debate in the UK and Europe', in J. Coulter (ed.), *Doing More with Less? Contracting Out and Efficiency in the Public Sector.* Public Sector Research Centre, University of New South Wales, Kensington, pp. 62–71.

Parsons, T. (1937), *The Structure of Social Action.* New York: McGraw-Hill.

Pateman, C. (1970), *Participation and Democratic Theory.* Cambridge: Cambridge University Press.

Pocklington, J., Lyons, M. and Onyx, J. (1995), *Data on Non-Profit Organisations: An Examination of Two Data Sources.* Working Paper no. 30. Centre for Australian Community Organizations and Management, University of Technology, Sydney.

Power, M. (1998), *The Audit Society: Rituals of Verification.* Oxford: Clarendon Press.

Pusey, M. (1991), *Economic Rationalism in Canberra.* Cambridge: Cambridge University Press.

Putnam, R. D. (1993), *Making Democracy Work: Civil Traditions in Modern Italy.* Princeton: Princeton University Press.

Putnam, R. D. (1995), 'Bowling alone: America's declining social capital', *Journal of Democracy,* 6(1), pp. 65–78.

Ranci, C. (1997), 'Return to (what) community', *Voluntas: International Journal of Voluntary and Nonprofit Organisations,* 8(1), pp. 81–8.

Raskall, P. (1993), 'Widening income disparities in Australia', in S. Rees, G. Rodley and F. Stilwell (eds), *Beyond the Market: Alternatives to Economic Rationalism.* Leichhardt: Pluto Press, pp. 38–52.

Rees, A. and Bulmer, M. (eds) (1996), *Citizenship Today: the Contemporary Relevance of T. H. Marshall.* London: UCL Press.

Rees, S. (1991), *Achieving Power.* North Sydney: Allen and Unwin.

Rees, S. (1995), 'The Fraud and the Fiction', in S. Rees and G. Rodley (eds), *The Human Costs of Managerialism: Advocating the Recovery of Humanity.* Pluto Press, Leichhardt: Pluto Press, pp. 15–28.

Reich, R. (1993), *The Work of Nations: Preparing Ourselves for 21st-Century Capitalism.* London: Simon & Schuster.

Repo, M. (1977) 'The fallacy of community control', in J. Cowley et al. (eds), *Community or Class Struggle.* London: Stage One.

Riddell, M. (1997), 'Bringing back balance: The role of social capital in public policy', in D. Robinson (ed.), *Social Capital and Policy Development,* Institute of Policy Studies, Victoria University of Wellington, Wellington. pp. 13–33.

Ritzer, G. (1996), *The McDonaldization of Society: an Investigation into the Changing Character of Contemporary Social Life.* London: Sage.

Ritzer, G. (1998), *The McDonalization Thesis: Explorations and Extensions*. London: Sage.

Robertson, R. and Turner, B. S. (eds) (1995), *Talcott Parsons: Theorist of Modernity*. London: Sage.

Robinson, D. (1997), 'Investing in the community', in D. Robinson (ed.), *Social Capital and Policy Development*, Institute of Policy Studies, Victoria University of Wellington, Wellington, pp. 13–33.

Roelofs, J. (1995), 'The third sector as a protective layer for capitalism', *Monthly Review*, 47(4), pp. 16–26.

Routley, R. and Routley, V. (1982), 'The irrefutability of anarchism in Australia', *Social Alternatives*, 2(3), February, pp. 23–9.

Runciman, D. (1997), *Pluralism and the Personality of the State*. Cambridge: Cambridge University Press.

Sabetti, F. (1996), 'Path dependency and civic culture: Some lessons from Italy about interpreting social experiments', *Politics and Society*, 24(1), pp. 19–44.

Salamon, L. M. (1997), 'The United States', in L. M. Salamon and H. K. Anheier (eds), *Defining the Nonprofit Sector: a Cross-national Analysis*. New York: Manchester University Press, pp. 280–320.

Salamon, L. and Anheier, H. (1992), 'In search of the non-profit sector, I: The question of definitions', *Voluntas*, 3(2), pp. 125–51.

Salamon, G. and Anheier, H. K. (1996), *The Emerging Nonprofit Sector: a Cross-national Analysis*. Manchester and New York: Manchester University Press.

Salamon, L. M. and Anheier, H. (1999) 'The third world's third sector in comparative perspective', in D. Lewis (ed.), *International Perspectives on Voluntary Action Reshaping the Third Sector*. London: Earthscan.

Salvaris, M. (1995), 'Jeff Kennett's anti-government', in S. Rees, and G. Rodley (eds), *The Human Costs of Managerialism: Advocating the Recovery of Humanity*. Leichhardt: Pluto Press, pp. 145–58.

Sanders, N. (1991), 'Who saved the Franklin?', in E. Baldry and T. Vinson (eds), *Actions Speak*. Melbourne: Longman Cheshire, pp. 56–75.

Sanderson, I. (1993), *Management of Quality in Local Government*. London: Longman.

Saunders, P. and Harris, C. (1994), *Privatization and Popular Capitalism*. Buckingham: Open University Press.

Scheaffer, R. L., Mendenhall, W. and Ott, L. (1985), *Elementary Survey Sampling*. Third edn. Boston: PWS-Kent.

Schmidt, J. (1995), 'Civil society and social things: setting the boundaries of the social sciences', *Social Research*, 62(4), pp. 900–32.

Scott, D. (1981), *Don't Mourn for Me – Organise*. Nth. Sydney: Allen and Unwin.

Scott, C. D. and Jaffe, D. T. (1991), *Empowerment: Building a Committed Workforce*, Los Altos: Crisp Publications.

Seibel, W. (1990), 'Organizational behavior and organizational function', in H. K. Anheier and W. Seibel, (eds), *The Nonprofit Sector: International and Comparative Perspectives*. Berlin: de Gruyter.

Seligman, A. (1992), *The Idea of Civil Society*. Princeton: Princeton University Press.

Semmel, B. (1973), *The Methodist Revolution*. London: Heinemann.

Smith, M. (1978), 'Australian women's health centres', *Social Alternatives*, 1(2), pp. 25–6.

Smith, J., Rochester, C. and Hedley, R. (ed.) (1995), *An Introduction to the Voluntary Sector*. London: Routledge.

Smith, S. R. and Lipksy, M. (1993), *Non Profits for Hire: the Welfare State in the Age of Contracting*. Cambridge, Mass.: Harvard University Press.

Squires, P. (1990), *Anti-Social Policy – Welfare, Ideology and the Disciplinary State*. Hertfordshire: Harvester Wheatsheaf.

Stilwell, P. (1993), *Economic Inequality: Who Gets What in Australia*. Leichhardt: Pluto Press.

Stilwell, F. (1994), 'Political–economic systems: A fourth way?', *Social Alternatives*, 13(3&4), pp. 5–11.

Stretton, H. (1996), *Poor laws of 1834 and 1996*. Occasional paper, Brotherhood of St Laurence, East Melbourne.

Summers, A. (1975), *Damned Whores and God's Police*. Ringwood: Penguin Books Australia Ltd.

Tam, T. (1998), *Communitarianism – a New Agenda for Politics and Citizenship*. London: Macmillian Press Ltd.

Taylor, M. (1982), *Community, Anarchy and Liberty*. Cambridge: Cambridge University Press.

Taylor-Gooby, P. and Lawson, R. (eds) (1993), *Markets and Morals: New Issues in the Delivery of Welfare*. Buckingham: Open University Press.

Theophanous, A. (1993), *Understanding Social Justice – an Australian Perspective*. Melbourne: Elikia Books.

Therborn, G. (1983), 'When, how and why does a welfare state become a welfare state?' Paper presented at the ECPR Workshops, Freiburg, March.

Thompson, E. P. (1963), *The Making of the English Working Class*. London: Gollancz.

Thorpe, R. (1985), 'Community work and ideology: An Australian Perspective', in *Community Work or Social Change?* London: Routledge and Kegan Paul, pp. 11–27.

Thorpe, R. and Petruchenia, J. (eds), (1985), *Community Work or Social Change?* London: Routledge and Kegan Paul.

Tocqueville, A. de (1969), *Democracy in America*. Garden City: Anchor.

Trachtenberg, Z. M. (1993), *Making Citizens – Rousseau's Political Theory of Culture*. London: Routledge.

Touraine, A. (1981), *The Voice and the Eye: an Analysis of Social Movements*. Cambridge: Cambridge University Press.

Turner, A. (ed.) (1975), *Black Power in Australia*. London: Heinemann Educational.

Turner, B. S. (1986), *Citizenship and Capitalism: the Debate Over Reformism*. London: Allen & Unwin.

Turner, B. S. (1989), 'Aging, status politics and sociological theory', *British Journal of Sociology*, 40(2), pp. 588–606.

Turner, B. S. (1992), 'Outline of a theory of citizenship', in C. Mouffe (ed.), *Dimensions of Radical Democracy Pluralism, Citizenship, Community*. London: Verso, pp. 33–62.

Turner, B. S. (ed.) (1993), *Citizenship and Social Theory*. London: Sage.

Turner, B. S. (1993), 'Contemporary problems in the theory of citizenship', in B. S. Turner (ed.), *Citizenship and Social Theory*. London: Sage, pp. 1–19.

Turner, B. S. (1994), 'The postmodernization of the life course: towards a new social gerontology', *The Australian Journal of Gerontology*, 13(3), pp. 109–111.

Turner, B. S. (1998), 'Aging and generational conflicts: A reply to Sarah Irwin', *British Journal of Sociology*, 49(2), pp. 299–304.

Turner, B. S. (1999), 'McCitizens: Risk, coolness and irony in contempory politics', in B. Smart (ed.) *Resisting McDonaldization*. London: Sage, pp. 83–100.

Van Parijs, P. (ed.) (1992), *Arguing for Basic Income*. London: Verso.

Van Gunsteren, H. (1992), 'Four conceptions of citizenship', in B. van Steenbergen (ed.), *The Condition of Citizenship*. London: Sage, pp. 36–48.

van Steenbergen, B. (1994), *The Condition of Citizenship*. London: Sage

Vaughan, G. (1994), *Classifying Welfare Services: a Preliminary Paper*. Australian Institute of Health and Welfare, Canberra.

Wade, D. A. (1991), 'Kurnell residents take on the giant Bayer', in E. Baldry and T. Vinson (eds), *Actions Speak*. Melbourne: Longman Cheshire, pp. 37–55.

Walker, A. (1981), 'Social policy, social administration and the construction of welfare', in *Sociology*, 15(2), pp. 225–50.

Walzer, M. (1992), 'The civil society argument', in C. Mouffe (ed.), *Dimensions of Radical Democracy: Pluralism, Citizenship, Community*. London: Verso, pp. 89–107.

Ward, J. (1993) *Australian Community Development: Ideas, Skills and Values for the 90s*. Partnership Press, Windsor and Community Quarterly, Oakleigh.

Watts, R. (1994), '"Fragment and riddle and dreadful accident": Rethinking the employment and citizenship link', Paper delivered at the Extending Democracy Conference. August, Deakin University, Melbourne.

Weeks, W. and Gilmore, K. (1996), 'How violence against women became an issue on the national policy agenda', in T. Dalton, M. Draper, W. Weeks, and J. Wiseman, (eds), *Making Social Policy in Australia: an Introduction*. St Leonards: Allen and Unwin.

West, R. (1991), 'How single mothers overcame discrimination', in E. Baldry, and T. Vinson, (eds), *Actions Speak*. Melbourne: Longman Cheshire, pp. 168–86.

Wijkström, F. (1997), 'The Swedish nonprofit sector in international comparison', *Annals of Public and Cooperative Economics*, 68(4), pp. 625–63.

Williams, R. (1963), *Culture and Society (1780 – 1950)*. Harmondsworth: Penguin.

Wiseman, J. and Watts, R. (eds) (1989) *From Charity to Industry: the Future of the Social and Community Services Industry*. Bundoora, Victoria: PIT Press.

Wittfogel, K. (1957), *Oriental Despotism: a Comparative Study of Total Power*. New Haven: Yale University Press.

Wright, E. O. (1995), 'Introduction', to J. Cohen and J. Rogers, *Associations and Democracy*. London: Verso.

Wuthnow, R. (1991), 'The voluntary sector', in R. Wuthnow (ed.), *Between States and Markets*. Princeton: Princeton University Press.

Wuthnow, R. (1991), *Acts of Compassion*. Princeton: Princeton University Press.

Wuthnow, R. (1996), *Poor Richard's Principle*. Princeton: Princeton University Press.

Xenos, N. (1989), *Scarcity and Modernity*. London: Routledge.

Yamamoto, T. (1998), *The Nonprofit Sector in Japan*. Manchester: Manchester University Press.

Yestman, A. (1994), *Postmodern Revisionings of the Political*. London: Routledge.

Young, I. (1990) 'The ideal of community and the politics of difference', in L. J. Nicholson (ed.), *Feminism/Postmodernism*. New York: Routledge, pp. 300–23.

Index